ALL ABOARD!

The fantastic story of Charlie "Choo Choo" Justice and the football team that put North Carolina in the big-time

50th

Celebrating the 50th
Anniversary of the
"Choo Choo" Justice Era

CHAPEL HILL

Bob Terrell

WORLDCOMM®

a division of Creativity, Inc.

Publisher: Ralph Roberts
Vice President/Publishing: Pat Hutchison Roberts

Cover Design: **WorldComm**®

Editors: Pat Hutchison Roberts, Samuel Garrison, Ralph Roberts

Interior Design and Electronic Page Assembly: **WorldComm**®

Printed in the United States of America

10 9 8 7 6 5 4 3

Third Printing, June 1996

Library of Congress Cataloging-in-Publication
Terrell, Bob
    All Aboard: The fantastic story of Charlie "Choo Choo" Justice and the football team that put North Carolina in the big time / Bob Terrell.
        p.   cm.
    ISBN 1-56664-094-6 (alk. paper)
    1. Justice, Charlie, 1924- 2. Football players--United States--Biography.
    3. University of North Carolina at Chapel Hill--Football--History.   I. Title.
GV939.J8T47   1996
796.332'092--dc20   96-6847
    [B]   CIP

The author and publisher have made every effort in the preparation of this book to ensure the accuracy of the information. However, the information in this book is sold without warranty, either express or implied. Neither the author nor WorldComm will be liable for any damages caused or alleged to be caused directly, indirectly, incidentally, or consequentially by the information in this book.

The opinions expressed in this book are solely those of the author and are not necessarily those of WorldComm.

WorldComm®—a division of Creativity, Inc.—is a full–service publisher located at 65 Macedonia Road, Alexander NC 28701. Phone (704) 252–9515 or (704) 255–8719 fax.

WorldComm® is distributed to the trade by **Alexander Distributing**, 65 Macedonia Road, Alexander NC 28701. Phone (704) 252–9515 or (704) 255–8719 fax. For orders only: 1-800-472-0438. Visa and MasterCard accepted.

This book may also be purchased on the internet in the **Publishers CyberMall**. Set your browser to **http://www.abooks.com** and enjoy the many other fine values there as well.

If you would like to a copy of this book autographed by both Charlie Justice and Bob Terrell, e-mail **author@abooks.com** or call, fax, or write WorldComm® (see addresses above). Limited quantities available.

Contents

FOREWORD

Here is a book some have waited fifty years for. Other books have been written about Charlie ("Choo Choo") Justice, the great North Carolina All-American of the late 1940s, and they were good books, but not any have contained a definitive history of the Asheville, North Carolina lad who rose to the top of the football world from severe childhood illnesses that caused his doctor to say he would never play the game.

Charlie Justice is one who played professional football before he went to college. Strange as that seems in the orderly athletic world of today, he came along at the only time in the history of football that a person could do that—during World War II. Fresh out of high school while the war was still young, he played two undefeated seasons with the Bainbridge (Maryland) Naval Training Station Commodores, a 19-year-old kid standing shoulder to shoulder with men who were either stalwarts of professional football or salty veterans of college football.

He bucked all odds, weighing only 155 to 160 pounds as a sailor and every week going up against behemoths in the 250- to 290-pound range, all of whom were bent on knocking out his brains. Yet the exploits of this young David among Goliaths were unbelievable then and legendary today.

In high school, he lived a fairytale existence, leading two undefeated Asheville High School teams to twenty-one consecutive regular-season victories over the cream of Southern high school football. College scouts who watched that team play found it difficult to put what they felt into words and wound up calling the team simply "the best high school team I've ever seen." Actually, that thought could be carried to one more level: the 1942 Asheville starters were probably the best high school starting eleven ever put together anywhere. Winning eleven games, they scored

441 points and held the opposition to six. Had the war not been on, Duke, a national football powerhouse, would have recruited the entire eleven.

There is one high school statistic that tells the Justice story. In 1942 he scored 27 touchdowns and averaged 41.37 yards per touchdown run. At the same time, he punted 19 times for a 42.74-yard average. Thus, his average punt traveled only one yard, thirteen inches farther than his average touchdown run.

In the truest sense, Charlie was a "triple-threat halfback," a variety of football player that is extinct today. He ran, kicked, and passed, and won games with all of those attributes.

Never has a man, be he athlete, statesman, entertainer, or whatever, more completely captivated a region. The years of 1946 through 1949, when Justice played football for the University of North Carolina, have become known as "the Justice Era," and today, half a century later, if you mention the Justice Era in North Carolina, folks know what years you are talking about. There are no other comparable eras in North Carolina history.

Not only did he captivate the people, but the press as well. It has been said that Charlie Justice had the best press (those were pre-television days, remember) anyone in any field ever had, and one reason may have been that the media as a whole was not so critical then as it is today. But Charlie met the press more than halfway. He was helpful and courteous, and he appreciated every word written about him, good or bad. The press was so much on his side that if Charlie had a bad day, it was attributed in so many words to "exhaustion from a tough season," "overwhelming concentration of a strong defense," or simply to "one of those days." The press credited Charlie with being human, capable of having as bad a day as anyone else. But when he had an off day, he was still spectacular, if for nothing more than being the breakaway threat that kept the defense always in a state of tension.

There was more to Charlie Justice, however, than football. The mark of a man is how well he gets along in life. Games like college football have blinded many a man in the glare of adulation—but the nation's focused attention upon Charlie's exploits on the gridiron never made the slightest dent in the man's character or his attitude toward others.

Gentleman, faithful family man, good friend, and all-around good fellow, Charlie has carried the same calm, unassuming attitude through life that he showed on the football fields of the nation during his All-Everything heyday. His tremendous fame never went to his head.

This is not just a book about Charlie Justice: it is also the story of those around him, those who played with him at Asheville High, at

Bainbridge, at the University of North Carolina, and with the Washington Redskins. To those of World War II vintage who remember those days, the characters in this book will be larger than life. But there are two generations today that weren't around when Charlie played football, who will read his incredible story and realize that this is not just a story of one of the best football players of all time, but also of a tremendously inspirational fellow, and they will profit from reading it regardless of whether they have ever played the game.

Finally, it was pure pleasure working with a man like Charlie Justice. His memory is still sound, his companionship was pleasurable, and he was professional in his approach to this book. He spoke what he wanted to say clearly, and without wasting words—and through all of our tape-recording sessions, he never had a bad word to say about anyone.

Bob Terrell
P.O. Box 66
Asheville, NC 28802
January 1, 1996

ALL ABOARD!

The fantastic story of Charlie "Choo Choo" Justice and the football team that put North Carolina in the big-time

AMAZING ADVENTURE

S tanding on Pack Square in pre-war Asheville, North Carolina, the brothers stared down the grade of Patton Avenue and saw only lines of buildings and thousands of bobbing heads of Christmas shoppers. The older looked at his brother and grinned. "You ready, Neil?"

Neil nodded. "Let's go," he said. Tucking imaginary footballs under their arms, they broke into a run down Patton Avenue, Neil a step behind his brother Charlie.

Astonished pedestrians watched them go, weaving in and out of crowds, dodging shoppers by the narrowest of margins, darting left and right, unaware of the consternation they caused those whose arms were filled with packages. They moved swiftly and sure-footedly with perfectly timed steps that took them two blocks to the intersection of Haywood Street, and around that corner they sped, still running, dodging, and laughing. At the head of Haywood, where the crowds thinned out, they stopped to get their breath, and after regaining composure, they were off again, retracing their steps, weaving, sidestepping, enjoying the ebullience of unbridled youth.

Why they ran that way neither could say, except that it gave them a feeling of freedom, of extending their wings in an effort to burst like rockets out of childhood into their teens.

What better place to practice running a football? Like other North Carolina cities, Asheville in 1937 was in the pre-mall era, and shoppers by the thousands clogged the streets, especially along Patton Avenue and Haywood Street where stores glittered with Christmas lights. In the days before Christmas, automotive traffic had trouble moving along those main city arteries because of teeming shoppers making their way from one store to another.

Sprinkled here and there in the crowds were uniformed policemen, twirl-ing billysticks when there was room, talking and joking with people, but at the same time keeping sharp eyes peeled for mischief makers. The crowds were so thick they were prime targets for pickpockets and thieves of every ilk.

Charlie, a spindly lad of thirteen, and Neil, two years younger, made their way downtown several times during the holidays, mostly to watch the sights, savor the pre-Christmas aura, and practice running a football. They came in from Shiloh, a poorer suburb south of town, and had little or no money in their pockets, but they loved the atmosphere and the throngs of people, all happy and smiling, shopping carefully but cheerfully because they could sense the end of the Great Depression was not far off. At that time, few had any idea the depression would turn into a second world war.

Months before, Charlie and Neil had begun to run in a pine forest near their home, dodging tree trunks, seeing how close they could come without hitting trees, and when Neil centered a pine one day and knocked himself goofy, and Charlie scraped layers of skin off his arms on the rough pine bark, they agreed to find a better place to run.

The first time they went downtown together at Christmastime and saw the opportunity, they looked at each other with smiles lighting their faces, and took off down Patton Avenue.

Burly foot policemen viewed their game with different eyes, however, and one afternoon a big cop reached out and grabbed the lead runner, which happened to be Charlie. Neil also stopped.

"Here! Here!" admonished the law. "What do you think you're doing? Have you stolen something?"

Thoroughly alarmed, Charlie managed to say weakly, "No, sir, we haven't stolen anything. We're just running."

After a cursory search turned up nothing incriminating, the officer warned the boys about running recklessly through the crowds and turned them loose. As soon as he turned his back to stroll on up the street... *Whiz!* the boys took off again!

Quickly, they were out of the policeman's sight, and approaching the corner of Patton and Haywood, Charlie angled to the right and cut the cor-ner close to the building. Neil, blindly following his brother, took a wider arc around the corner – and hit a large, plump woman head-on.

"I heard a splat and looked back," Charlie Justice said, "and saw this huge woman rocking back and forth on her heels, and Neil lying on his back in Patton Avenue wondering what had hit him."

That was the first portent of times to come.

On a crisp autumn afternoon eleven years later – November 20, 1948 –

Charlie's parents, P.W. and Nell Foster Justice.

under bright skies in Kenan Stadium, Chapel Hill, North Carolina, Charlie Justice lined up at tailback for the North Carolina Tar Heels, who had the ball on arch-rival Duke's 43-yard-line. Charlie tugged at his leather helmet and looked across the line to see a solid wall of navy blue jerseys, and thought the blocking back would check off the call for 365, a play on which the fullback handed off to Charlie who went around right end, hopefully behind good blocking. The Duke defense was aligned to stop that particular play, but to Charlie's surprise, the blocking back went on with the count, and the snap was made to Hosea Rodgers, the fullback, who spun and handed off to Justice.

The flow went right. The Carolina end, Bob Cox, crashed in on the Duke end, Johnny Clements hurtled across the line from wingback to take out Duke's left linebacker, and behind the wingback came Paul Rizzo, the blocking back, and both guards, Sid Varney and Bob Mitten, with Justice building steam, moving swiftly in hand-touching distance behind them.

Around the end they thundered, and the blockers fanned out on their assignments. A bruiser from Duke came through the flow and hit Charlie a glancing blow, knocking him off balance, but Charlie touched the ground with his hand to steady himself, and when he came up he saw an alley open to the right. He went for the alley and the defense closed in from his left, but he dipped his shoulders and faked the tacklers back, and then saw Varney picking off two of the defenders. He cut quickly behind Varney, angling to the left toward the goal line, and suddenly a wall of Duke blue rose ahead of him. There was Mitten, the other guard, polishing off two more defenders, but the Duke tacklers bounced back up and came at Charlie again.

Justice cut to his left, angling this time across the field toward the left sideline. Dodging a tackler at midfield, he turned slightly right, faked a man and went by him with almost clear sailing ahead. As he crossed the fifteen, only one man was between him and the goal line, and Charlie gave him a glance as he checked off the positions of everyone else near him. He usually had no problem faking and getting by one tackler, and that was the case this time. With a wiggle of his hips and a nod of his head, Charlie went around him and sped into the end zone. Turning, he looked back upfield toward the carnage and saw that the last man he had faked was his own center, Chan Highsmith. Charlie started back upfield and Highsmith came roaring down to grasp him by the shoulders.

"Sorry, Chan," Charlie laughed. "I didn't know that was you. I was so pooped all I could think of was getting into the end zone."

Highsmith pounded Charlie on the back, laughing. "You little rascal," he howled. "That was a great run."

After the game, a 20-0 victory for the Tar Heels in which Charlie also passed to Art Weiner for a touchdown, Justice trudged into the dressing room and sat on a bench, head hanging in fatigue.

Suddenly he thought of dodging those pine trees in Shiloh so long ago. He chuckled.

Someone looked around to see what he was laughing at, and Charlie said, "They fell just like pine trees, didn't they?"

At that moment the thought went through his mind that he had just made the greatest football run of his life.

Today, a half century later, though many disagree, Charlie hasn't changed his mind.

Charlie Justice, the Carolina Choo Choo, was in his element at the University of North Carolina, at the apex of his football life, a champion not only for Carolina but for the nation. Military veterans, who had fought the toughest war in history, had just returned home and were looking for something – anything, really – to take their minds off the hell they had encountered in Europe and the Pacific. When they saw this pint-sized, boyish-looking, 22-year-old war veteran running wild with a football, many of them remembered him from the last three years playing for Bainbridge Naval Training Station and the Hawaiian Navy All-Stars, and they knew they'd found their diversion. They could identify with him, and they loved what they saw, likening Justice on a football field to a flea among elephants – and it was their nature, as it is with all Americans, to pull for the little guy.

Charlie Choo Choo Justice was a known name and familiar face from coast to coast; his picture had been on the covers of magazines and would later grace the biggies, *LIFE, The Saturday Evening Post, Sport, Pic,* and *Collier's.* There was no television in those early post-war days, but newsreels of his magnificent runs with a football were shown in theaters across America, and he was destined to have an era named for him. There were many great players of his day and time – Doak Walker, Kyle Rote, Charlie Trippi, Doc Blanchard, Glenn Davis, Slingin' Sammy Baugh, Hugh McElhenny, Johnny Lujack, Y. A. Tittle, Bobby Layne, Elroy Crazy Legs Hirsch (household names of America's football heroes) – but only Blanchard, Davis, and Justice are remembered as having created eras: Davis and Blanchard with the great Army teams of 1944 and '45, and Charlie Choo Choo with North Carolina from 1946 through 1949. People around West Point still dream with pleasure of the days of the Davis-Blanchard Era because they haven't seen the likes since, and folks in North Carolina still refer to the late forties as the Justice Era. For them, Charlie replaced World War II. He was the biggest news in Carolina, making headlines almost every day – big, bold ones on weekends – and his name was on the tongue of every Carolinian. Everybody knew Charlie Choo Choo.

It is no less amazing that almost everyone in North Carolina recognizes him on the street today. His fame has dwindled little since he played his last game for Carolina in the 1950 Cotton Bowl, for he is still the greatest athlete ever to run a football for the University of North Carolina.

Charlie was all-state, all-conference, all-star, All-American, all-everything. Twice he was runner-up for the coveted Heisman Award, which ostensibly goes to the nation's best college football player. He lost to his good friend, Southern Methodist's Doak Walker, in 1948, and in 1949 he lost to Leon Hart of Notre Dame in a ballot that to this day, Charlie is convinced, smacked of politics. Charlie played in the first Senior Bowl and was a terrifying runner and most valuable player in the College All-Star Game.

He came from that day and time, just after the war, when college football was at its all-time height, and he had been fortunate to play on one of the greatest high school teams ever in the South, the 1941-42 Asheville High teams that steamrolled through two seasons of undefeated regular season play, defeating a couple of college teams along the way.

Those who remember how easy it was to bend college football rules back then will also remember that high school rules in many instances were practically non-existent, and players could grab the ball and run, on and on and on. There were few eligibility rules in high school, and those they had were easily fractured. Tough players came from miles around to enroll at

Asheville High so they could play against the best competition in the South. Other teams played local schedules, but Asheville played only three or four North Carolina teams, some of them junior colleges, and drew the bulk of its competition from Knoxville, Kingsport, Atlanta, and several South Carolina cities. Veteran college and professional coaches said the Asheville High team of 1942 was the best they had ever seen.

Thus, coming out of high school seventeen months after Pearl Harbor, just as America was reaching the apex of its military might, Charlie was privileged to play service football – on an equality level with the professional game – and actually signed a professional football contract before enrolling in college.

His, indeed, was an amazing, and, in many respects, strange football adventure. ...

Charlie and his oldest brother, Jack.

TOO PUNY TO PLAY

Charlie Justice was born May 18, 1924, the fourth of five sons and one daughter, to Parley Wittington Justice and Nell Foster Justice. He was born at home in West Asheville on Westwood Place, a community just across the French Broad River from downtown Asheville. Fortunately, the Justices did not follow their first whim in naming the new baby boy. They initially thought of naming him Junior.

Can you imagine? Parley Wittington Choo Choo Justice, Junior! Or, worse still, Junior Justice.

Parley, Senior, went by his initials, P. W. So, how about P. W. Choo Choo Justice, Junior?

They settled on Charlie Justice with no middle name.

Charlie was a puny boy. He had various ailments all along, including the normal childhood diseases like mumps and measles, and he was hyper, frail, and wan. He missed his first two years of grammar school because of illness, often lying sick in bed. He was anemic, had bad tonsils, and suffered from the shingles. When he was ten, his right leg locked. He could neither walk nor bend the leg and had to be carried to the table and the bathroom. With no surplus of money on hand, the Justices did not call a doctor, and in about a month the condition went away and never returned.

Charlie ate like a horse but could not gain weight. He recalls being skinny as a rail.

"A great part of my problems were probably mental," Charlie said, "influenced by my timidity. I was really a shy person. I'd fuss every morning at having to get up and go to school. Mama would have to make me go, and finally I got to playing sick. All of that brought me down with a nervous stomach, which was an illness; at least I thought it was.

"What I was trying to do," he added, "was wait till my brother Neil caught up with me in school, and when he did that in the second grade, then I went on to school without argument. I kinda leaned on him. I was two grades behind my age group and was probably as old or older than anybody else in the class."

Early in Charlie's life, P. W. moved his family to Emma in the northwest part of Asheville, and when Charlie finished grammar school the family moved to the Biltmore area on the south side of Asheville in 1936. They moved in with Charlie's father's uncle–Dan Justice–who had a nice home and some money. He lived on Caribou Road in the Shiloh district, about a mile and a half from Hendersonville Road, the main artery into Asheville from the south. After Charlie entered high school, the family moved to Boston Way in Biltmore, a pretty street of European style homes.

"We moved around a lot," Charlie said. "I was born in that house on Westwood and my brother was born across the street. They used to say that every time the rent came due we moved."

Charlie's brothers were turning out to be good athletes, and each played football at Asheville High School in his own turn, but Charlie didn't seem to be destined for football. The family physician, Dr. Joe Sevier, told P. W. that Charlie would never be strong enough to play and suggested that the family channel his interests in another direction.

But there was no way to switch Charlie to another interest. And in the end it was football that helped him overcome all his childhood illnesses.

With all of his brothers playing football at Asheville High, no one or no thing could have deterred Charlie from that path, not even his frailty. Despite his peakedness, he was determined to follow his three older brothers, Jack, Joe, and Bill, on the Asheville team, and then his younger brother, Neil, would succeed him.

Heeding the doctor's words, Charlie's older brothers tried to dissuade him. "You won't be able to play," they told him repeatedly, and usually added, "You're too puny."

In school, he didn't knock the top out of his class's averages, but he managed to hold his own and make all the grades. And between playing with his brothers and running through those pine trees and the downtown foot traffic, he did learn to play football. To everyone's surprise, he became quite adept at the game, although folks and family continued to try to pull him along other paths. His childhood ailments had disappeared, at least partially because of playing football; he had gained weight and felt up to playing football on a competitive basis.

"I found that in athletics," Charlie said, "I could outdo anybody in my grade. I could run faster and jump farther than anybody in class, and my teachers took a liking to me. I learned through sports that I could be somebody other than the puny kid down the street."

Shiloh was just across Hendersonville Road from the exclusive Biltmore Forest section, and in the late 1930s, pre-high school boys from both places came together to form a sandlot football team. Another group in the Grove Park section of North Asheville organized a similar team, and on Saturday mornings the two teams would play each other.

Charlie rushed his work in order to be free in time to play in the games. His mom had made him her household help. While his brothers did the outside chores, which were considerable in the 1930s – chopping stovewood, bursting coal, push-mowing lawns, trimming the edges, milking, and a myriad other jobs – Charlie learned to make beds, clean house, wash dishes, and wax floors. Waxing floors was his Saturday morning task.

A couple of Rutledge girls, twin sisters Ann and Ruth, of Biltmore Forest, went to the games every Saturday, taking cold drinks and snacks for the Biltmore Forest players. Two other girls, Barbara and Dolly Lockeran, had horses and would ride up Caribou Road on Saturday morning to the Justice house. Charlie, on hands and knees, waxing the porch, would stop and watch them approach.

"Charlie," one would ask, "you gonna be able to come this morning?"

"Yeah," he would grin, "just as soon as I get through shining floors."

Charlie remembers those sandlot games well. "I found that I could play better than the other boys, and that's what a kid needs," he said, looking back through the years. "We ran the double-wing. Rollins College came here every summer and trained for the season, and my brothers, Joe and Jack, were on the Rollins team. They ran the double-wing and that's how I learned the formation, by watching Rollins practice. We would line up with a tailback, a fullback, and two wingbacks. Bobby Miller was our tailback and Everett Wilkinson was the fullback. Johnny Creasman and I were wingbacks.

"On the first play of every game my brother Neil would snap the ball to Wilkinson, who would spin and give the ball to me, and I would hand it to Creasman coming around on a double reverse – and Creasman could fly. He'd wear their tails out going down the sideline for touchdowns. Our linemen would say, 'What are we supposed to do?' and I would tell them, 'I don't know. Just pick out somebody and hit him.' Neil was the only boy on our team who could snap the ball. He was smaller than everybody else but he could make his snaps accurately. He still ribs me, 'If you hadn't made me a center on that Biltmore Forest team, I would have been a good back like you.' "

Charlie looked up to his brothers with admiration. Jack, the eldest, was like a father to him, and Charlie needed a father figure because his own father, P. W., was seldom there for him. P. W. was a hard drinker.

"Jack had to take charge and turn us around," Charlie said. "We were going backward. Jack went to Emma High School and was a heck of a basketball player. Then he found out that Lee Edwards (Asheville High) was the place to go because players there got recognition through the newspapers, *The Asheville Citizen* and *Times*. Jack transferred to Asheville High for one reason: He knew that Joe was going to be a great athlete and thought he needed the recognition he could get playing for Asheville." Jack was looking ahead with college in mind, figuring Joe would need a scholarship since the family finances were not great enough to educate the boys in college.

"Jack got Joe to Asheville High when Price Leeper was the coach. Joe had already finished high school at West Buncombe, but he played two more years for Asheville. He was going to the University of North Carolina on a basketball scholarship and was packed and ready to go when Jack McDowell, the Rollins coach, talked him into going to Rollins on scholarship. The move turned out for the best, though; Rollins was good for Joe."

Jack was graduated by Rollins College and came home to Asheville to work for Carolina Power & Light Company. Charlie depended on Jack to take him to David Millard Junior High at the corner of College and Oak streets in downtown Asheville.

"Sometimes," Charlie said, "if we missed Jack, we would hitch-hike to school in the mornings, my brother Neil and me, and then we would thumb back home in the afternoons. Jack watched me play ball for David Millard, and it didn't matter how good a day I had, it was never good enough for Jack. He kept my head on my shoulders. In the end, it was he who persuaded me to go to Chapel Hill by threatening to disown me.

"A fellow named Roy Starnes, who owned a paint store uptown and lived farther out than we did, usually stopped and picked up Neil and me and drove us to school. He didn't care that it was out of his way. He was a good man, glad to befriend us. Roy would drive up and stop and open the car door. 'Hop in, Charlie,' he would say. We depended on him, me and Seat."

That's what Charlie called Neil – Seat. Years before, when Charlie tried to say that Neil was sweet, the word came out "seat," and that name stuck to Neil.

For eleven years, Asheville had a Justice on its high school football team. Jack played from 1933 to '35; Joe in '34 to '36; Bill from '37 through '39; Charlie from '39 through '42; and Neil from '41 through '43. All were outstanding football players.

Jack was a good all-around athlete, a fine football halfback who also played well on the basketball squad. In 1934 he won the North and South Carolina middleweight boxing championship. Enrolling at Rollins College, he was shifted to guard where he became a terror in Florida football. Later, he spent many years as director of Champion YMCA in Canton, North Carolina, and then became commissioner of Pop Warner Little Leagues of America.

Joe was All-State quarterback at Asheville High in 1935 and All-State in basketball in 1936. He, too, went to Rollins and became a Little All-America football player as a triple-threat quarterback. Joe was also a good baseball player who toured Cuba in 1939 with the All-American baseball squad. Later he coached in high school and then joined the Rollins coaching staff and wound up spending several years as athletic director there.

Bill was a football star. He was an All-State halfback at Asheville High in 1935, and set a Shrine Bowl record in Charlotte after his senior season in 1939 by scoring three touchdowns. The record stood unmatched for three years until brother Charlie tied it in the 1942 game. Bill played at Rollins College and later turned to high school coaching. He became principal at Clearwater High in Florida, then assistant superintendent of the Pinellas County School System.

Charlie's brilliant high school career began with one game in 1939 and continued through a 6-4-1 season at Asheville High in 1940, and then he blossomed into the greatest running back in the state during the undefeated seasons of 1941 and '42.

Neil played at Asheville High from 1941 through 1943, paralleling Charlie's tenure, but unfortunately was known as Charlie's brother. Neil didn't play a lot in high school because of his size – he was smaller than Charlie – and seemed to have little interest in football. But he could kick the ball a mile and a half. He served in the navy and finally compiled a strong record as a college athlete. He was a punter for Rollins College, and his punting average was higher than Charlie's, which gave him something else to chide Charlie about. He was also a good baseball player.

He would say to Charlie after their high school careers, "I don't understand how you get all this recognition. I can out punt you." He would then tell what each of their punting averages were, and his was always higher than Charlie's.

"Well, Seat, let me ask you something," Charlie would retort. "When you punted into the end zone, did they take twenty yards off your punt when they brought the ball back to the twenty?"

"Oh, no," Neil would answer.

"Well, there's the difference right there," Charlie would gouge him back. "They took the twenty off of my punts."

Beginning with those sandlot games in Grove Park and running through college and the pros, Charlie received level-headed guidance from his brothers. For many athletes, a little conceit or swell-headedness would have been natural, but Charlie's brothers saw to it that he kept both feet firmly on the ground. Charlie saw his brothers get a measure of fame before his day, and saw that it didn't alter their personalities. Thus, when his time came, his brothers' attitude toward stardom served as a model of steadying influence for him.

Actually, their influence served Charlie in another, perhaps more important way. His brothers kept kidding him, telling him that he should watch them closely and enjoy what he saw because he was too puny to play football or basketball himself. Their needling only spurred him on with an I'll-show-you determination that he carried to the end of his playing days.

Joe was a fine all-around athlete, and he loved to rib Charlie. He would stand before a mirror combing his hair just so and Charlie would stand admiring him. Joe would turn and say, "Kid, you ought to be proud to be my brother and live in the same house with me."

"You just wait!" Charlie would come back, his determination deepening a little more. He never approached football with anything but the most serious attitude, and never made a mistake on the field that he didn't try to correct the next time.

Charlie's confidence was bolstered over the years by his brother Seat.

"I was the shyest and most timid person who ever came down the pike," Charlie confessed. "I had to have somebody with me, and Seat was the one who was always there. I was really backward for years, and Mom gave me hell about it. I sucked my thumb and rolled up my hair with the other hand, and pulled it. In the sixth grade, I got my face slapped for pulling hair. I was in class, sucking my thumb, and reached up to twirl my hair, but it had been cut short and I couldn't get hold of it, so I reached and twirled the hair of the girl in front of me, and she slapped the fool out of me.

"I was afraid of people," he said, "and even after I started playing football I couldn't understand why I was given so much publicity when it was the team that was winning games. It really never occurred to me that I was doing anything special. I enjoyed doing it, don't get me wrong, but I was only doing the best I could do."

Two teachers helped Charlie with his confidence. At the age of ten, in the third grade at Biltmore School, he learned he could play football well. His teacher, Mrs. Buckner, recognized his ability and maneuvered him into playing situations. She encouraged him to play baseball, and soon he could outplay all others on the team. His athletic ability came naturally, and Mrs. Buckner recognized that. So did Mrs. Hoffman, his seventh grade teacher, a sister of Mrs. Buckner. She encouraged Charlie to play and develop the talent he had, which by that time was consider-able.

"Mrs. Hoffman could throw a baseball harder than most boys," Charlie said, "and she pitched to us. I could hit her better than anyone else.

"No one will ever know how much confidence I gained when those two sisters encouraged me."

In basketball, owing to his small size, he played as a guard. The problem that defeated him in basketball was that he seldom differentiated between basketball and football. "I'd rough it up," he explained, "and I got the hell beat out of me a couple of times. I'd rough up some bigger guy and when he told me to stop I would bristle and keep it up until he manhandled me. I suppose deep down inside, I wanted to play football so badly that I carried those skills over to other games — blocking, tackling, bumping, piling on."

Charlie played baseball wherever he went to school. His natural skills lay at second base, but when he got to Asheville High and made the team in the spring of 1941, the Maroons already had a second baseman and Charlie was put on third, the hot corner.

"That corner was so hot it sizzled," he laughed later. "I booted nine balls in one game. Those hard grounders came down the line, bouncing every which way, and when I missed them I thought Coach Sadler would take me out, but I guess he didn't have anybody else who wanted to get in front of artillery like that, so I kept playing."

One reason Coach Bill Sadler, who also assisted the football coach, kept Justice playing was the way he swung the bat. In his first at-bat he arched a home run over the outfielders' heads, batting eighth in the lineup, and be-fore the season ended he was hitting third and rifling base hits all over the outfield and beyond.

That one season ended his high school career in baseball; the school dropped the sport for the duration of World War II.

Charlie also calmed down enough to play high school basketball that winter, and became a three-letterman.

Baseball and basketball were only side attractions and Charlie knew it. He was never that serious about either, although he gave a hundred percent on the court or the diamond. He knew deep down that his sport was football.

When Jack transferred the family to Asheville High, his ploy worked. Each boy in turn received the recognition he needed to attract college scouts, and each one in turn received a free education for playing sports.

The first mention of Charlie's name in *The Asheville Citizen* was on Sep-tember 16, 1939, after Asheville High had beaten Greeneville, Tennessee, 13-6, in the season-opening football game in Asheville's Memorial Stadium, a football field with only a few hundred seats. It was located on the hill above the baseball park, McCormick Field. The game story did not mention Charlie, but the name of Justice appeared in the small six-point type game summary. Little did anyone at that time realize how large that type would grow by the time Charlie finally got to college.

When he played that game, Charlie was only an eighth-grade student, not yet in high school. His school was David Millard Junior High on Oak Street near the city's domed First Baptist Church. Hardly able to wait to play football until the next year, his first in high school, the fifteen-year-old Justice had asked permission of David Millard principal Dutch Leonard to try to make the high school team. Leonard, knowing the Justice family's reputation on the football field, said, "Go ahead," and gleefully Charlie headed for the high school daily to practice following his last class at junior high.

He walked and hitch-hiked the mile to Asheville High to practice with Coach Lee Stone's team, and his skills were good enough to make the team – or perhaps Coach Stone put him on the team because of the Justice predominance of Asheville High football.

At any rate, Charlie played as a substitute in the Greeneville game and apparently played his position well, though not spectacularly enough to merit mention in the game story.

For that year, Charlie's high school season ended there. On Monday when he came to school, Leonard called him to his office and unceremoniously said, "Charlie, you can't practice and play with the high school any more."

"Why not, sir?" Charlie asked politely, though inside he was crestfallen.

"Because we're going to have a team over here starting today," Leonard said, "and you're going to play for us. It will be good for you because you'll get a lot more playing time and learn more football this way."

"Yes, sir," Charlie agreed. The idea pleased him.

Leonard drove Charlie to Lee Edwards High that afternoon and up in the attic where old, discarded football gear was stored, they dug out enough to equip a team with some semblance of uniformity. A man named Sandy Graham, who knew little about football, was chosen to coach the team.

At the first practice session, Graham chose eleven boys almost at random, including Charlie, and told Charlie to take them to the far end of the field and give them four plays. Those were the only plays the team ran when it made its debut a week or so later at Sylva High School in Jackson County. With plenty of mountain-grown beef on its side, Sylva easily defeated David Millard, 37-0, and the team was rather discouraged when it regathered for practice the following Monday.

However, coming back into its own class, David Millard began to win. The team defeated all the junior high teams it played, including two from Charlotte, and beat the varsity of Blue Ridge School for Boys in Henderson County. In a game against Charlotte Piedmont Junior High, Charlie intercepted a pass on Asheville's one-yard line and returned it 99 yards for a touchdown, giving Asheville its first real hint of things to come.

After Justice and most of his teammates went on to high school the next year, junior high football in Asheville fell victim to the war effort. It wasn't until 1947 that it returned when a team was organized jointly between Asheville's two junior highs, David Millard and Hall Fletcher, called the Millard-Fletcher Mighty Mites. For three or four years this team slaughtered the bulk of its opposition, including various high school teams. The man who built this team and coached it was Max Spurlin, who played at the University of North Carolina with Justice in 1946.

Charlie began to lose his puniness one high school summer when he got a job. He and Seat went to work for a teacher named Alder who operated a small dairy farm. "Seat got to ride the truck, making milk deliveries, and while he was driven around the countryside, looking for sales, Charlie shoveled out the cow stalls."

The experience was helpful to Charlie. It led him to getting a job at the sprawling Biltmore Dairy on George Vanderbilt's estate. The dairy had a softball team playing in the Asheville City League and hired young men in the summertime who could play softball. Jack and Joe got jobs there and played softball, and later Bill did the same. When Charlie got a job there, it was not one of playing softball but doing general chores around the dairy.

He had to carry loads of popsicles into the hardening room, and would always come back out eating a popsicle.

His appetite picked up and he exercised greatly, and he ate so much ice cream that one man commented, "Justice, you're gonna eat us out of house and home. You can eat more than we can make!"

At the end of that summer he had gained twenty pounds and weighed 145 rather than the 125 at which he started the summer.

Charlie—punting in high school.

HIGH SCHOOL JUGGERNAUT

Never before and never since have the Carolinas seen a high school football team like the 1942 Asheville High* Maroons. This team easily rolled over nine regular season opponents, scoring 441 points to 6 for the opposition. Their closest game was a 22-0 victory over Kingsport, Tennessee, which fielded powerhouse teams in that era. Such was this team's might that it played only four North Carolina opponents, and one of those was a junior college. The Maroons played two teams from South Carolina, two from Tennessee, and one from Georgia. Few high schools in the South got the opportunity to play against the competition that Asheville did. Most great teams have a spearhead, and on this team it was a slightly-built young man named Charlie Justice, who ran through opposition as if it were smoke and compiled records that may never be touched by any other Tar Heel high school runner.

Any reader not familiar with that team and that running back will be astonished at the state records Justice still holds from the era that ended more than fifty years ago. Running from the tailback position in the single-wing offense, Justice averaged 265 yards for each of the nine games, a record that has never been approached. The feat becomes even more phenomenal when you consider that Justice played only half of each game. He split his time at tailback with a speedster named Billy Britt who was so fast he was

---

*In 1935, Asheville High was renamed Lee Edwards High School after its late principal. However, the school's sports program continued as Asheville High in all sports so it wouldn't have to change its logo. The Asheville newspapers, *The Citizen* and *The Times,* continued this policy in the sports departments until after World War II, even though the news department used Lee Edwards.

often just a blur going by, and by playing Britt half of each game, Coach Ralph James proved to the South, and indeed to the nation, that he had more than one man who could run a football.

Charlie's records form an incredible chapter in the annals of North Carolina schoolboy football. Like Cy Young's 511 pitching victories in major league baseball, some of Charlie's high school records will never be broken.

In the nine games, Justice ran from scrimmage 128 times, only 14.2 times per game, but he totaled 2,385 yards for the season. Every time he carried, he gained an unbelievable 18.63 yards, a record that defies all efforts to surpass it.

His most amazing records, however, are those he set scoring touchdowns. He no longer holds the record for most touchdowns scored in a season, but he crossed the goal 49 times in his three-year high school career and averaged a record 28.63 yards on his touchdown runs for those three seasons.

The 1942 season produced an even more incredible record. Justice scored 27 touchdowns and averaged 41.37 yards on the 27 runs. These included some long yardage runs on kickoff and punt returns – but he had to run through the defense on those, too, the same as on runs from scrimmage. Justice punted 19 times that season for an average of 42.74 yards, so his punts on the average measured only one yard and thirteen inches more than his touchdown runs!

Britt, who also played only half the time, scored 18 times, giving the tailback position a total of 43 touchdowns, almost five for each game.

One thing that helped the Maroons build those teams was the relaxed rules of the day. Players were not restricted to playing in their home high schools, so if a really promising player began at Swain High School in Bryson City, 70 miles west of Asheville, he could eventually find his way to Asheville High. Asheville had players in 1941 and '42 who lived in the nearby towns of Bryson City, Weaverville, Candler, Canton, Black Mountain, Swannanoa, Biltmore, and other locations. Until the days of busing and consolidation of high schools, most were too small to have football teams.

A big, bruising fullback, Glenn Painter, played four years for Sylva High School and then played the 1940 season for Asheville High. After playing four years in the army and four years at High Point College, Painter said the best "scholarship" he ever had was to Asheville High. "They put me up in a nice home," Painter said. "You can't imagine how nice that home was and how much we had to eat."

"Nobody paid much attention to age then," Charlie remembered. "As long as the fellows showed up without long beards and wrinkles around their necks they got to play." A team that didn't recruit as Asheville did was soon left behind in the tremendous competition among upper echelon football high schools in the South.

Scheduling was also relaxed in those days. Teams could arrange their schedules any way they wanted and add games at midseason in open dates. Asheville always played an Armistice Day game on November 11, and in 1941 that created a schedule that included three games in eight days, all of which the Maroons took in stride and won easily.

Preceding the 1942 team, which many veteran football coaches called the best high school team they had ever seen, Asheville was also unbeaten in 1941. That year, in eleven games, the Maroons scored 348 points to 32 for the competition.

In regular-season play, team totals for that 1940-'42 team showed a 21-0 record from the final game of 1940 (a 28-0 win over Children's Home), and 811 points scored against 38 opposing points.

Dick Kaplan, a long-time writer for *The Asheville Citizen* who saw every high school game Justice played, looked back over the Justice years and wrote of the 1942 team in an October 1961 story: "This was predominantly a great first team and in the minds of many of the game's cognoscenti — including famed college coaches, officials, and sportswriters fortunate enough to see it — was probably the finest starting eleven ever seen in high school anywhere. ..."

Primarily that starting line, which was big and fast and hard-hitting, included Carl Perkinson at center, Ed Williams and Don McCurry at guards, Bill (Footsie) Williams and Phil Bennett at tackles, and Carl Tipton and Richard Knapp at ends. "Most of them went to High Point College," Justice said, "because that's where Coach James was coaching after the war. Tipton could run like a deer. Perkinson went on to Duke because his daddy was a Duke man." In that high school backfield were Justice at tailback, Jim Pinkerton at fullback, Forrest Maney at wingback, and Captain Norman Harris at blocking back. "Pinkerton had never played football before," Charlie said. "He was a natural who went on to play for South Carolina after the war."

Britt backed Justice. When he was sent in to replace Charlie it was like a pitcher switching from a curve to a fastball. They were different type runners, but each was effective in his own way. In some games, Britt carried the ball more than Justice.

Biggest man on the team was Phil Bennett, who was called "Fat" by his teammates and is remembered by them as having weighed somewhere between 240 and 270. He was a brutish tackle. "He looked fat," Justice said, "but he was quick and he could run. He was so tough that he won the heavyweight boxing championship of Western North Carolina."

The only disappointments for that team were two defeats in two bowl games, an exaggerated 44-0 loss to Boys High of Atlanta in the January 1, 1942, Milk Bowl in Atlanta, and a 13-7 defeat by Miami High on December 12, 1942, in the High School Orange Bowl in Miami.

That era from the early 1930s through the early years of World War II probably was the best ever for Southern high school football. Interstate rivalries were keen, and certain schools in every state played on a plane above most of the others. Asheville High was one of those on the elevated plane with Charlotte Central, Greensboro, Knoxville, Chattanooga, Columbia, Miami, Atlanta Boys High....

Lee Stone was the Asheville coach when Charlie Justice started to high school as a ninth grade student in the fall of 1940. He looked forward to his three seasons* with the Maroons. Justice had played the opening game for Asheville High in 1939, and then played the remainder of the season for David Millard Junior High. However, he was permitted to take spring football practice with the high school in April of 1940, two months before finishing at the junior high.

He opened the 1940 season as second string tailback, playing behind Joe Sawyer, a transfer from Weaverville High School whom everyone called "Cip." In Asheville's opening game against Lenoir, Coach Stone put Justice and the second team in at the start of the fourth quarter, and Charlie showed his heels to Lenoir on "two of the prettiest runs of the evening for two touchdowns," wrote Paul Jones, sports editor of *The Asheville Citizen*.

> When the final quarter started, in came Justice, with several other second team players, and within two minutes he had brought the crowd of 1,500 to its feet with a sparkling 64-yard touchdown return of a Lenoir kick. He picked up the booted ball, looked over the field, and lit out up the middle. After going about 15 yards he cut for the sidelines and was going away when he crossed the goal line. Later, Justice faked a pass and sprinted around left end for a 10-yard touchdown. He copped the spotlight with his fine dashes. ... He was the best back on the field Friday night.

Charlie, who weighed between 145 and 155 through high school, was in and out of every game that season. He caught a pass and sprinted for a 30-yard touchdown against Gaffney (S.C.) High. After Greenville (S.C.) High beat the Maroons, 14-0, in the seventh game of 1940, Jones was prompted to write: "Had Coach Lee Stone a back of (Greenville's) Monty Byers' caliber the Asheville high combination probably wouldn't be beaten by any of the teams on this year's schedule." Little did Jones know what fortunes lay within

---

* High school in North Carolina only went through eleven grades until 1946 when there was no graduating class, making the Class of 1947 the first twelve-grade class.

Asheville's grasp in the 145-pound package of dynamite sitting on the Maroons' bench! Charlie Justice played so well the next two years that he was named to the mythical All-Southern high school team after both seasons.

Stone vacated the coaching job after that 1940 season and went into military service. He was succeeded by Ralph James, a former All-State player in football and basketball both at Columbia (S.C.) High and Asheville High during the 1920s. He was the only player to ever make All-State in both sports in two states.

James did not teach at the high school but was an employee of the City of Asheville as manager of the City Auditorium. His transfer to Asheville High as football coach probably was the first time Charlie Justice influenced a major decision.

J. Weldon Weir was Director of Public Works in the Asheville city government. He and Ralph James had been football teammates both at Asheville High in the early twenties and at Wake Forest College in the middle twenties. Recognizing Justice's potential greatness and thinking two years ahead, the two worked it out for James, an excellent tactician who had coached at Western Carolina Teachers College, to replace Stone and influence Justice to play his college football at Wake Forest, barring, of course, America's entry in the shooting war which had begun more than a year before in Europe.

Regardless, by that stroke of political fortune, James succeeded Stone for the 1941 season, and proved to be the perfect man for the job. He knew how to get the most out of his players, and, realizing the tremendous potential of Asheville High's physical material – especially its starting eleven -- he did not over-coach but instituted a simple version of the single-wing that would not interfere with anyone's thinking process on the field. He figured if his players blocked, tackled, ran, and passed to the best of their abilities, it would make no difference what plays they ran. He knew his most effective play would be a simple give-Charlie-the-ball-and-turn-him-loose.

James knew the Maroons' personnel well, having been referee in five of their 1940 games and umpire in another. The same names – Ralph James, Hal Weir, Nemo Coleman, Jack Alexander, and Bob Swicegood – appeared as officials in most of Asheville's home games in 1940.

"Every team had its own game officials," Justice laughed, "and there was a lot of home-cooking around. Sometimes you had to play against eleven men and four officials, so you had to have an extremely good team to win on the road.

"We ran the single-wing right," Justice said, "and sometimes when we got to the right side of the field, we would have to run a reverse to get the ball back to the left side. We had the basic plays: spinners, slants, sweeps, reverses, double reverses, the usual line bucks, the regular punt, and the quick kick, which was sometimes our best weapon. Coach never overwhelmed us by giving us an extensive playbook to memorize. Heck, he didn't have to. About all he had to do was throw the ball on the field and get out of the way while we went for it. We knew what we were doing, and we had the timing down, and the power and finesse to execute."

Charlie added: "Coach James knew how to inspire us. He gave us a special lift and a great desire to win."

James was an average-sized man, perhaps 5-feet-10 and 160 pounds. His face had a sly, foxy appearance, and his eyes reflected deep intelligence. He combed his thinning hair straight back, and as most coaches did in those days, always wore a hat. Before pre-season practice was a week old that fall, the team bore the James touch. Without giving away his secret to any of the players, James, a shrewd tactician, emphasized blocking and tackling, and combined power, speed, and deception in his offense. He had no problem doing that because the team was big and burly, fast, intelligent, and hard-hitting.

Before the 1941 season began, James wore a constant smile and his gray-blue eyes, crow-footed from exposure to direct sunlight, twinkled with delight. In a pre-season game, the Maroons slapped a 12-2 defeat on Mars Hill College, and a week later opened the season at Children's Home in Winston-Salem. In his first game as a junior, Justice scored two touchdowns on five-yard runs and Jordan Maynard plunged two yards for a third, and the Maroons left with a 21-7 victory. *The Asheville Citizen* reported next morning that "Asheville played a swell game from start to finish and Coach Ralph James appeared more than pleased with the performance."

A week later the Maroons opened their home season with a 21-0 victory over Kingsport, Tennessee, at McCormick Field. Forest Maney, Joe Penland, and Justice scored the touchdowns, and *The Citizen* saw fit to describe Justice's 61-yard punt return the next morning:

> Kingsport's Hagan Bright kicked from his own 20 and Justice grabbed the ball on the run just before he reached Asheville's 40. Going north, he cut to the west sideline where a half-dozen mates picked him up to form excellent interference. However, after sprinting well into Kingsport territory he was blocked, so he cut straight across the field, shaking off at least three tacklers, and then cutting towards the goal line again near the east sideline, he went over standing up. ...

Justice's mates cut down Indian after Indian with precision blocking.

Wingback Forrest Maney blocked out one man soon after Justice started his run, and while Charlie was cutting across the field Maney picked him up on the other side and promptly eliminated the last of Kingsport's defenders.

Paul Jones, the sports editor, wrote in his Sunday column, "In Charlie Justice, the Maroons have a grade A back, and in Bill Britt they have a relief man for Justice who can step with the best of them. ... The odds of going undefeated may be too big, but the games they might lose certainly won't be by wide margins."

After that game, the Maroons took on four consecutive South Carolina opponents and polished them off one by one: Gaffney, 38-0; Columbia, 25-0; Sumter, 54-0; and Greenville, 19-6. Justice scored three touchdowns and passed for another against Gaffney; and Britt highlighted the Columbia game with a 66-yard touchdown run off tackle. He shot through the left side of the line and was in the secondary before the Caps had a chance to locate the ball. Outrunning a trio of Columbia defenders Britt scored without a hand being laid on him. Against Sumter, Justice scored five times on runs of 41, 7, 43, 16, and 45 yards, and Britt scored twice on 41- and 60-yard runs.

Early in the Greenville game, the Maroons found themselves behind a 6-0 score, the first time they had trailed anyone in that 1941 season. But the Maroons pulled their act together and put three touchdowns across to win handily. Proving that old-fashioned football was still in vogue, Bailey drop-kicked the only extra point the Maroons made.

Then the Maroons played three games in eight days, sandwiching a November 11 Armistice Day game between two regular games. They polished off Riverside (Ga.) Military Academy, 20-6; Biltmore High School, 39-6; and Andrews, 39-0.

The last two games, then, were waltzes, 19-0 over Charlotte Central, and 53-7 over Blue Ridge School for Boys. Justice scored twice in the Blue Ridge season-closer and ran his point total to 114, highest in the state. Soon after that game, he was named to the mythical All-Southern team. Thus an eleven-game 1941 season ended 11-0.

The 1942 team was more mature, tougher, faster, harder-hitting, more skilled, and certainly more relentless that the 1941 Maroons.

After Asheville whipped Greenville, South Carolina, 55-0, Scoop Latimer wrote in *The Greenville News:*

> The biggest and best high school team this corner has seen is the Asheville Maroons, who should apply for membership in the Southeastern college conference, where they might find competition. Clad in scarlet jerseys, the Tar Heel hefties looked like a forest fire burn-

ing their way around and over the lighter Greenville Raiders. In size, power, and capabilities the Asheville team would be superior to many college outfits.

Two weeks later, the Maroons slaughtered the Brevard College football team, 67-0.

In those days of the pre-war era, leading up to the first year of World War II, folks took football seriously. Because Asheville was the biggest, strongest, and most widely known team in the Western North Carolina mountains, it attracted the largest following. So did certain other teams in their areas, like Kingsport and Knoxville, Charlotte Central and Greensboro, Boys High of Atlanta, and three or four teams in South Carolina.

On the twenty-fifth of September, 1942, Asheville played at Kingsport and the East Tennessee fans demonstrated in a foul way just how serious they were about their football team. Both teams were undefeated going into the game. Asheville had already clobbered Tech High of Atlanta, 34-0, in the 1942 opener. Thus, the Kingsport game was billed as a "Battle of Unbeaten Teams," though that title was a little strong, considering the fact that each team had played only one game.

Asheville took command of the game immediately and with Justice at the controls, rolled to a 22-0 victory. Justice scored once on a six-yard sweep, passed 25 yards to glue-fingered Carl Tipton for another, and fooled the Kingsport defense by handing off to wingback Forrest Maney on a razzle-dazzle reverse for a 13-yard score. Then the Maroons tackled a Kingsport runner behind the goal line for a two-point safety.

As the game wound down, Kingsport tempers rose. Among such rabid fans there are always some who believe their team is incapable of losing and blames the other side for winning. That attitude surged to the surface late in the game when, on an end sweep, Justice was knocked out of bounds at the yard markers. He looked up and grinned at the young man carrying the downs marker, and the youth, who had played for Kingsport the year before, balled his fist and hit Justice in the mouth, splitting his lip.

On the sideline, trying to stop the flow of blood, Justice warned Coach James: "Coach, you better get ready. We're gonna have a darned free-for-all when this thing's over with."

"Nah," James replied, and redirected his attention to the field for the final series of downs.

"Well, don't put me back in," Justice said. "I'm not going back in this game."

Working themselves into the frenzy of a mob, the Kingsport faithful followed the Asheville team to its dressing room, taunting and threatening, and milled outside for hours, waiting for the Maroons to emerge. Asheville stayed in the dressing room until 3 a.m. when Tennessee police decided the team had been punished enough for winning, rescued the Maroons, and escorted players and coaches through Johnson City, Erwin, and Flag Pond to the state line at the top of the mountain. Carloads of Kingsport people followed the cavalcade, but turned back with the police at the state line.

Such were the fortunes of football in some of the games the Maroons played. By and large, though, opposing crowds stood in awe, not anger, watching the Maroons click off yardage and touchdowns with precision plays.

The week after the Kingsport game, the Maroons played at Columbia, South Carolina, and the stands were packed with newly-enlisted G.I.s from Camp Jackson. Some were taking basic training and others were awaiting assignment.

In a 47-6 demolishing of Columbia High, the big story probably should have been the touchdown scored by the Capitols – the only points allowed by Asheville that season. The Columbia touchdown came after Justice fumbled on the Caps' 17. A penalty against the Maroons put the ball on the 12, and a bruiser named Jackson hit the line twice, the second time bursting into the end zone. Afterward, Asheville so completely dominated the game that Columbia did not threaten again.

The Maroons blocked like scythes, and Justice ripped off two long touchdown runs, 70 yards on a punt return and 80 yards on a sprint from scrimmage. He also scored on a six-yard sweep, and actually had a hand in all seven Asheville touchdowns. *The Columbia State* reported next morning that "Asheville's blocking on Justice's two long runs was the prettiest any ball carrier ever received." Coach James called Charlie's performance "his greatest."

On a fake reverse with Justice carrying, he so skillfully faked and hid the ball under his arm that after he crossed the line of scrimmage and slipped and fell on a cutback, tucking the ball beneath him, the Caps defense was still concentrating across the field on Forrest Maney, the wingback who faked receiving the reverse, and finally Maney threw up his empty hands and laughed. "See," he shouted, "I don't have it!"

On the punt return, Charlie went up the right side to about the 50, cut to the left sideline for another 20 yards, and then back to the middle of the field and straight into the end zone. The soldiers went crazy. Taken out to rest, Charlie heard a chant start from the army crowd and swell in volume – "We want twenty-two! We want twenty-two!" -- and when Coach James relented and sent Charlie onto the field again, as if in appreciation he ripped off the 80-yard run from scrimmage.

Justice's performance was so brilliant that a wall of soldiers stormed the field at the end of the game, hoisted Charlie to their shoulders, and paraded around the field, then out the stadium gate to the adjacent capitol building,

The starting eleven for Asheville High's undefeated, once-scored-on football team of 1942 included left to right: line—Richard Knapp, Phil Bennett, Bud Williams,

Carl Perkinson, Don "Duck" McCurry, Footsie Williams, and Carl Tipton; backs—
Forrest Maney, Team Captain Norman Harris, Jim Pinkerton, and Charlie Justice.

marching around it. Frightened at this attention from strangers, Charlie was crying, "Let me down! Let me down!" but the celebrating G.I.s carried him back to the field and turned him loose, shaking his hand and thanking him for the great show he had put on. They gave him a resounding cheer, did an about-face, and went back to their barracks.

Asheville added a game to its schedule after the 1942 season was underway. Hickory High had won its first five games and decided it would like to try the unbeaten Maroons. Both teams had an open date on October 16, and the Hickory coach, Ed Scarborough, who had been a teammate of Coach James at Wake Forest years before, asked James for the match-up and James agreed to play the game in Asheville's McCormick Field. James had trouble filling Asheville's schedule because of the strength of his team. Few teams wanted to play the Maroons. James gave his consent to play because the Maroons had had an open date the weekend before and James didn't want two open dates in a row with tough Charlotte Central coming up the following week.

So methodically did the Maroons demolish Hickory that evening, winning 94-0, that the Hickory coach intimated after the game that he was pulling for Asheville to score a hundred points. "Shucks, I'd never seen anybody score a hundred," he said. "I thought it would have been good to see that just for the record."

Asheville's tailbacks, Justice and Britt, dubbed the "Touchdown Twins," lived up to that billing, making nine of the fourteen touchdowns. Britt had his best night, scoring five times on runs of 37, 46, 3, 57, and 76 yards. Justice scored four touchdowns on runs of 21, 85, 22, and 92 yards. Britt carried the ball eleven times for 281 yards, an average of 25 per carry; and Justice ran from scrimmage only five times for 165 yards, an average of 33. Three of the five times Justice carried, he scored touchdowns. His fourth score came when he returned the second-half kickoff 85 yards to the end zone.

James played every man on his squad of twenty-seven, giving the reserves most of the playing time, and the Maroons ran only 28 ground plays. Eleven went for touchdowns. Asheville rang up 565 yards rushing and 60 passing. The Maroons did not have to punt and were not once held for downs.

The Asheville Citizen reported that "the Hickory boys were fine sports and took the shellacking in stride. They said after the game that they had learned something."

The score was a record number ever scored by a Maroons team, but one previous Asheville eleven had had more scored against it.

In his Sunday column following the Hickory game, sports editor Paul Jones wrote in the *Citizen-Times:*

Thinking of the 94-0 victory over Hickory, someone re-called the 117-0 pasting the 1914 Asheville High team suffered in the state championship game with Raleigh. Gene Coston (later an Asheville real estate man), a half-back in '14, remembered most of the horrible details of the alleged contest played in Chapel Hill.

Asheville had defeated Huntersville, 6-0, at Davidson to reach the finals.

"George Mears, our right end, scored the game's only touchdown on a pass," Coston said. "However, Roy Jordan, our captain and quarterback, suffered a broken neck just before the game ended and we didn't have him at Chapel Hill. In those days we only had a couple of substitutes — and no coach. (The team captain did the coaching.) When Roy was hurt it forced a complete shifting of players.

"As I remember, we had to pick up a couple of high school boys who had never played football, but they played at Chapel Hill."

The remainder of the 1942 season was merely a clicking off of victories. Charlotte Central fell 35-0, Greenville's Red Raiders 55-0, Knoxville 27-0, Brevard College 67-0, and Children's Home of Winston-Salem 60-0.

Not only did Charlie run, pass, punt, return punts and kickoffs, and play defense, he also called signals.

"Actually," he said, "Coach James called many plays from the sideline. We worked out a communictions system in which he would signal plays by taking off his hat or keeping it on, crossing his legs one way or another, crossing his arms , or by the way he turned his body when I looked at him."

Not only did Justice play well, the whole Asheville team was spectacular that year. Blocking and tackling worked to perfection, and every man took pride in his blocks to pave the way for Justice and Britt. Other ball carriers gained yardage by the gallop, and more often than not it was difficult for the defense to follow the ball, so skillful were the Asheville backs at sleight-of-hand.

This was a team of heroes, not just Justice (though he was the greater part of the offense), but Tipton, Pinkerton, Maney, Britt – all scored time and time again in an offense that was all but unstoppable.

The Maroons were also a great defensive team, proven by the fact that only six points were scored against them, and that touchdown was set up by a recovered fumble, which was hardly the fault of the defense. Normally, the enemy would score a few points accidentally, but the Asheville team was not prone to accident. Asheville's defense held opponents to minimum yardage, sometimes minus yardage, while rolling up huge hunks of turf themselves.

In a nutshell, here is a summary of that 1942 season, which was the making of an All-Service and All-American star:

TECH HIGH, ATLANTA, 34-0 – Justice scored three times, once on a 74-yard punt return. Britt returned a kickoff 57 yards for a touchdown and went 64 yards off tackle for another.

KINGSPORT, 22-0 – Justice accounted for 157 of team's 291 yards rushing. Tipton took a 25-yard Justice pass for a touchdown and scored another on an end around. Forrest Maney scored the last touchdown on a 13-yard reverse.

COLUMBIA, 47-6 – Justice's three touchdowns were complemented by two Maney scores, and one each by Britt and Pinkerton.

HICKORY, 94-0 – Five touchdowns by Britt, four by Justice, two by Tipton, and one each by Pinkerton, Karambelas, and Harris.

CHARLOTTE CENTRAL, 35-0 – Maroons gained 302 yards and held Charlotte to 37. Included in Justice's 183 yards were three touchdowns. Tipton scored two more and Maney one. (After this game, Paul Jones finally called Asheville High a "juggernaut" in the newspaper.)

GREENVILLE, 55-0 – With 8,000 spectators looking on, Justice went 64 yards off tackle for a touchdown on the first scrimmage play, but Pinkerton, the fullback, stole the show with four touchdowns, one on an 80-yard run with a pass interception, and the others on short, powerful bursts through the line.

KNOXVILLE, 27-0 – Justice ran 99 2/3 yards from scrimmage for a touchdown, and added two more on runs of 33 and four yards. Maney passed 32 yards to Tipton for a score.

BREVARD COLLEGE, 67-0 – Justice and Britt scored four touchdowns each, and Maney and Eckel Bradley scored the other two. Asheville rushed for 396 yards and passed for 42 more.

CHILDREN'S HOME, 60-0 – Asheville gained 556 yards through a helpless defense. Justice scored five times and had two other touchdowns called back. Tipton caught three touchdown passes. Pinkerton set up a score with a 68-yard run, and Maney scored on a 75-yard dash. The Maroons showed a pesky persistence after an 85-yard Justice touchdown run was called back by Referee Charlie Munday who ruled that Justice's knee had touched the ground at the 30. Two plays later Justice went 70 yards for a touchdown, and this one was called back because of a clip. Then, with the ball on the 23, Maney hit Tipton for a 77-yard touchdown that counted.

Herman Hickman, then line coach at North Carolina State and eventually head coach at Yale, saw that game. "I must admit that I had to see them play," he said, "before I could believe all the things I had heard about them. I was amazed in more ways than one. I had wondered how Justice could have made such a record gain on his touchdown runs alone, but after seeing him go against Children's Home, it no longer is a mystery.

"It's too bad," the 300-pound Hickman added, "that such a team had to come along at a time when we're at war and the boys cannot take full advantage of their great team and of their chances to capitalize on their record. I may have seen at some time or other a better high school team than Asheville, but I can't remember one. And if I ever saw a better all-around high school back than Justice I don't remember him."

Possibly Charlie Justice's greatest run in high school came against Knoxville at McCormick Field. With the Maroons backed up to their own one-foot line, Justice raced an amazing 99 2/3 yards before a capacity crowd that included J. B. (Jock) Sutherland, erstwhile head coach of the Pittsburgh Panthers and professional Brooklyn Dodgers.

Tennessee's No. 1 ranking high school team, Knoxville, came to Asheville undefeated. "They thought they were going to wear our tails out," Justice said later. "The first time they had the ball they drove to our one-yard line, gaining a good bit of yardage over Dick Knapp, one of our ends. Fat Bennett, our huge tackle, could almost stop a freight train, and when Knoxville came within a yard of the goal, Bennett quietly swapped positions with Knapp — and the fourth-down play came straight toward him. He stopped the Knoxville runner dead in his tracks on the one-foot line and we took over."

In the huddle, Justice said, "We've got to punt out of here. Let's kick it back upfield and get some room."

The others looked at him with shock on their faces!

"Hell, no, don't punt," said Norman Harris, the team captain and blocking back, who called signals. "Take it and run, Charlie; we'll clear out for you."

The Maroons went into punt formation, and Justice ran a fake punt the length of the field to score. Right field at McCormick Field then had a slight incline, and Charlie came charging down the hill to the amazement of the Knoxvilleans, burst through the entire team, and fled goalward.

About thirty yards out he came upon the Knoxville safety, faked him to the left and went by him on the right for the touchdown.

The Asheville Citizen reported next morning:

> The lengthy jaunt, which definitely eliminated Knoxville's chances of overtaking the undefeated Maroons, was the longest scoring run from scrimmage ever made on the field and was a great one in every respect, yet it could not match the show of expert broken field running Justice delivered in the final quarter when he slashed off tackle and ran 33 yards to score.

Maney passed 32 yards to Tipton for a touchdown. Justice scored again from the four, and in the fourth quarter went 33 yards off tackle for a touchdown on a run that found Justice shaking off one tackler after another. Twice he appeared hemmed in, but on each occasion he squirmed his way through. Adept in picking up blocking, he did this in A-1 style and dashed over the goal line while a big crowd roared in approval of a truly great run.

Justice carried 14 times for 244 yards in Asheville's 18th straight victory (Actually, it was the 19th, counting the last game of 1940).

Knoxville coach Bill Cox met Coach James on the field after the game and said, "You've got the best ball club I ever saw."

Sutherland (very reserved), a lieutenant-commander in the navy in command of the rest and recreation center for naval officers at Grove Park Inn, congratulated Coach James after the tilt. He gave James a verbal pat on the back by saying that the Maroons were well drilled and that the best team won. He said, too, that he believed the difference between the teams was Justice.

Burt Frel, manager of Grove Park Inn, who was coach at Asheville High from 1921 to 1924 when James quarterbacked the Asheville eleven, was an interested spectator that evening. He thought the Asheville team was excellent, better than any other team he had seen.

Charlie Justice recently said that he regretted never having won a bowl game and never having scored in one. He played in five bowls, two with Asheville High and three with the University of North Carolina Tar Heels.

Actually, he played in eight, and he did win three — the 1942 Shrine Bowl in Charlotte, which matches senior football players from North Carolina high schools against those from South Carolina, the first annual Senior Bowl of 1950, and the 1950 College All-Star Game in Chicago's Soldiers' Field.

At the end of his senior season at Asheville High, Justice and Carl Tipton and halfback Stan Henry of Waynesville were named to represent the western part of the state in the Shrine Bowl and Ralph James was to be its coach. Player selections were limited to two from a school.

Charlie wasn't the first Justice to play in the Shrine Bowl. His brother Bill beat him to that honor.

The Shrine Bowl team of 1938, for which Bill Justice scored three touchdowns, had featured a lineup studded with Asheville High players. Six Maroons were chosen on the North Carolina team: Herb Coman, Bobo Carter, Fred Lytle, Tom Jones, Gene McCrary, and Bill Justice.

"They had five of us in the starting line, and I was the fullback," Bill said. "All but McCrary started the game, and when he came in there was a Maroon in every line position except center and guard."

Bill played fullback. He turned out to be a great utility man later at Rollins College, playing every position at one time or another. "We only had sixteen players," he explained, "and when somebody was out, I played his position."

North Carolina football in 1938 was tough from top to bottom. That was the year Duke went undefeated, untied, and unscored on in the regular season and lost to Southern Cal, 7-3, in the Rose Bowl. Two Asheville men, Dan Hill and Gordon Burns, played center on that great Blue Devil club. Hill made All-American, but Burns started in the Rose Bowl because Hill was injured.

When only two Maroons were chosen for the Shrine Bowl in 1942 Paul Jones was prompted to wonder in *The Citizen,* "We don't see why the Maroons as a whole aren't asked to represent the state in the Shrine game. It's certain that South Carolina's eleven won't be meeting a team made up of the best Tar Heel talent."

But the talent was good enough to demolish South Carolina, 33-0, in the December 5 game. Justice scored three touchdowns, tying his brother Bill's record of three in the 1938 Shrine Bowl. Charlie went off tackle from the one for a score, raced 25 yards with a pass interception for another, and scored from 24 yards on his famous fake reverse. In adition, newspapers reported that "he kicked and passed in All-American style."

Tipton scored a touchdown on an 11-yard pass from quarterback George Clark of Rocky Mount, who went to Duke and played against Justice for four years.

So dominating was the North Carolina team that South Carolina did not cross midfield once in the game. North Carolina had 281 total yards to South Carolina's 55.

In two high school bowl games with his team, however, Justice struck out.

On January 1, 1942, soon after he had been named to the All-Southern team in late 1941, Justice led the Maroons against Boys High of Atlanta in the Milk Bowl in Atlanta's Ponce de Leon Park where Georgia Tech played at the time.

The Maroons faced three overwhelming obstacles – driving rain, ankle-deep mud, and a Georgia runner named Clint Castleberry – and came away on the scoreless end of a 44-0 margin. Once fortune began to flow to Boys High, the game became a runaway.

It began innocently enough. The Maroons failed to move with the opening kickoff, and Justice punted to the Atlanta 35. Castleberry took the ball and returned it 41 yards to the Asheville 24. On the next play he outran Justice to the end zone to take a touchdown pass from Jenkins. Running from the single-wing, Castleberry scored again on a 38-yard reverse, and a third time on a 70-yard punt return.

"I kicked the ball to him," Justice said, "and he was so fast that by the time my feet got back on the ground he was already by me and headed for the goal."

Charlie laughed. "Castleberry was a character. He had battery-powered taillights on the seat of his pants, and when he passed you you could see those taillights flashing – just to show his tail, I guess, which he frequently did in that game."

It was proof of Castleberry's greatness that in the next game he played, he helped Georgia Tech beat Notre Dame. That was in the 1943 season opener. Castleberry made second-team All-America that fall of his freshman year in college.

"Castleberry was a small fellow," Charlie recalls. "He stood about five-feet-seven and didn't weigh more than one-fifty. But he could fly! He came by me once and I grabbed at him up close, timing my tackle, and all I got was air. It was too bad he got killed in the war. His coach, Bobby Dodd, told me later that Clint was the greatest runner he ever saw."

Size did not matter as much in football then as it matters today; people weren't as large then. Many college basketball teams were anchored by six-foot centers. Some of the greatest football players in history were small guys. Justice never weighed more than 165, but he carried the mail just fine. The Four Horsemen of Notre Dame – Harry Stuhldreher, Don Miller, Jim Crowley, and Elmer Layden – each weighed less than 165. Layden, the fullback, was 162, and Stuhldreher weighed only 152 and stood five-feet-eight.

Mobility more than size was the measure of a winning football team. Teams looked for beef in tackles, height in ends, and good size in blocking backs. For the others, weight did not matter as long as they were quick and mobile and had the guts to play the game. Coaches wanted players who were fast and heady and would knock the fool out of you.

The 1942 Asheville team played Miami High in the Orange Bowl on December 12, and the game was billed for the mythical national high school championship. The game matched Justice, destined to be an All-American at North Carolina, against Miami quarterback Arnold

Tucker, who became an All-American quarterbacking the famous Army teams of Glenn Davis and Doc Blanchard.

Asheville lost the game, 13-7, in a pouring rain; and Coach James played only two substitutes, owing to the team's lack of depth. Justice still feels that Asheville received a lot of "home cooking" from the game officials. The Maroons turned in an iron-men performance that rated the highest praise from Coach James.

In that, Justice's final high school game, he accounted for 133 of his team's 206 yards gained. He threw the pass that gave the Maroons their touchdown, aiming a pass at Tipton who went into the air to catch the ball, but Tucker batted it away at the last second — directly into the arms of Asheville's Dick Knapp, who caught it and scored standing up on a 60-yard play.

Tucker made both Miami touchdowns on short sweeps.

James refused to comment on the officiating after the game. The Maroons had complained to the officials that they were being held on every play, but Justice said the officials penalized Asheville fifteen yards for "unnecessary griping."

Probably no other high school team has been blessed with two tailbacks like Justice and Britt. They battled it out for the starting position and Charlie won. He was a triple-threater who could run, pass, and punt with the best. Britt was a runner, but not a good passer, and he didn't even try to kick. He never mastered the art of holding his kicking foot just right.

Britt had blazing speed on straight runs, and hit the line powerfully, built low to the ground as he was, but he never got the hang of using the whole field on cutbacks. On the other hand, Justice was not as fast as Britt, but was fast enough. He could stop on a dime, give you change, and instantly be on his way at full speed in another direction.

A three letterman at Asheville High, Justice, a guard on the basketball team and third baseman on the baseball squad, made the All-Southern football team his last two seasons. He was also All-State and all-everything-else those years. Tipton, easily one of the greatest ends ever seen in Asheville, made the All-Southern team in 1942.

In 1941 and '42 Asheville had the kind of seasons that teams and towns dream of but few attain. Asheville High's games took precedence over the ten-cent war movies cranked out by Hollywood; over listening to the war news on radio; over everything. Friday nights in the falls of 1941 and '42 were reserved by Ashevilleans for the Asheville High football games. McCormick Field's 3,500 seating capacity was stretched to 5,000 or more on many occasions.

Charlie made one other major move in high school. He met his future wife, Sarah Hunter, while horseplaying in the hall, and he moved in quickly. He and Everett Wilkinson, manager of the football team, were scuffling one morning and Charlie ran into Sarah and knocked her flat on her back.

Charlie apologized profusely – he was a polite boy – and Sarah came up smiling. Charlie liked her immediately because she seemed to be such a good sport. In those days, schools often gave parties in which girls had to ask boys for dates – Daisy Mae style, as adapted from Al Capp's cartoon strip, Li'1 Abner, in which Dogpatch girls got to chase the boys on Sadie Hawkins Day – and Sarah invited Charlie to be her escort to a dance. Charlie thought he had struck out on that first date because he couldn't dance a lick and refused to be drawn onto the dance floor where he was certain he would make a fool of himself.

They stayed at the dance about ten minutes and Sarah suggested, "If you're not going to dance, let's get out of here." She liked him, though, and within a few short weeks they were going steady.

She must have wondered how a boy could be so nimble on the football field and such a clod on the dance floor.

In the late 1950s, a reunion of the Asheville High football teams for which Charlie Justice played included, left to right: first row — Hal Weir, a game official; sportswriter Charlie Chakales; sports editor Paul Jones; Joe Penland, Billy Bridgewater; second row — Neil Justice, Alvin Vick, Carl Tipton, Coach Ralph James, Don McCurry, Charlie Justice, Ed McKinney, Malcolm Arthur, Billy Britt; third row — Richard Knapp, Jesse Jayne, Phil Bennett, Emmett Maney, Donald Maney, Norman Harris, Eckel Bradley, Bob Vines, Footsie Williams, Gil Maney, Bill Robinson, and Walter Brank.

A DAVID AMONG GOLIATHS

A t the end of the 1942 football season, all the guys who played on the James teams at Asheville High knew they were ripe for the draft. Some volunteered for the military to be able to choose their branch of service, and others, like Justice, waited for the draft. Charlie was deferred from December, 1942, until June of 1943 to finish high school, but he didn't quite make it. He lacked one credit, which he earned in the navy, and became a high school graduate eligible to play college football, if and when he was able to go to college because of the uncertainty of war.

Charlie's choice of service branches was the Army Air Forces, which would be changed after the war to the United States Air Force, a separate branch of its own. He didn't want to be a foot soldier in the army, but would have preferred that to the navy. He couldn't swim and was determined to somehow escape induction in the navy if he was chosen for it. He couldn't fly, either, but his choice, like that of thousands of other youngsters, was to be a fighter pilot. There was something glamorous about flying fighter aircraft in that war, and in wearing wings on your chest and walking with a swagger. Few boys gave thought to the cannonfire that was to be directed at our fighter planes.

"I had a friend named Mac Duncan," Charlie said, "who became a fighter pilot. He was a good football player, a big tackle, and would have attained greatness if he had survived the war. But he was shot down over the English Channel and never found."

In June Charlie answered the call, and when he left Biltmore on the bus for induction at Charlotte, he told his mother, "There's one thing for sure, Mom: I won't be in the navy when you see me again. I don't like the navy or the water, and I can't swim, so I'm hoping they'll put me in the air force."

In true military fashion, when he passed the physical exam, a tough old sergeant stamped his papers NAVY ONLY.

"Oh, Lord, Sarge," Charlie protested, "please let me go to the air corps."

Gravelly-voiced, the sergeant growled, "You're going to the navy and like it, kid."

"Well, it looks like I'm going," Charlie replied, "but I'm not going to like it. I can't swim."

"Don't worry about that," the sergeant said. "They'll teach you."

With others, Charlie was sent directly to the Bainbridge, Maryland, Naval Training Station and put in boot camp. Finishing boot training Charlie was ordered to Physical Instructors School at Bainbridge, and on completion of that school he was assigned to a boot company as physical instructor.

Early in the program, Charlie's boot company was asked who couldn't swim. Charlie raised his hand, as did others, including Johnny Mize, a huge first baseman the St. Louis Cardinals had traded to the New York Giants in 1941 for three players and $50,000. At that moment, Charlie thought he was suddenly living in high cotton. Mize had hit forty-three home runs for the Cardinals in 1940.

An instructor named Adolf Kiefer was assigned to teach this group to swim. An excellent teacher, Kiefer knew his business. He had won the 100-meter breaststroke in the 1936 Berlin Olympics while Hitler watched. For several days Kiefer put the group through its paces in the pool, trying to teach the backstroke, and he couldn't help but notice that Justice and Mize made no progress at all.

One day he turned to watch them flounder in the water, and when they came up, Kiefer yelled: "I'll be damned if I know what it is with you two. Every time I look around, you're both on the damned bottom. Get the hell out of here!"

Justice and Mize grabbed their clothing and fled.

He could never stand being in water that deep, probably owing to an incident that occurred when he was just a lad. The Justices lived in Emma, and almost every day the neighborhood boys sneaked over to a rock quarry in nearby Bingham Heights to swim. Charlie would sit on the bank and watch and laugh.

One day several boys grabbed him and threw him in the pond, yelling, "Sink or swim!"

Frantically, Charlie began thrashing at the water, and down he went. He came back up, down again, and back up – and just as he was going down for the third time, his oldest brother, Jack, jumped in and pulled him to safety.

"From that time on," Charlie said, "I was scared of water. I wouldn't go near it. I don't know what I would have done if the navy had sent me to sea instead of letting me play football."

"They passed us anyway," Charlie recalled fifty years later, "but I still can't swim."

Charlie pushed boots through boot camp for a year. He was called an exercise specialist and those in that category were placed in a Specialist-A bracket. Most attained the rank of Chief Petty Officer, but Charlie, being so young, only attained the rank of 2nd Class Petty Officer.

"The commander of the camp at Bainbridge was responsible for putting me in that category," Charlie said. "He forced them to

Charlie, the sailor.

put me in the program because he wanted to keep me a year so I could play for Bainbridge in 1944."

Pushing boots meant that Charlie exercised them, marched them, took them to classes, and did many other things for them.

"The first class I had," Charlie recalled, "was made up of much older men than I was. Remember, I was nineteen, and a lot of them were so old they wouldn't let us put them through a lot of the stuff others had to endure. Remember that forty-five year old men were allowed to enter service in World War Two. When those old-timers found out how old I was and that I played football, they laughed and would say, 'Why, you're just a kid!' Some of them were old enough to be my daddy. We called them senior citizens."

Charlie once came close to a court-martial in that job.

"I had duty one night," he said, "and had to take a group to the theater and bring them back. When I got them back, I wanted to get home real quick, so I dismissed them and left. What I didn't know was that one of them had passed out on the way back and was still lying out there somewhere.

"If I hadn't been one of the base commander's favorites, I'd have been gone. The commander told the lieutenant who was dressing me down, 'That's my boy! You don't touch him!'"

Fortunately, the guy who had dropped out was all right the next day and nothing more ever came of the incident.

Sarah was employed at Bainbridge. Dick Sisler, who had played baseball for the Asheville Tourists, was a major leaguer serving time in the navy and was at Bainbridge to play baseball. His wife and Sarah had jobs overseen by the base commander. They made portraits of new recruits at the base.

Boot camp had ended and sailors were waiting for orders when the Bainbridge call went out for football players to report for equipment. Charlie asked his officer if he could try out.

The officer looked at Charlie's small frame, grinned, and said, "Sure, kid, go on out."

Charlie reported to the equipment room and got in line with a crowd of huge, towering, brutish-appearing sailors, and when he got to the counter and asked for gear, he was shunted to the end of the line. Twice more he gained the counter only to be sent back. Finally, when all others had been equipped, he asked for equipment and was given a practice uniform but no shoes.

"What about cleats?" he asked.

"Sorry, kid," the equipment manager told him, "we're fresh out."

Charlie had been qualified for aerial gunnery, which increased his determination to make the team, so he went out in uniform, but barefooted. The team coach, Joe Maniaci, former Fordham University and Chicago Bears fullback, took pity on Justice and rounded up a pair of beat-up, too-large shoes. He put Charlie far downfield to shag punts for a pair of punters, Don Durden and Harry (Hippity) Hopp.

Durden, an Oregon State punter-quarterback who had starred against Duke in the 1942 Rose Bowl in Durham, a 20-16 win for Oregon State, and Hopp, brother of St. Louis Cardinals' first baseman-outfielder Johnny Hopp, were punting to Justice, who stood about fifty-five yards away.

On impulse, Charlie, who had averaged 40.5 yards on fifty punts in high school, said to another shagger, "I'm gonna kick one back."

"You'll get in trouble."

Nevertheless, he put his foot into one that sailed far over the heads of Durden and Hopp, a 75-yard beauty. Suddenly, the field quieted down and all heads turned toward the shaggers downfield. Maniaci came out of a huddle, looked downfield, and yelled, "Who kicked that ball?"

"Uh, oh," Charlie muttered to himself, and thinking he was in trouble, slowly raised his hand.

"Come up here," Maniaci yelled, and when Charlie jogged up, Maniaci asked, "Can you do that again?"

"I guess so," Charlie replied, and boomed another 70-yarder downfield.

He spent the next ten minutes launching punts into orbit while Maniaci watched with growing pleasure.

"Where've you played before?" the coach asked Charlie.

"I played in high school."

"What high school?"

"Asheville High School."

"Where's that?"

"That's in North Carolina."

"What kind of team did you have?"

"Pretty good," Charlie said. "We didn't lose a game the last two seasons."

"Did you punt?"

"Yes, sir."

"How well?"

"I averaged over forty yards for two years," Charlie answered.

"Well, I'm gonna have to have a kicker," Maniaci said, "and you're going to get a chance to be it, kid. I'll even buy you a set of new cleats."

"Gee, thanks, Coach," Charlie said, thinking that this scenario was straight out of Hollywood. He also thought that coming to the navy may have been the best break he had ever had.

"Don't think you're gonna play," Maniaci said, looking over Charlie's 155-pound frame, "because you won't be able to play in this league. But I guess we can protect you enough to let you be our kicker."

Scrimmaging the Washington Redskins one day, Charlie pestered Maniaci into letting him run the ball.

He gained forty-five yards on three runs. On defense he intercepted two passes and made a tackle or two. He shanked the only punt he tried, and at the end of the game, Maniaci laid a hand on Charlie's shoulder and laughed, "Good thing you did something today besides kick. You'd be at sea by now."

The personnel roster for that Bainbridge team read like a Who's Who in College and Professional Football: Buster Ramsey, 1942 William & Mary All-American guard who later signed with the Chicago Cardinals; Lou Sossamon, South Carolina and the New York Yankees; Carl Tomasello, New York Giants; Carl Mulleneaux, Green Bay Packers; Howard (Red) Hickey, Cleveland Rams; Don Durden, Oregon State; Harvey (Stud) Johnson, William & Mary; Bill de Correvont, Redskins; Harry Hopp, Nebraska; Dewey Proctor, Furman; Hilliard Cheatham, Auburn and the Chicago Cardinals; Lou Rymkus, Notre Dame and Cleveland; Phil Regazzo, Philadelphia Eagles; Jim Gatewood, Georgia; Leonard Aiken, Baylor and the Chicago Bears; and several other names that glittered like gold to Charlie.

It was not long, however, before the star-studded Bainbridge lineup began looking up to Justice, the "little guy" from the mountains of North Carolina. The pros in the Bainbridge lineup took an immediate liking to Charlie, who had a great competitive flair and an even and controlled temperament mixed with his natural talents. On the practice field, Charlie had enthusiasm to spare and an attitude of total cooperation and self-sacrifice. His good nature and fine spirit were always present.

In scrimmage games against the Redskins and the U. S. Naval Academy, Charlie won his spurs, running wild, eating yardage in huge bites, and, despite his size, playing well on defense. After the Redskins game, Maniaci allowed, "He could play for a pro team right now."

Before the real season began, Charlie had taken a starting berth in one of Bainbridge's two elite backfields. He loved the T formation, which was strange at first to his single-wing sensibilities. "The first time I saw the T," he said, "we went down and practiced it, and I thought, 'My goodness, what is this?'" It was altogether a different world for him, quick-opening plays, sprints rather than thundering crashes through the line. He soon discovered he didn't get beaten up as badly playing the T as the single-wing. The difference was that of finesse against brute strength.

Charlie found an independence that he had never seen before among the players, especially the pros. More often that not, when Maniaci called a play from the sideline, the pros would nix it in the huddle. "Aw, hell, he don't know what he's talking about," someone would say. "We're gonna do it this way: Kid, you run here, and you run there. ..." Charlie always thought the coach was boss, but at Bainbridge the guys reworked and refined the coach's plays to their own taste. Maniaci recognized what they were doing and gave them leeway, because what they did worked.

Bainbridge was undefeated for two seasons, 1943 and 1944, and Charlie led the way as the team's leading scorer and ground-gainer. Of Justice's capabilities in service, Dick Kaplan wrote in in *The Asheville Citizen*:

> His sixth sense in the open field — ability to anticipate situations before they developed — combined with wonderful timing and change of pace were marveled at by the pros. But he was fast, too. Bainbridge's pair of backfields found Justice heading the "pony unit."
>
> It is a popular misconception among the uninformed that he lacked speed since his cutbacks and shiftiness overshadowed it. But Charlie was the fastest runner on the Bainbridge squads of 1943 and 1944 in the 50-yard wind sprints. The T-formation requires more speed in quick line thrusts than does the single-wing. His quickness and timing easily enabled him to make the transition from high school single-wing to the Bainbridge T.

As a national powerhouse – the elite of military service football teams – Bainbridge won all seventeen of its games in two seasons, and while doing so, Justice's fame began to spread across the nation. College football became watered down because of the military draft taking most of the well-conditioned athletes, and the media began to follow service football closely. The great college and pro football players wound up playing service ball.

Maniaci called Justice "the best back I've ever seen at his weight," and other knowledgeable observers nodded and agreed.

The Commodores played seven games in 1943 and no one came close to them. Bainbridge scored 313 points and allowed but seven, and gained an average of 304 yards rushing and 163 passing.

Justice had deep respect for all the linemen in front of him and special respect for two. He said of Red Hickey, an end for the Cleveland Rams, "When Red hits 'em they bounce!" and of Buster Ramsey, Charlie said, "He was the greatest guard I've ever seen. He was best at pulling out on interference and had the quickest charge in the business." He still holds that opinion fifty years later.

As in high school, Charlie played only half the time. With so many great runners in camp, Bainbridge divided time equally between its two crack backfields. Charlie led the offense with 482 yards on 132 carries, an average of 15 yards. He scored touchdowns on runs of 45, 43, 41, 40, 33, 22, and 14 yards. After Charlie became his star runner, Maniaci let others do the punting, but Charlie kicked twice that 1943 season -- for 62 and 54 yards from scrimmage. He caught nine passes and intercepted four, and his blocking and tackling were superb.

Charlie's nickname, Choo Choo, came out of a Bainbridge game. An officer in the stands commented that Justice ran "like a runaway choo choo," and a sportswriter for *The Baltimore Sun* overheard and used it in his game story the following day. The name had a ring to it: Charlie Choo Choo Justice, and others began using it. Soon, everyone knew of the Carolina Choo Choo, and even today, a half century later, when someone mentions Charlie Justice, someone else will invariably say, "Oh, you mean Choo Choo."

Bainbridge was tabbed number one team in the nation after the 1943 season and the Associated Press named Justice the service "rookie of the year" in the Mid-Atlantic district.

Charlie celebrated his season by returning home to marry his high school sweetheart. On November 23, dressed in navy blue, he wed Sarah Hunter in a ceremony at Trinity Episcopal Church in Asheville. Some say the age of 19 is "too young" for matrimony, but the marriage changed the course of Charlie's life for the better in more ways than one. In early 1944 he was ordered to report to the Annapolis Preparatory School as a midshipman in the United States Naval Academy, where he would have played his college career, but the orders were nullified when Charlie revealed his marriage. The service academies did not accept married men. Thus freed, he played a second season for Bainbridge, the nation's fourth largest naval training center with 35,000 personnel.

In 1944 both Bainbridge and Charlie Justice had better seasons than in 1943. Playing a full and much tougher schedule of 10 games, the Commodores went undefeated again, scoring 331 points to their opponents' 70, and shared the nation's service championship with power-laden Randolph Field of Texas.

Charlie was the team's major offensive weapon again. He gained 629 yards on 48 carries, and his 14 touchdowns, good for 84 points, were second in the nation to the 120 points made by Glenn Davis of Army. He averaged a touchdown for every four times he carried the ball.

In two seasons at Bainbridge, Charlie ran 80 times for 1,011 yards, an average of 12.6 per carry. He scored 21 touchdowns. His total rushes are in contrast to football today when a running back having a good day may carry thirty times.

His performances were spectacular, and perhaps his best single game came against Camp Lejeune, the Marine Corps base in North Carolina. He scored four touchdowns, one on an unbelievable 83-yard run. He remembers that run well, for it was one of the greatest runs he ever made on any level.

"I was having a hot day," he said. "We ran a sweep to the right from our 17-yard line and I twisted around John Younger, a big end from Notre Dame, cut back across the field and found no opening there, so I cut across to the right sideline again and when the way closed up there I cut back across the field for the third time, found a lane over there, and went on in for the touchdown."

The last man Charlie had to pass was Elroy (Crazy Legs) Hirsch, later a star pass receiver for the Los Angeles Rams. He faked to the left and when Hirsch countered the move, Charlie sped by him on the right and reached the end zone untouched.

On November 5, 1944, not realizing he was playing at his future home, Justice and the Commodores crushed the North Carolina Navy Pre-Flight at Chapel Hill, 49-20. Even Otto Graham, Pre-Flight's great passing star, was no match for Bainbridge. Justice was the star with a 42-yard run for a touchdown and a 47-yard sprint to set up another.

At game's end, the Bainbridge team whooped onto the field, hoisted Charlie onto big shoulders, and carried him off the field to admiring cheers from the crowd. Overwhelmed at the sight of this diminutive back directing such brutal blockers as Ramsey, Rymkus, and Leonard Aiken, the crowd stood in awe as Bainbridge bowled over Pre-Flight tacklers like ten-pins. That was one of the secrets to the success of the Commodores — their great teamwork. Each man knew his job and did it, but when Justice or any other ball-carrier ordered them this way or that in the heat of a high-powered run from scrimmage, they responded and chopped down the enemy like stalks of sugar cane.

Those blockers taught Charlie a lesson he never forgot. He employed what he learned to make himself a better ball player year by year. At Maxwell Field, Alabama — which had Charlie's high school "twin," Billy Britt, in its backfield — Charlie decided to solo on one play. He cut away from his blocking, thinking he saw a better lane to the left, and a big Maxwell end hit him so hard he saw every star in the sky. Determined not to let anyone know how badly the tackle had momentarily stunned him, almost unable to breathe, Charlie hoisted himself to his feet with difficulty, and limped his way back to the huddle.

Ramsey looked him straight in the eye. "Uh, huh," he said, "we told you! You wouldn't listen to us, but we told you, didn't we? Stay with your blocking, kid, and we'll clear a way for you."

"I will," Charlie promised, nursing his wounds. "I'll never do that again!"

Buster was gruff in his praise but the twinkle in his eye gave him away.

"I had run back and forth crossing the field three times in this game," Justice said, "and when we came to the bench Buster stood in front of me with hands on hips glaring down at me for a moment, and then he grinned and said, 'Kid, you're the craziest son of a bitch I ever saw in my life. When you get that damn ball in your hands you don't know where in the hell you're going.' I had passed him three times on that play, passed him this way, passed him that way, then passed him this way again and he said his head was going from side to side like he was watching a tennis match."

At Cherry Point after Justice scored four times to beat the Marines, 34-0, Ramsey said to John Yoniker, a Notre Dame All-American who played for Cherry Point, "Damn, Yoniker, I thought you were an All-American. You just let a little high school boy make a fool out of you."

Yoniker shook his head and grinned and watched the Marines, who appreciated a good performance, carry Justice off the field on their shoulders.

Justice had such a great day against Maxwell Field that at the end of the game Leonard Aiken, who had played ten seasons with the Bears, said to him, "Kid, I've seen a lot of football in my time, but that was the greatest exhibition I've ever seen." Charlie has always cherished that word of praise as highly as his All-American status in college later.

Football people found it hard to believe that a small kid straight out of high school could run so well with all the pros.

Charlie wore number 23 at Bainbridge, the only time in his career he wore anything other than 22.

The Associated Press, whose post-season all-everythings were considered the ranking picks in the country, had a dilemma. Justice had gained 629 yards and scored 84 points, but was still relatively unknown to most of the AP's readers across America. He was only twenty years old and had nothing behind him but a high school career, which did nothing to deter him in outpointing proven professional and college stars, but the AP put him on the second All-Service team.

On the first team were Otto Graham (Northwestern) North Carolina Pre-Flight; Charlie Trippi (Georgia) Third Air Force; Bill Dudley (Virginia) Randolph Field; and Len Eshmont (Fordham) Norman Navy. The second team had Justice with Indian Jack Jacobs (Oklahoma) Fourth Air Force; Glenn Dobbs (Tulsa) Second Air Force; and Bill Daley (Michigan All-American) Fort Pierce.

Editorially *The Bainbridge Mainsheet* protested: "If you ask us, the second string backfield is better than the first."

The war ended just before the 1945 football season, and the military shifted athletic personnel to Hawaii to perform for war-weary veterans returning home for discharge and taking R&R on Oahu. Justice was among the navy football personnel transferred there to play for the Navy All-Stars in a four-game round-robin competition with the Army, Air Force, and Marine Corps all-star teams. The teams were to play each other twice.

When Charlie was shipped from Bainbridge to Schumacher, California, in December of 1944, he thought he was going to be assigned to sea duty so he went to California by way of North Carolina and took Sarah to Schumacher with him.

"The commander shipped me out of Bainbridge," Charlie said, "because the Navy Bureau was wondering why I was still around there after two years. Schumacher was a shipping-out point for sea duty. After I got there, though, the football people found out I was there and were going to keep me to play the 1945 season there."

"We were lying in bed early one morning," Charlie said, "when someone knocked on the door. It was a shore patrolman who said unceremoniously, "You've got one hour to get your stuff together and be at this place." He handed Charlie a piece of paper with a military address on it.

"What is this?" asked the startled Justice.

"All I know is that you're going to Pearl Harbor on the first available air transport out of San Francisco. The orders came down from the Naval Bureau in Washington."

Charlie looked at the orders and then at the shore patrolman. "I don't have any choice, do I?"

"No," the man replied, "you have no choice."

Charlie packed his sea bag, kissed Sarah goodbye, and went to the mentioned address. From there he was quickly shuttled to the airfield in San Francisco, and a few hours later was winging over the Pacific en route to Hawaii.

The airplane was filled with officers with scrambled eggs on their hats, and Charlie was an ordinary seaman. Upon arrival in Honolulu, a jeep met the plane and as the crowd descended, the driver yelled, "This is for Justice."

"Right here," Charlie called, making his way to the front, and while the startled officers watched, the enlisted man climbed in the jeep and departed, giving the officers a cursory salute. A bus was approaching to take the officers to their destinations.

The jeep took Charlie to Pearl Harbor and he was housed in a barracks with other athletes. The baseball season was ending and he found himself in the same barracks with Ted Williams, Joe DiMaggio, Lou Boudreau, and a horde of other major league baseball players.

"I was just a high school kid," he said, "but, man, I was in heaven! I don't know if they knew exactly who I was, but they knew I had played some good football at Bainbridge."

He found that Buster Ramsey, Lloyd Cheatham, Lou Sossamon, and Dewey Proctor had been sent from Bainbridge to Hawaii at the end of the 1944 season to play in the post-war games and had asked their coach to get Justice transferred so he could play with the team.

The teams played every Sunday with 45,000 to 50,000 troops watching and screaming, glad to have something to yell about other than the war.

The teams played each other twice. The Air Force went through its four games undefeated. Justice and the Navy won two and lost two, and the Marines lost all four.

Alvin Dark, future major league baseball player and manager, played single-wing tailback for the Marines, on the same team with a big fullback named Hosea Rodgers. Hosea had also played for the V-12 program in Chapel Hill during the war. Justice and Rodgers would get to know each other better at North Carolina after the war. The Navy team also included George McAfee and Steve Lach of Duke, Bob Sweiger of Minnesota, and Jackie Crain of Texas.

Justice teamed with McAfee at running back on the Navy team. Against the Marines he ripped off a long run on a punt return to set up the first touchdown. Navy won the game, 13-0. In a game against the Army, Justice scored three times.

When the football season ended, the Navy players were shipped on a destroyer escort back to the states for discharge, so Charlie finally got a six-day taste of life at sea. He didn't like it; he was happy that he knew how to play football.

In San Francisco, the Navy All-Stars played one more time, against a Main Fleet Marines team in a war bond game in Kezar Stadium.

"They beat the fool out of us," Charlie said. "Buddy Young and Harry Hopp ran all over us. Our boys weren't interested in playing the game; they wanted to get home. In fact, at least ten of our players went out on the town the night before the game and got drunk. They weren't feeling like playing football the next day."

After that game, the Navy team's personnel were broken up and discharged.

"That was the navy's way of getting us out of Pearl Harbor," Charlie said. "Those football games were so popular with the returning war veterans that the service branches eased us out of Hawaii without creating a furor."

Buster Ramsey was a handsome, blond-haired young man who, Charlie thought, looked like a movie actor.

"Women were crazy about him," Charlie said. "As we came back from Pearl Harbor, we got stuck in San Francisco, Buster and his wife and Sarah and me. We couldn't get on a train for Chicago. Buster walked up to the girl at the ticket window and turned on the charm and she became so shaken she sold him not only tickets but Pullman berths as well. Buster turned to me and said, 'See, I can fix you up.'

"Buster was one of the nicest guys you've ever seen, but he loved to drink. He loved his whisky. Had a nice wife, a beautiful girl, and boy! she could make him walk the chalk line. Nobody else could, but she knew how."

When he was discharged Charlie had no inkling of what awaited him at home.

All the college recruiters were making plans to gather in Asheville to welcome him home, each armed with a scholarship, and some with other offers.

A VERITABLE HELL

O wing to the nature of the times and circumstances, and to his abilities and potential, Charlie Justice was perhaps the most widely recruited player in the history of football.

In the navy, he had been a pint-sized, fleet-footed flea running among elephants. Most of the players on service football teams were former professional players and the top stars of college football. Since Justice, fresh out of high school, had become a brilliant runner in this league, he was subjected to the recruiting pressures not only of college football, but of professional football at the same time.

The opportunities were so attractive, the temptations so inviting, and the pressures so great that for many months he lived in a veritable hell, a pressure cooker almost beyond imagination, as colleges sent recruiters to his door in droves and found the professional recruiters already there with checkbooks in hand. How could colleges compete against the "big money" of the pros? They soon discovered they could, but only because of the nature of the man. Choo Choo was determined to go to college. He did not want to go into the pro ranks; he didn't think he ever wanted to play professional football.

Duke, one of the great powers of American football, which itself had gone unbeaten, untied, and unscored on in the 1939 season and lost the Rose Bowl to Southern Cal, 7-3, expressed interest in Justice in 1942, but the interest was feeble because Duke knew what happened to healthy high school football players at that time: They were drafted into military service. From the time he went to the navy in June of 1943 until he signed to go to Chapel Hill in the spring of 1946, he was under tremendous recruiting pressure.

After Justice and the Asheville High Maroons finished those unde-feated seasons of 1941 and '42, Duke wanted to sign the entire Asheville starting eleven to college scholarships and take the team en masse to Durham.

"We voted to take the offer," Charlie said. "We wanted to see what we could do against the best college competition, and I'll tell you right now that I think we would have done all right. We would have been a good college team. The only thing that prevented us from doing it was the war. We were all prime for the draft and not any of us knew whether we would ever again play football. Times were very uncertain then."

The pros actually got the first serious recruiting crack at Justice when he played service football. But all those like Justice who had never been to college and played service sports during the war were eligible for college athletics after the war. Thus Charlie was free to make his own choice: pro or college.

So he became one of a handful of players in history who was recruited by the pros before the colleges – except one college: the United States Na-val Academy at Annapolis, Maryland, which in 1943 was looking for some-one to counter the great Army duo of Davis and Blanchard. Justice was the only man on the horizon who even halfway fit that bill; so, with the power of the U. S. military forces behind it, the Academy tried to pick a plum.

Justice took leave from Bainbridge and Sarah took leave from her job at the Naval Observatory and the two went home to Asheville and were mar-ried on November 23, 1943. They didn't wed because Charlie was afraid of being assigned to Annapolis, but because of the uncertainties of war, and they wanted as much time together as they could get.

The Bainbridge team had gone to Annapolis to scrimmage the Naval Academy team before the regular 1943 service season began in September, and the Commodores were invited to eat lunch with the plebes.

"They marched in and sat down on orders," Charlie said. "They relaxed on an order, and began eating what they called a 'square meal.' They carried forks full of food from their plates to their mouths by steps, forward first, then upward, and finally straight into their mouths, lowering their forks in a straight line, and all of that formed a square."

After the meal, the Bainbridge players laughed about the square meal, and someone asked Charlie if he wouldn't like to come to Annapolis.

"No," Charlie said. "I don't want any part of that kind of foolishness."

In the afternoon scrimmage, Bainbridge ran all over the Navy team, and Charlie had a great day, attracting the full attention of Navy coach Bill Walsh, who suddenly began to dream of having a team spearhead like Justice. When Davis and Blanchard came from the Army camp to slay the Navy's Philistines later in the season, Coach Walsh concentrated his efforts in having Justice transferred to the Academy.

In November, then, as soon as Charlie returned to Bainbridge, he was summoned into the base commander's office.

"Are you really just a high school boy?" the commander asked.

"Yes, sir."

"You've never been to college or anything like that?"

"No, sir."

The commander smiled, arose from behind his desk, and walked smugly around it to sit on the edge of the desk, facing Justice.

"How would you like to go to Annapolis?" the commander asked, and a bolt of fright shot through Justice.

"I couldn't, sir," Charlie stammered. "I couldn't pass the work."

"Oh, don't worry about that," the commander said. "You'll do just fine."

He dismissed Charlie, and a week later the summons came again.

Reporting to the commander's office, Charlie sat in the same chair. The commander came quickly to the point.

"Mr. Justice," he said, "you have been ordered to Annapolis to further your education." Charlie knew that his commander really meant "to play football" but couldn't say it, and Charlie liked the idea even less.

"But, sir," Charlie protested again, "I couldn't pass the work."

The commander laughed again and said, "Oh, yes, you can. Go pack your bag, everything you've got. You're going over here to Annapolis Preparatory School and brush up on your school work."

"I don't want to go, sir," Charlie tried to be adamant without disrespect.

"You have no say in it," the commander snapped. "You don't have any choice whether you go or not. I have your orders here and they are in order. These are orders from the navy, and you must obey them."

But Charlie had one more shot to fire. He had been told that married men were not accepted at Annapolis.

"May I ask one question?" Charlie inquired. "What if I'm married?"

The commander's mouth fell open. He stared hard at Charlie and finally said, "You're not married, are you?"

"Yes, sir," Charlie replied. "I got married two weeks ago."

A look of consternation crossed the commander's face, and without uttering a word he tore the orders to bits and dismissed Justice with a wave of his hand.

Next came the pros.

The Chicago Bears and Philadelphia Eagles tried to sign Charlie before he left the navy. His potential was so great that the pros could not resist.

The first to get to Justice was Philadelphia, which actually tricked him into signing a professional contract at Bainbridge in 1944. Phil Rigazzo of the Eagles, an officer based in Bainbridge, called Justice to his office one day, invited Charlie to sit down, and began to discuss this and that. On the desk before Rigazzo lay a stack of one-dollar bills.

Finally, Rigazzo got around to the reason for the summons. He told Charlie that the Eagles wanted to sign him.

"I don't want to sign with anybody," Charlie said. "I'm going to college. I've made up my mind."

Rigazzo looked at the stack of money, and Charlie's gaze moved there also.

"Now, Charlie," Rigazzo said, "the Eagles want you to play for them when you decide to play with the pros. This contract is our insurance that you will play for us when the time comes. You can go to college if you like and play college football, but we want to make sure of your services after that. All you've got to do is sign this contract and you'll be our property after college. We'll then pay you $450 a game."

Charlie's eyes were on the dollar bills. He couldn't remember ever having seen that much money in one place.

"That's your money, Charlie," Rigazzo said. "All you have to do is sign this contract, then you can walk out of here with that money in your pocket." He emphasized these words: "That's one hundred and fifty dollars, Charlie, a hundred and fifty smackers."

Justice felt his resolve sliding away.

"Let me get this right," he said. "I'm definitely going to college. I don't even know if I'll want to play ball after that. If I don't you'll lose your money."

The stack of bills had Justice wide-eyed by that time. It was, indeed, a lot of money in 1945, enough to tempt a young man into doing something drastic.

"Well," Rigazzo mused, "it's good that you want to get an education, and if that's what you want to do, it's what you ought to do. Still, the money's yours whether you go to college or not. Take it. We just want you to sign, and we'll take our chances. This contract will only bind you to Philadelphia in case you decide to play in the pros."

Justice still had doubts, and he voiced them. "I'll still get to go to college," he said, "and I won't have to play with the Eagles until I'm finished. Is that right?"

"Right as rain," Rigazzo said, finally feeling the fish take the worm.

Suddenly, Charlie reached for the money and Rigazzo turned the contract toward him and handed him a pen.

"Sign right there," he said, pointing to the line, and Charlie scratched his name on the contract.

Overjoyed and feeling flush with the money in his hand, Charlie walked out of Rigazzo's office into the hall and came face to face with Joe Maniaci, his coach.

Seeing the money and Charlie's grinning face, Maniaci asked, 'What the hell are you doing?"

"Look there, coach," Charlie said. "That's a lot of money."

"Whose is it?"

"It's mine. I just signed with the Eagles."

"You what?" Maniaci exploded. "Give me that money." He took the bills from Charlie and nodded toward two chairs. "Sit down and tell me what this is all about."

Charlie told him the story, and Maniaci, fiercely angered, took the money to his office and telephoned Elmer Layden, one of the Four Horsemen of Notre Dame who was then commissioner of the National Football League. He told Layden the story.

"How old is this young man?" Layden asked.

"He's twenty," Maniaci said.

"Well, then, don't worry about it," Layden said. "He has to be twentyone to sign a valid contract."

When Layden received the contract from Rigazzo, he voided it.

Maniaci, like Rigazzio, wasn't entirely dealing to Charlie from a full deck. He had his own plans. When the war ended Maniaci was scheduled to coach Fordham University and wanted to take Justice with him. But that coaching dream of his was never fulfilled.

Once before Maniaci had showed his real intentions. When the Commodores played at North Carolina Pre-Flight and afterward the Bainbridge team was invited to go to Durham and see a Duke football game. Maniaci took the team and stuck to Justice like a mother hen. "He didn't let me out of his sight," Charlie laughed in later years. "He wouldn't let me talk to anybody from Duke or Chapel Hill."

Charlie's next offer came from George Halas and the Bears in Hawaii in 1945.

Justice had become friends with George McAfee and thought the Duke ace was the greatest back he had ever seen. His admiration ran so deep for McAfee that he suspected nothing when McAfee told him that Halas had telephoned and asked him to bring Justice over.

"Halas was a commander," Justice said, "and I was an enlisted man, so I knew this wasn't going to be a social call. Because of his rank, I guess he thought he could buffalo me into signing with the Bears."

Most of the time, Charlie was big-eyed and therefore vulnerable to the overtures of the pros. Remember, he lived in the same quarters and rubbed shoulders with Joe DiMaggio and Ted Williams and other big-league baseball players who were in Hawaii to play baseball.

Halas was blunt. "Ain't no use your going to college, Charlie," he said without preamble. "You don't need to go to college right now. I'm going to offer you a lot of money to sign with the Bears, and you'll make enough money playing professional football that when the time comes you can pay your way through any college in the United States."

"I don't know, commander," Charlie said. "I'll have to think about it. I've got my mind set on going to college."

"Let me put it this way," Halas said. "What I'm about to say to you will be the best offer I've ever made. I've never paid anybody this kind of money."

When Charlie didn't respond, Halas continued: "I'm going to pay you a thousand dollars bonus for signing and five hundred dollars a game for as long as you play for the Bears."

He peered closely at Charlie to see the dollar marks in the youth's eyes, but they weren't there. Charlie had learned his lesson at Bainbridge when he signed with the Eagles.

Charlie stood and said, "I'll think about your offer, commander," and walked out.

Halas then called McAfee in and closed the door. Charlie waited until McAfee came out, and as McAfee drove Charlie back to his quarters, he asked, "What did he offer you, Charlie?"

"A thousand to sign," Charlie said, "and five hundred a game."

"Aw, he'll go up on that."

Charlie was surprised, but did not mention that Halas had said it was the best offer he had every made anyone.

"What about you, George?" Charlie asked.

"I went ahead and signed."

"How'd you come out on money?"

"Twelve hundred a game," McAfee said.

To himself, Charlie said, "He lied! Halas lied to me!" Silently he swore that he would not go back to see Halas, not even if the commander ordered him to, and that he would never play for Halas.

If Justice thought the pros had pressured him, he hadn't seen anything yet. When he was discharged in January, 1946 – here came the college recruiters! For weeks Charlie and Sarah saw no peace. Recruiters knew everywhere they went, and when they went on invitation to check out a university, rival recruiters found them on campus and tried to persuade them to come to their schools.

No one but Sarah, not even his mother and father, knew how and when Charlie was coming back to Asheville. He rode the train, seeking privacy in a Pullman. When he stepped off the train in the Asheville station looking for Sarah in the crowd, the first person he saw, standing at the foot of the train steps, was Dan Hill, Asheville's first All-American at Duke and the chief recruiter for the Blue Devils. Charlie was amazed that Hill not only knew which train he would be on, but also knew the number of the coach he would be riding.

"Hello, Charlie," said Hill. "Welcome home."

"Thanks," Charlie answered, sweeping the crowd for Sarah and finding her standing off to the side.

Hill insisted that Charlie talk to him. He invited Charlie to come to Duke the following day to talk with the coaching staff and was so insistent that he wouldn't let Charlie pass to get to Sarah before he got an affirmative answer.

"All right," Charlie finally said. "We'll come tomorrow."

If Charlie is anything at all, he is a loyal man. He and Sarah spent three or four days at Duke. The Blue Devils coach, Wallace Wade, like Justice, had just returned from the war, and Eddie Cameron had been Duke's coach in the interim. The Duke people privately told Charlie that Wade would resume the coaching position immediately.

During one conversation with Wade, Charlie said, "Coach, I played over at Pearl Harbor with one of your boys who was one of the greatest players I've ever seen."

"Who was that?" Wade asked.

"George McAfee."

Wade spat. "Pffftt! George McAfee wasn't a football player. Steve Lach was my kind of football player."

Lach, also considered one of the greats at Duke, had been at Pearl Harbor, and Charlie, a high school boy, had played more than Lach. McAfee, on the other hand, was the greatest player Charlie had ever seen. "He fielded some punts," Charlie said, "and got away from people the slickest I've ever seen. I never saw anybody run like that. He was the greatest. The pros always ranked him high."

When everything had been said and Charlie and Sarah left, they stopped on the sidewalk outside, and Sarah smiled. "I know one thing," she said. "We're not coming to Duke, are we?" She knew what her husband thought of George McAfee.

Charlie looked her in the eye. "That's the truth," he said. "We're not coming to Duke."

Later he confided, "If they'd left Cameron there, I might have come, but they slipped around and thought they were doing me a favor by telling me Wade was coming back. He did take over again the next week."

While the Justices were visiting Duke, Charlie received a call from Tom Young at Chapel Hill. Young had been head coach of the Tar Heels in 1943 and was assisting Carl Snavely as chief recruiter in 1946. Before the beginning of the school year in the fall of 1946 Young took the head coaching job at Western Carolina Teachers College (now University) and built the team into the 1949 North State Conference champions with a crop of huge World War II veterans and the single-wing.

Fate apparently smiled on Carolina's side in the recruiting of Justice. Had it been left to Snavely, Charlie would have had the same opinion of Carolina as he had of Wallace Wade at Duke. But Carolina had Tom Young.

Young had gone to the navy after the 1943 season and was stationed at Bainbridge. He and Charlie knew each other there. Young was a likeable man, and as gregarious as Charlie was, the two of them struck up a lasting friendship.

When Young called Charlie at Duke and invited Charlie and Sarah to Chapel Hill, he said he would bring Crowell Little, one of Snavely's assistants who was from Asheville, and pick them up.

But Charlie said no. "I wouldn't feel right doing that. We came down to visit Duke and I don't think I should come over there until I am away from here."

He told Young when they were leaving Durham and that they were going to visit Charlie's sister, Frances, in High Point. "You can pick us up over there if you want to," he suggested.

When the car arrived in High Point from Chapel Hill, Chuck Erickson, athletic director of the University of North Carolina, was driving, and Coach Snavely came with him.

As they approached the car, Erickson said to Sarah, "Let's you and me sit in the back seat and put Charlie up front with Coach."

From High Point they drove to Winston-Salem for lunch with North Carolina alumni, and returning to Chapel Hill, Snavely asked Charlie one question: "How much do you weigh?"

"A hundred and fifty-five pounds," Charlie replied.

Snavely grunted, and from there to Chapel Hill said no more to Charlie.

On campus, Erickson put them in a fraternity house for the night, and early next morning Snavely called Charlie and said, "I have to go to Pennsylvania to do some recruiting. You can come on down to the office and someone will be here to look after you."

Arriving at the office, Charlie and Sarah discovered that Snavely was already gone. "Nobody paid much attention to us for about an hour," Charlie said, "so we walked uptown and took a bus to High Point." After spending a couple of days there, they rode the train back to Asheville.

At that point, Charlie wrote North Carolina off his list. "I don't think Snavely wants me," he confided to Sarah.

Later, Crowell Little came to Asheville to talk with Charlie and brought George (Snuffy) Stirnweiss with him. Snuffy, who had played football at North Carolina and been in the V-12 program there during the war, was second baseman for the New York Yankees for eight years, playing in three World

Years after their football careers ended, Asheville's first two All-Americans posed for a stunt shot. That's Dan Hill at left, All-American center at Duke, and Charlie Justice at right. Hill was the man who tried to recruit Justice for Duke.

Series. Charlie thought Little brought Snuffy along to impress him, and if that were true, it worked. Stirnweiss certainly impressed him, but not enough to cause him to make a commitment to Carolina.

Charlie shot from the shoulder with them. "Coach didn't seem to care one way or the other," he said, "and I really have no further interest in Chapel Hill."

"That's just Coach Snavely's way," Little attempted to explain the incident away. "He is a man of few words and he's pretty brusque at times. He really wants you."

"If he wanted me, he would have paid some attention to us," Charlie said. "But I'll give it some more thought."

At their home in Biltmore, No. 8 Boston Way, the Justice family did not have a telephone. Sarah's family across town had one, but before the recruiters decided to go that route to reach Charlie, they found out the phone number of the Arakas family, the Justices' neighbors across the street, and the recruiters almost drove the Arakases nutty, answering the phone for Charlie.

"We weren't home much," Charlie said. "We spent some time visiting colleges."

Charlie counted more than two hundred colleges and universities that made overtures to him. Notre Dame, Southern California, South Carolina, Tennessee, Georgia, Duke, UCLA, Fordham – all the biggies tried to snare him, and they put relentless pressure on him.

"We saw no peace," Charlie said, "not at home and not on the road when we visited some schools. I've always felt sorry for our neighbors because every time I went uptown or anywhere and came back home the neighbors had two or three numbers for me to call."

Charlie and Sarah became rather well traveled. They visited South Carolina, Tennessee, Georgia, and a lot of other schools, some large, some small. Ralph James, Charlie's high school coach, wanted him to come to High Point College where most of the rest of the 1941-42 teams at Asheville had come after the war, but Charlie told him he wanted to play football at a higher college level.

At the University of South Carolina's invitation, Charlie and Sarah went to the first Gator Bowl in Jacksonville, Florida, in 1946. South Carolina played Wake Forest, and while there, Wake Forest Coach Peahead Walker found out their room number and took time away from his team's preparation to call and ask Charlie and Sarah to meet him in a park across the street so he could talk with them. Just as they had refused to let Carolina coaches pick them up at Duke, they turned down Peahead's invitation. They didn't think it would be fair to South Carolina.

South Carolina had great recruiters and a campus that would rival any other anywhere, neat and clean, and the students gave that appearance also.

"They treated us royally," Charlie said. In contrast to the opinion he had formed of Carl Snavely, Charlie thought South Carolina Coach Rex Enright was one of the finest people he'd ever met. "We fell in love with that place," Charlie said. "Thought it was the finest place in the world."

"There was so much ballyhoo over what I was being offered," Charlie said, "that it got funnier and funnier. People said I was being offered thousands of dollars and new cars and paid-for homes, and this, that, and the other, and not any of it was true. Oh, some schools made ridiculous offers, but we wrote them off the list very quickly because their offers were extravagant and we knew they couldn't live up to them. The major schools offered me scholarships and stayed within the limits established."

Two factors in reaching a decision, Sarah said, were what type of people Charlie would be playing for and with, and whether he would be able to complete his education if he got hurt.

"In some schools," she said, "if you got hurt, you were out. They wouldn't run you off, but would treat you so badly you'd quit."

"I never had any trouble at all," Charlie said. "I never asked for anything except that Sarah's way be paid, too. I was never paid a salary under the table, as some people claimed. In that day, we played primarily for the love of the game. We expected our school to live up to the promises it made in the scholarship, but no more."

After all the sorting and sifting was done, Charlie and Sarah made up their minds to go to South Carolina.

"They had us all set up," Charlie said. "Had us an apartment. Had me a job where all I'd have to do was go to the legislature once or twice a week and be a page. I thought that was great. And with Rex Enright coaching, they had a good football program."

So, showdown time arrived, and the principals of the drama gathered in the Justice home at the same time.

An Asheville alumnus of the University of South Carolina, Herb Coman, who had played for Enright and had become football coach at Asheville-Biltmore College, drove a car over to take Charlie to Columbia to enroll. He parked in front of the Justice home.

At the same time, Tom Young, accompanied by an ardent Asheville alumnus of North Carolina, Pierce Matthews, was parked in back of the house.

Charlie didn't know that the drama was developing so. "I didn't even know the recruiters were in town," he said. "I didn't suspect that anything was going on."

The Justice brothers, who did know what was coming down, gathered in the family home.

When Jack Justice, the oldest, looked out the front window and saw Herb Coman sitting in the parked car, he drew Charlie to one side.

"The time has come," Jack said. "It's decision time. There's a South Carolina car out front and a North Carolina car out back, and you've got to make up your mind. Now."

"Well, I'm going to South Carolina," Charlie said.

Jack took his younger brother by the arm. "Charlie, I have only one thing to say. If you leave the state of North Carolina, I'll disown you. You belong here. Chapel Hill is your school."

Charlie hesitated for only a moment. He looked up to Jack and had always been grateful that Jack had taken the family under his wing in the absence of their father, and hoisted them up a notch or two on the ladder of life. The bond between them was like a father-son relationship. And deep down, Charlie must have felt that Jack was right.

"Well, I guess I'd better go," Charlie said, and went out the back door and climbed in the sedan with Young and Matthews. And deep down, Charlie must have felt that Jack was right.

"When Charlie came out the back door," Young said years later, "it felt as if a great weight had been lifted off my shoulders. That was the first inkling I had that we had won."

Thus ended one of the greatest manhunts the South had ever seen.

The die was cast. At that moment, Charlie didn't feel good about the decision he had made. He really thought South Carolina would be the best place to go, but he agreed to Jack's wishes because there was an uncertainty within his own mind and Jack had never once misled him.

Nine years later, when Charlie was doing television color work for the Washington Redskins, Rex Enright came to Washington to try and hire Jim Tatum, the Maryland coach, to take South Carolina's coaching reins. Justice was working with North Carolina alumni in an effort to get Tatum to take the Tar Heel coaching job.

The trails of Justice and Enright crossed, and they exchanged pleasantries.

"Charlie," Enright said, "I've thought a lot about the decision you made back there in forty-six, and for a long time I have wanted to tell you that I think you made the right decision when you went to North Carolina."

What class! Justice thought. *After what I did to him, if he can still say that to me, I know what a gentleman he really is.*

At last, Charlie felt that the old score was squared.

Justice enrolled at Carolina on St. Valentine's Day, February 14, 1946, just five weeks after his discharge from the navy on January 9.

When Snavely received a telephone call from the admissions office telling him that a Charles Justice from Asheville had just enrolled, he uttered his now famous statement: "I hope he comes out for football."

THE GREY FOX

A mong the sharpest and most orderly minds in Chapel Hill in 1946 was that of Carl Snavely, the football coach, and no wonder! Snavely was once a prep school chemistry and mathematics teacher.

Employing preciseness in an analytical approach to football, paying sometimes severe attention to minute details, Snavely figured that mountains really were made of mole hills, and if he could conquer the small things that went wrong, he could certainly overcome the larger. In seasons past, because of minute oversights in his coaching procedure, he felt sure that his teams had lost games he thought they should have won.

Collier's Magazine reported that no man ever lived who devoted more time to football than Carl Snavely. "The sport is his whole life," the story read. "Aside from a little golf he plays occasionally in the summer, he has no recreation."

Except eating ice cream. He loved ice cream, and sometimes demolished a quart while watching game films in the evening.

His attention to detail was so phenomenal that he wanted the grass in Kenan Stadium cut to exactly one inch on game day to give his runners better footing. He checked the field often with Raymond Hutchins, the head groundskeeper, and Hutchins seldom cut the grass without Snavely's approval.

Snavely's weather eye was always peeled and focused on the clouds because weather has so much to do with the performance of a football team, especially a single-wing team. Athletic director Chuck Erickson fed long range and immediate weather reports daily to Snavely. If rain was forecast for game day, Snavely had his managers keep practice balls

Carl Snavely at the height of his coaching career.

soaking in buckets of water so his players would get the feel of wet footballs all week before the game.

To further reduce the chance of misplays with a wet ball, Snavely had his managers pack several dozen pairs of thin, white cotton pallbearers' gloves for his ballhandlers. Dusted with rosin, these gloves were worn to prevent fumbles in wet games.

Snavely hired a student to keep track of all classroom work of his players and report to him daily so he could quickly move a tutor into position when a player's grades began to slip. All players were required to maintain a C average.

After every practice on Navy Field, Snavely had trainer Chuck Quinlan weigh each player, and if the weight of some fell too far that day he slowed the pace of practice the following day.

He was a coach who used all available aids – movies, Dictaphone, blackboard, charts, statistics, newspapers – to drill his system into his players until each could repeat it backward. He wanted no mistakes on the field from a player who didn't understand his role in any play.

During a season, Snavely's cameramen shot more than 40,000 feet of movie film which the coach watched at night, usually with his assistant coaches. He once said he didn't know a thing about football until he started filming it.

Snavely was always aware of how folks in his players' hometowns felt about his team, and he was aware of what was going on in the enemy camps for the entire season. He gleaned this information by subscribing to more than two dozen daily newspapers – those in the major cities in North Carolina, certain papers from Pennsylvania, West Virginia, Virginia, New Jersey, Maryland, and Ohio, where most of his players were recruited, and the newspapers in the hometown of each opponent. He assigned newspapers to assistant coaches to read daily and report to him any mention of the Tar Heels or their opponents. In this way, he also kept himself and his staff abreast of any college football prospects developing in the high schools covered by those papers.

Though Snavely's teams ran from the single-wing formation, it wasn't just any single-wing. It was dubbed the "black and blue single-wing" by his opponents who were often darkly bruised by Snavely's hard-hitting blockers and tacklers. In that respect, Charlie Justice was thoroughly acquainted with procedure; he had run behind bruising blockers all the way through high school and service football.

The advent of the quick-hitting T-formation and its evolution into the quick-opening split-T changed the whole face of football. The single-wing, already considered archaic by consensus, appeared to most coaches to be far outmoded. But Snavely's single-wing was more massive and explosive than others, prompting Oklahoma's Bud Wilkinson, beginning to build his reputation as one of the nation's finest coaches, to say of the Tar Heels, "I've never seen a single-wing team do more with a ball than Carolina."

Two events of significance that helped mold Snavely's stalwart reputation and earned him the respect of the nation's coaches occurred during the 1940 season when Snavely coached the Big Red at Cornell.

The first was an accusation made against Snavely after his Cornell team defeated Ohio State on November 2, charging that Snavely had called signals from the sidelines, an illegal procedure in that day before free substitution. The Ohio State athletic director, L. W. St. John, issued the charge and breached football's ethics by releasing his letter of accusation to the press before it was received by its addressees, James Lynah, director of athletics at Cornell, and Asa Bushnell, commissioner of the Eastern Intercollegiate Football Association. By doing so, St. John opened himself to criticism not only by Cornell but also by others in college football across the country.

Taking the bull by the horns with a strong grip, Lynah dressed down the Ohio State athletic director in a letter of pointed protest, which read in part:

> I take decided exception to your releasing for publication a complaint based on 'unreserved convictions' before your complaint had reached the one to whom addressed and before any of those concerned in your complaint had been made aware that you would submit a complaint.
>
> In other words, you chose to attempt to convict in the eyes of the public, on a charge of violating the letter of the rule and the code of sportsmanship, a man of unimpeachable character and of the highest standards of sportsmanship, who enjoys the respect and confidence of the entire university community, before placing a charge against him. ...
>
> At home games Coach Snavely sits at a table just in front of the press box in plain view and directly opposite from where I sit in the Crescent. ... I frequently focus my glasses on Coach Snavely to see how he reacts to certain situations encountered by the team. It is a restless period for the coach and he changes his positions frequently, and whatever he is holding in his hand, a rolled-up program or sheets of paper (St. John charged Snavely signaled with a 'cylinder'), goes through many gyrations.
>
> Not once at the Ohio State game or in any other game have I detected any actions that could be construed as signaling from the bench by Coach Snavely. ...

The controversy prompted Columbia University coach Lou Little, after losing to Cornell the following week, to call Cornell "a mighty football team."

A United Press report told the story in a way that appeared to castigate Ohio State without mentioning names:

> ... (Little) didn't charge Carl Snavely with spiking the water bucket with gin. He didn't claim the Ithacans had reinforced their hip pads with stove lids, nor did he indict the trainers for giving the Cornell quarterback hashish to smoke between halves. He did none of these things because he was too busy hailing the Big Red as one of the best football teams ever. To Little, the connoiseur, Cornell was a masterpiece in motion. ...
>
> Cornell is a team excellently coached by a man with a genius for method and detail. ...
>
> Poise is a word you find more often in a drawing room than a dressing room, but Little holds that it is poise which puts poison in the Big Red attack. ...
>
> It isn't just confidence and certainly not cockiness but rather a sureness and certainty of action. The boys have worked together long enough to sense their abilities and capabilities, and that pulls them through the pinches.

Six years later, coaching at Chapel Hill, Snavely, if innocent then, like most coaches of the day had changed his tactics and, indeed, was signaling plays from the bench.

"Snavely had a certain way to signal what he wanted," Justice said in a lengthy interview. "He would get in a certain position and cross his hands or arms, or, if sitting down, cross his legs like Coach James did it in high school. Everybody did it. They said you couldn't signal a play in, or send one in, but everybody did it, everybody had their own signals, just like a third base coach talking to batters in sign language. They carried papers in their hands and rolled them up and beat them in their hands. So many beats meant one thing, and another number of beats meant something else."

The other 1940 incident, one that proved Snavely's integrity beyond the shadow of any doubt, occurred the day after Cornell's come-from-behind victory over Dartmouth. Watching films of the game on Sunday, Snavely discovered that Cornell had unwittingly taken a fifth down to score the winning touchdown. He immediately wired Red Blaik, the Dartmouth coach who later gained monumental fame as coach of Army teams at West Point, and forfeited the victory.

Snavely was a dignified and scholarly man who stood stiffly erect. He cut a different figure from most coaches of the day. Snavely's deep-set eyes beneath shaggy brows bored into those with whom he spoke, and he had a deliberate manner of speech.

But on the sidelines during a football game, he became an animated man, jumping up and down, stalking back and forth in front of his bench, chewing gum furiously, and bellowing the names of substitutes who always came back with a loud, "Yes, sir!" so Snavely would know they had heard and responded.

In 1949, his kicker missed an extra point and Snavely threw his hat in the air and yelled, "Dog gone it! We shouldn't miss a one of those all year! Not a single one!"

No detail of play escaped him; neither did any oversight, nor any error by a player.

Snavely was born in Omaha, Nebraska, in 1894, the son of a Methodist minister. He was named Carl Grey Snavely, and later his name and his Dutch ancestry prompted writers to dub him "The Grey Fox" and "Dutch Master," and similar sobriquets.

His father moved into a Pennsylvania district of the Methodist Church when Carl was an infant, and he spent his boyhood in several Pennsylvania towns where his father was assigned to preach.

Snavely was a three-letterman in sports at Lebanon Valley College, graduating in 1915. After graduation he played three years of professional baseball as a first baseman.

But even while playing baseball, he reverted to his first love – football. He coached high schools and small colleges in Pennsylvania and Ohio after the baseball season.

Ready for tougher competition by 1927, and knowing he wanted a life of football coaching, he accepted the head coaching job at Bucknell. His love for football was so deep, and his desire to field as fine a team as possible was so great that he volunteered to coach baseball and made sure that his football players made the baseball team. This was not always entirely fair to the school's baseball-only players, but the practice is continued in certain schools today. When Snavely coached baseball, then, many baseball patrons were surprised when they showed up early for a game and saw Snavely's baseball team killing time by running football drills in the outfield.

His coaching career at Bucknell lasted six years, and in 1934 he received a request to move to Chapel Hill and coach the University of North Carolina team, a decided step upward from his position at Bucknell. He took the job and set about building his version of North Carolina football around an excellent guard, George Barclay, who in 1934 became the first Tar Heel ever named to an All-American first team. Jim Tatum, who, like Barclay, later coached the Tar Heels, was an all-conference tackle on that 1935 team.

In his first season, Snavely coached the Tar Heels to a 7-1-1 record, losing to Tennessee, 19-7, and tying North Carolina State, 7-7. In the Carolina-Duke game in six-year-old Kenan Stadium the Tar Heels eked out a 7-0 victory, which would have satisfied some Tar Heel afficionados had the team won no other games.

Using players left from 1934 as a nucleus, Snavely built another powerhouse in 1935, finishing 8-1. The Tar Heels won their first seven games and folks in Chapel Hill were singing Rose Bowl tunes, but on November 26 in Durham, Duke dashed Carolina's bowl hopes with a precisely-engineered 25-0 victory. A record Southern Conference football crowd of 47,000 watched the game. UNC games were seen that year by 149,500 fans, another attendance record for the Tar Heels.

Virginia was the unfortunate next opponent for North Carolina and the Tar Heels took out all their frustrations on the hapless Cavaliers, winning 61-0. North Carolina wound up eighth in the Associated Press final rankings that year, its highest ranking ever to that time.

With a record of 15-2-1 after two seasons at Carolina, Snavely abruptly departed for Cornell after the 1935 season, prompted by what he considered to be a blow that would wreck the Carolina football system. Frank Graham, then president of the University of North Carolina, presented a "Graham Plan" to the sixteen-team Southern Conference which called for the virtual abolishment of subsidization of athletes, ostensibly aimed at putting sports in the conference back on a simon-pure footing but more likely it was designed to combat the depression-ridden times when universities, like individuals, had to pinch pennies to make ends meet. The conference adopted the plan, Snavely left for the Ivy League head-coaching job at Cornell, and after two dull seasons of football without scholarships, the Southern Conference abandoned the plan and returned to subsidizing players. Unfortunately for North Carolina, Snavely was long gone.

In five seasons at Cornell, Snavely built an undefeated, untied 1939 team, but by that time the clouds of global war had spread darkly across the world, and Snavely found himself facing the same situation at Cornell that had set him packing at Chapel Hill. Because of the war, Cornell abolished scholarships after the 1941 season. Snavely weathered the war with the Big Red, though very sadly after his only son, Carl, Jr., a navy flier, was lost at sea in 1944.

Thus, when Snavely returned to Chapel Hill in 1945 he was a different man, more introspective and reclusive, though he held a job of high visibility. There was within him a deep emptiness caused by the death of his son, and he relied on his football players to help fill the void inside him. Snavely buried himself in his work, often laboring relentlessly around the clock.

"He was a very cold man," Justice said, "who rarely said anything. He seldom made a comment on the practice field except to snort. I never heard him use a curse word, and on Sunday after Saturday games, he would watch movies of the Saturday games and grade each player as if he were grading mathematics papers."

Snavely's second tenure at Carolina was blessed with an influx of war veterans eager to get their college education and willing to play football to pay for it. The team had lost eight games and won only one (beating the Cherry Point Marines) in 1944, and Snavely turned the team around, winning five games and losing five in 1945 when only a sprinkling of war veterans had returned.

Johnny came marching home in force early in 1946, and grizzled veterans and a handful of pink-checked boys immediately went to work on Navy Field in Chapel Hill, building a football team for the fall season. For the next four years, North Carolina ruled Southern Conference football with as devastating an attack as the single-wing formation could generate, which in this case was huge and formidable.

The team, Justice included, had deep respect for the Grey Fox. Being, in the main, war veterans who hadn't had the opportunity to think a lot for themselves during the four years of war, many disagreed with some things Snavely did on the field and exercised their right of dissent. Snavely took no umbrage at those who questioned him but forced his way by exercising his own iron will and using assistant coaches who had been through the war and knew how to handle military-minded veterans.

Coaches were firm with the players who as veterans understood discipline, and soon they saw the logic of the moves Snavely made, for he had applied the depth of his logical mind to his approach to football.

In four post-war seasons (1946-49) Snavely and his talented players – the Justice-Weiner-Rodgers crew – raised Carolina football to a new level of national prominence, but in 1950 the departure of Justice and the remnants of the great 1947 and '48 teams left a void in North Carolina football that was impossible to fill at the time. The situation was almost that of having to start the program all over. The 1950 team, still under Snavely, finished 3-5-2; in 1951, 2-8; in 1952, 2-6 – a combined 7-19-2 – proving, Snavely thought, that if you didn't have the horses you couldn't pull the wagon.

Under the heat of increasing pressure from the university and its alumni, Snavely was forced to scrap his old faithful single-wing in favor of the quick-opening, quick-hitting split-T. Snavely did not want to change offensive formations for one that would take him years to learn to operate; so when George Barclay, the 1934 All-American guard who knew the split-T, was brought in as an assistant, the Grey Fox saw the handwriting on the wall. He took his medicine like the man he was, taking consolation in the thought that he had had the pleasure of coaching the Tar Heels through their most magnificent era.

Snavely's employment was terminated at the end of the 1952 season. Taking some of his assistants, he moved to Washington University in St. Louis.

Barclay became head coach at Carolina, and for three years, he fared about the same as Snavely in his last three years, winning 11, losing 18, and tying one.

In 1956 Barclay was succeeded by Jim Tatum, whom Justice helped lure away from Maryland. Tatum had won a national championship at Maryland and was one of the outstanding coaches of the day. He was also a 1935 North Carolina graduate who played football for Snavely during the Grey Fox's first term in 1934-35. After working as a freshman coach at Carolina from 1939 through 1941 and wartime head coach in 1942 (5-2-2), Tatum always said he wanted to come back home to coach the Tar Heels. So he succeeded Barclay, and working under increasing pressure from alumni to rebuild Carolina to national prominence, he was making good progress when, after three seasons, he died suddenly in 1959 of Rocky Mountain spotted fever. Tar Heel football fortunes immediately dropped back into the chasm of mediocrity.

Thus, for twenty years after the departure of Justice and the crew with whom he played, North Carolina's football team scraped along the bottom. From 1950 through the 1962 season, the Tar Heels had only two better than .500 seasons, both 6-4 and both under Tatum.

Snavely stayed in St. Louis and died there in his 80s. He was fifty-two when he came back to Chapel Hill to coach in 1946, and when he left in 1952, he was fifty-eight.

Snavely was a straight-laced man, which brought him grief at times because many other coaches felt he was a perfect butt for jokes.

Once at a coaches meeting, about fifty coaches took time after a day-long session to attend a burlesque show and see the girlies. A coach from Illinois, no doubt a joker, had a telephone receiver with a long cord attached. He shoved the cord in the ticket office window and spoke into the dummy phone. When Snavely approached the window, the coach called, "Carl Snavely?"

"Right here," Snavely replied. "I'm Coach Snavely."

"Telephone for you, Carl," and the coach handed Snavely the receiver.

"I wonder who could be calling me here," Snavely furrowed his brow. Then he put the receiver to his ear and said, "Hello, Coach Snavely here."

There was no answer, but Snavely had identified himself loud enough that all eyes were on him, coaches and other spectators, too.

"Coach Snavely here!" Snavely said a little louder.

The crowd began to chuckle, and Snavely pulled the cord out of the ticket office and saw that he had been taken. He simply smiled.

He was not completely immune from humor, however. He could also dish it out when he felt in a jovial mood.

Sometime in the 1949 season, Red Miller, tall, red-haired, rather pompous sports editor of *The Asheville Citizen*, decided to telephone Snavely one evening for information to use in his column.

He picked up the phone at his desk and when the company operator answered, he said, "Red Miller here. Would you get Snave on the line for me?"

"Who?"

"Snave," Red replied. "Snavely. Coach Snavely in Chapel Hill."

In a couple of minutes she dialed Red back and had Snavely on the line.

Bill Hensley and Al Geremonte, two other sports writers at work in the office that evening, stopped what they were doing and listened.

"Hello, Snave," Red said. "I wanted to ask you...."

Red was silent a moment, then, "Red. ... Red Miller! .... M-I-L-L-E-R.... Sports editor, *Asheville Citizen*."

He held the phone at arm's length and glared at it. Replacing it to his ear, he yelled, "Miller! Miller! Red Miller! From Asheville! That's right. I want to ask you a few questions about...."

He stopped in mid-sentence and listened a moment.

"MILLER!!!" he screamed. "RED MILLER! ASHEVILLE! Yes, of course that's in North Carolina. ..."

By this time Red was so overcome with consternation he didn't even see Hensley and Geremonte rolling in the floor in laughter.

RUNNING, RUNNING, RUNNING

A fter a few practice sessions in 1946, Snavely knew he had the nucleus of a great team – and he also realized that Justice's hand must be on the throttle. Choo Choo was a runner like Snavely had never seen before.

He had pegged Charlie correctly.

After Carolina lost the 1949 Sugar Bowl to Oklahoma, 14-6, the Sooner coach, Bud Wilkinson, commented: "There's no question about Justice being a great back. He was the player we feared most and he showed us why."

Early in 1948 Wake Forest knocked Justice out of bounds hard and the Carolina fans screamed in protest. After the game, Peahead Walker, the Wake Forest coach, was asked about the play, and he said, "What do you expect my boys to do – watch the yard markers go by when they're chasing Justice? Next thing you know somebody will suggest asking his permission, like being at a dance. Heck, this is war and Justice has got most of the ammunition."

Tom Anderson, sports columnist for *The Knoxville Journal*, wrote after Justice's great 1946 run against the Tennessee Volunteers: "But what, now we ask, in the devil are you going to use for words to describe young funks like Charlie Justice even half-adequately? You simply cannot do it without resorting to the stereotyped superlatives because he is undoubtedly one of the greatest ball carriers of all time."

And Wally Butts, the Georgia coach, once warned his players: "Watch him close. He'll outrun you, outpass you, outthink you. He'll fake you out of your shoes in a broken field. Take no chances with Justice."

People used to ask the question, and writers sometimes headed their columns with a hackneyed phrase: "What makes Charlie run?"

What, indeed? He didn't have ground-blistering speed. He wasn't big enough to bulldoze defenders out of his way. But he could run.

Few others ever ran as Charlie did. One reason was because he had certain physical attributes that the average person didn't have: He was blessed, for example, with tremendous peripheral vision like an ultra-wide camera lens, with which he could see almost the entire field. He had the surefootedness of a mountain goat, enabling him to fake a guy out of his jock strap, and such balance and great control of his body that he could stop on a dime and in the next split-second explode into full speed. He could cut and run, dodge and run, fake and run with no loss of motion. He could change speeds that fooled tacklers as certainly as Bob Feller's changeup fooled batters.

And wherever he played, he always had devastating blocking. "Anybody can run," says the modest Charlie, "who has blocking like I had."

Possibly his vision and his razor-sharp mind had as much to do with his success as his legs. With peripheral vision stretching far wider than that of an ordinary person, Charlie could see every defender on the field at most times. Unconsciously he counted them, noted where they were, and calculated where they would be by the time he got to them. Working like a computer before computers were born, Charlie's mind instantly flashed onto his mental screen the move he needed to make – and he had the reaction time and body control to make the move.

Very simply, he outthought the opposition first, and then outmaneuvered it.

Seldom did a tackler slip up on him, and the only times he got blindsided was when he was already tackled and going down. He does not remember many cheap shots, but does recall numerous late hits.

He thanked the Good Lord every day for his football-oriented mind. He was no genius in class, but he was an Einstein on the field. And he thanked Him for his vision. Those two factors did not show in his movements on the gridiron, but they triggered the moves that did show.

"I don't know why God gave me those abilities," he often said. "I didn't develop them; they were inborn. God gave them to me for a purpose, and I used them to the best purpose I could."

Was that purpose beating Duke? The Tar Heels beat their arch-rivals in all four of Justice's seasons.

One coach, whose name has been lost in antiquity, summed up Charlie's play this way: "I think I know what Justice does. Defensive players to him are like standing tenpins. They appear upright and steady. When they make a move, he notes that movement; if they don't move, he fakes, and that half second when they commit themselves registers with him. He runs at them in that instant when they are thinking – and he outthinks them. I know what he does, and so do others know, but we can't teach our players to think with him. I wish I could."

Mechanically, Charlie was a wizard on the field. Starting on a 43-yard run, like the one he made in a 20-0 victory over Duke in 1948, Charlie would take the ball and scan the line and secondary quickly, looking for open space. There was a hole he was supposed to go through – through guard, off tackle, up the middle – but if he saw another hole open first he went through it and depended on a pattern of broken blocking to clear the way. His blockers knew he ran this way, and when they got through the line if they saw that Charlie had cut through earlier they simply cut behind him to keep the defenders from getting him from the rear or the side.

"I could see the whole field," Charlie said. "I could see things others couldn't see, and I don't understand why or how, but I could see what developed around me. That was the peripheral vision at work. I didn't realize what it was until a doctor told me when I was in college. It was natural to me. I was born with it; I didn't develop it. God gave me the ability to see things in a way that no one else on our team could see, and I used everything he gave me. At the same time, these things wouldn't have worked at all if the other ten guys hadn't used their abilities to get their job done."

Extraordinary vision is something many of the greatest athletes of all time had. Babe Ruth could read the label on a spinning 78 record; Ted Williams saw the ball so clearly he could tell you whether he hit it on the seam or the skin. Williams once walked into the Hillerich & Bradsby room at a baseball meeting in Fort Lauderdale, scanned a row of 200 bats, all of different sizes, picked one out without checking the size, hefted it, and said, "I believe I could hit with that." He handed the bat to the H&B man and walked out. Checking the bat, the man said, "I guess he could. That's the bat he used."

Ruth and Williams had adjusted their tremendous sight to suit what they did on the baseball diamond; Justice did the same – he adjusted his to fit what he needed to see on the football field.

Charlie free-lanced at times. He would follow the set play called in the huddle until he saw a better opportunity, and then he would cut away and try to go where the opposition didn't. "I just cut," he said. "If I saw a hole, I went for it. Sometimes I was wrong, but mostly I was right."

When his blockers came back in he would make his cut off their tails as they picked off defenders. "That was instinct," he said. "Once we got away from the set play, everything ran on instinct. I've heard others say they did what they were supposed to do, but we didn't run that way. If I saw blockers I went for them. I never wanted to get out front by myself until I was by all the tacklers. That's a naked feeling, running without anybody looking for

Breaking through crushing blocking, Charlie heads goalward.

someone to block. If I stayed with my blockers I knew they would pick 'em off for me."

Instinctively, Charlie could read his blockers' intentions from behind. "I'm not saying their brains were in the seat of their pants," Charlie laughed. "I followed the blocker to see which side of the defensive man he put his head on. If he put his head on the defense man's left, I'd cut to the right behind his head. The tackler couldn't come through the blocker's head to get at me. So wherever he put his head, I'd cut that way off his tail."

That, too, came instinctively. No one taught it to Charlie. Coaches, recognizing the ability he had, helped him refine it, but the original gift was God-given. It was born with him. Still, as instinctive as the moves were, they were far more complex than that.

"I don't think anybody could explain it," Charlie said. "I don't think you

could get any good runner who ran the way I did to tell you that he was taught. The coaches helped fine-tune my instincts. They would say, 'Now, Charlie, go the right way on your cut, and be sure you use the blockers. Wherever his head is, cut that way.' That's what they were teaching, to cut off his head or his tail. So, in teaching, they were simply reminding me of what I had to do instinctively. Of course, part of the success of the runner-blocker relationship is timing. If I cut away from the blockers too soon, I was dead. It had to be timed just right."

In high school, Charlie could get away with leaving his blockers more than in the navy, in college, and certainly in the pros. He only cut back when the way was closed up or when he saw good blocking in the other direction. Buster Ramsey, the William & Mary All-American guard with whom Justice played at Bainbridge, emphasized to Charlie the importance of staying with his blockers.

The Commodores were playing the Marine Corps team at Camp Lejeune in North Carolina and Justice was having a great day. Like scythes, his blockers cut down the Marines and his path was usually open. Once he cut away from the blockers and headed goalward and a defensive back ran him down from behind and tackled him on the ten.

Justice was getting up off the ground when Ramsey suddenly pounced on him, grabbed him by the back of the shoulder pads and under the breeches, and screamed, "You little high school son of a bitch! You think you're the greatest runner in the world, don't you? You just made a damned fool out of me in front of all these Marines, and I don't like it!"

He scooted Charlie along until they reached the bench. Justice sat down and occasionally cut his eyes toward Ramsey. Buster glared back.

In the huddle, the next time Bainbridge got the ball, Ramsey, still glaring at him, asked, "What makes you, Justice? Who makes you?"

"You do, Buster," Charlie returned. "You do."

That was the day Charlie learned to stay with his blockers. He didn't want to face Ramsey's ridicule again.

"Buster Ramsey was the greatest guard I ever saw," Justice said. "In more than fifty years since, I haven't seen another like him. He could run, he was fast, and he hit like a ton of bricks. I mean, he'd kill you!"

After Justice had played with a team for a while and he and his blockers got their timing down, Charlie's running style, lateral almost as much as forward, often gave his blockers more than one opportunity to help him on a play.

Once in high school, Asheville High's blocking back, Forrest Maney, blocked out an end, and when Charlie went by, Maney regained his feet, ran downfield, and blocked the last two men between Justice and the goal line. Maney loved to block; that was his bread and butter. He would say in the huddle, "Charlie, cut back for me, just cut back and I'll get 'em."

Cutback running was the most natural way for Charlie to run, and the style earned him touchdowns, national headlines, and widespread fame.

His blockers never lingered back. One block usually wasn't enough. They knew Charlie's cutback style, and as soon as they made their initial hits, they went on downfield looking for more.

Justice used the entire field, back and forth, criss-crossing sideline-to-sideline, always with an eye forward toward the goal. His style was the thing that prompted the oft-quoted story about Ted Hazelwood blocking the Duke lineman as Charlie sailed by, and pinning the lineman to the ground.

"Get up, Ted," the lineman said. "He's already by."

"Hell, no, I'm not getting up," Hazelwood replied. "He may be back this way two or three more times."

Charlie's lack of blinding speed never hurt him because he was fast enough for the systems he played. In the T-formation at Bainbridge and later for the Redskins, he was fast enough to hit his holes on the quick-opening plays, but from the single-wing, which he ran in high school and college, quick-starting speed was not a requisite.

"We didn't need to turn on the afterburners in the single-wing," he said, "and really didn't need power. I never depended on either. We would hit as quickly as we could, but remember that in the single-wing the ball had to be snapped five yards back to me or four and a half yards to the fullback, so we could never hit the line really fast. Too, I had to hesitate a split-second while the guards pulled out and got by in front of me. We always had to hesitate on the tackle traps. We'd take two steps and then hit in there pretty fast behind the linemen, going through right off the guards' tails."

In the T, blockers opened holes quickly, sometimes by brushblocking, and runners burst through like the snap of your fingers. In the single-wing the holes had to be kept open while the blocking back, the fullback, both guards, and the ball carrier went through like a cavalry charge. The guards lined up side by side in an unbalanced line so one wouldn't be three or four yards behind the other when they pulled out to block.

Charlie liked both offenses. He had no preference, except that in the single-wing he had more room to run and more time to pick up his blockers.

Reverses were run off the single-wing more easily than off the T. At Bainbridge, a reverse was known as a Sally Rand. "I'd start one way," Charlie said, "and turn around and come back and Don Durden would give me the ball."

Running the single-wing at Chapel Hill, the reverse was a surprise and very deadly play. On single-wing right, the fullback would take the ball and fake it to Justice who went on up the middle, trying to draw the defense to the inside. The wingback, coming left, would take the ball from the fullback, and then slip it to the left end, the weak-side end, who was usually Art Weiner, coming back to the right. Weiner played on the weak side because he was the biggest end on the team and his job usually was to knock the tackle down.

Both guards pulled on reverses and went the way the play was going. That was a hint to the defense which way the play was going, but in the heat of battle the guards were hard to detect.

Charlie did most of the passing from the pocket. Seldom would he come out of the pocket to pass.

"I would take one step like I was going to run," Charlie said, "then stop and cross over, look for my receivers, and throw." The fullback would come across and block to the left to protect Charlie from being blind-sided, and the blocking back would assume the protection to the right. Both ends and the wingback would run the pass patterns.

"We didn't split the ends at all," Charlie said. "We played them in tight."

Most who observed Justice consider his 74-yard run against Tennessee in 1946, easily the most exciting play in Knoxville that year, to be the best run he ever made, but a 43-yard dash he ran against Duke in the 20-0 win in 1948 was the play that Justice thought was his best. He has thought that for almost fifty years.

In Knoxville, Justice broke through the hard-charging Tennessee line at Carolina's 26 and cut toward the sideline. Behind brutal blocking, he picked his holes carefully and side-stepped and outran the entire Tennessee team, several of whom had more than one shot at him.

Folks who saw the run still talk about it, and occasionally a Knoxville television station will break out that old film and rerun the play for their viewers. It was, indeed, spectacular; General Bob Neyland, the Tennessee coach, always called it the finest run he had ever seen.

The Duke run was shorter, only 43 yards. Blocking in the secondary was crisp, and Charlie followed it down to about the 20 where he suddenly found the traffic situation bothersome. He wheeled to his left and cut across for the sideline where he found an open lane to the end zone, and he went through before it could close again.

Running, of course, wasn't Charlie's only attribute. He could pass and punt, making him a bonafide triple-threat every time he took the ball.

His high school punting was legend, and he boomed kicks all the way through college. Punting, remember, got him on the Bainbridge team, which was possibly the biggest break he ever got.

He was embarrassed in his first college game against Virginia Polytechnic Institute when VPI blocked two of his punts for touchdowns and tied the Tar Heels, 14-14.

After the game, Charlie swore in the dressing room that he would never have another punt blocked. In thirty-eight more college games, no one ever blocked another. By shortening his kicking style to a step and a half, he sped up his kicking speed until Tennessee scouts, timing him, reported to General Neyland that there was no way the Vols could block him. "With his kicking speed," they said, "it's not possible."

Often, single-wing teams ran from punt formation, trying to fool the opposition, or from short-punt formation.

Charlie loved to punt, and he was picture-perfect at it, but his favorite style of punting was the quick kick.

Generated from the single-wing, it was primarily used on third down to surprise the enemy. Often Charlie's quick kicks went for 70 to 80 yards.

"I would take a long step back with my right foot," he explained, "then a step with my left, coming forward, and kick the ball quickly before the linemen could crash in."

In 1949, the Tar Heels beat Duke, 21-20, with a quick kick. In three previous games with Duke, Carolina had never used a quick kick, so at an opportune moment Justice booted one out of bounds on the Duke one-yard line. Billy Cox of Duke retaliated with a quick kick, which he had never done, and Carolina tackle Dave Wiley blocked it into the end zone where Carolina recovered for a two-point safety. Had the safety not been scored, Duke could have won 20-19.

START OF AN ERA

The first day Charlie Justice went through spring football practice in 1946 at Chapel Hill, he was besieged with doubts.

Oh, Lord, he thought, we're in trouble.

At home afterward, he confided in Sarah, "I don't think we'll have much of a team at all. Nobody took practice seriously; they were all out there just having a good time."

"Why?" Sarah asked. "Why are they acting that way?"

"I don't know," Charlie said. "Maybe it's because the war has just ended and everybody's still letting down, trying to enjoy themselves. But I'm worried."

At that point, Justice had never played a season on a losing team. Two undefeated seasons of high school football and two more great years with Bainbridge were immediately behind him, and he had no desire to play on a mediocre team in college. He had no doubts about his own ability, but he always thought football was a serious business and couldn't understand the cavalier attitude taken toward the game by some of the players from whom much was expected.

The squad spent the spring getting to know each other and learning the intricate single-wing offensive system Coach Snavely used. Charlie had not played the single-wing in three years, not since high school. At Bainbridge in 1943 and '44 and at Hawaii in 1945 he had been a halfback in the T-formation.

Snavely had a fine coaching staff, including backfield coach Russ Murphy, who knew the single-wing intimately. He knew how to operate the formation to best effect. Max Reed was a line coach whom Justice called "probably the best line coach of that day." He had coached Snavely's lines at North Carolina in 1934-35. "Reed said very little," Justice said, "but when the time for talking came, he knew how to teach linemen what he wanted them to know. He was, perhaps, the most firm coach with the war veterans on the Carolina staff."

George (Snuffy) Stirnweiss, a Carolina graduate who played baseball for the New York Yankees, was a backfield coach in 1946. Crowell Little coached the freshmen and jayvee squads. He was an Asheville man who had been a fine back in his own right at Carolina from '35 through '37, the first year for Coach Snavely and the latter two seasons under Coach Ray Wolf. Little later worked several years as head coach at Davidson. Jim Gill was an outstanding coach who knew how single-wing ends should perform. He and George Radman coached the ends. Eddie Teague was a coach in 1946, too.

In the last three or four years of his stay in Chapel Hill, which ended after the 1952 season, Snavely had two from the great Carolina teams on his staff, fullback Walt Pupa helping with the freshmen in 1948-49, and wingback Jim Camp working with the varsity backfield from 1949.

In 1950, the departure of Justice and the other remnants of the great 1947 and '48 teams left a void in North Carolina football that was almost impossible to fill.

Charlie thought he might also have some trouble adjusting to the team because of the heavy buildup by the press. His enrollment at Chapel Hill had made headlines across the state, and he knew that much was expected of him.

"I didn't ask for the buildup," he said, "but it was there and I couldn't do anything about it. I could feel resentment in several players; I know human nature that well. I felt the best thing I could do was to meet all the players quickly and get to know them."

Two days after his introduction to the squad he could call most of the players by first names, and that meant a lot to the others. As the players got to know him better each day, as they saw his work ethics, the sweat he poured into the game, Charlie felt the resentment silently slipping away. Before spring practice ended, he was no longer the big star of high school and navy football who had earned headlines across the nation. The players saw that all the ballyhoo behind Charlie had no effect on him. He adopted the attitude that he was a freshman halfback trying to make the team, and that counted heavily with his fellow players and coaches. He was the only one in the state who thought that way. Everyone else thought the pressure was on the coaches and the team to perform up to Charlie's standards, and if they did this Carl Snavely had no doubt that his team would be a winner. His teammates saw that there were no stars orbiting around Charlie's head, but those who had never seen him play quickly learned that he could do wonders with a foot-

Charlie visited Tom Young at Cullowhee in 1948. Young, who recruited Charlie for the University of North Carolina, had become head football coach at Western Carolina Teachers College.

ball. He simply became one of the boys – a very special one, yes, but he felt as if he were just one in a crowd.

The first time Charlie was introduced to Chan Highsmith, the rugged center from Georgia, Highsmith looked him up one side and down the other and finally said, "So you're the son of a bitch they're paying so much money to. Well. . . we'll see."

Oh, boy, Justice thought. *I've got to get him on my side.* So he joined Highsmith's fraternity, Beta Theta Phi.

Years later, Charlie was traveling for the American Oil Company through Georgia and stopped to have dinner with Highsmith.

"Charlie," Highsmith said, "there was just one damned thing wrong with you."

"What was that?" Charlie asked.

"You tried too damned hard to please your teammates. You didn't have to, you know."

"I didn't let him know it, but that did me more good than anything," Charlie said later. "The more I thought about it, the more I realized that a person is only as good as the people around him. There was a saying in World War Two that a convoy was only as fast as its slowest ship. Applying that personally, a football player is no better than the people who surround him on the field -- and in life it's the same way."

The Tar Heels were deep into spring practice before Justice really began to feel that he was accepted by players and coaches alike. Until that point he felt that Snavely thought he was too small for a single-wing tailback at a major school, and Snavely showed him little attention until a scrimmage with Guilford. Neither team was doing much when Snavely beckoned and asked Justice if he'd like to run a play.

He ran one – 80 yards to the end zone, clicking off moves to dodge tacklers like clockwork.

The rest is history, but he never felt unaccepted after that.

Another way Charlie gained acceptance was by working extremely hard on the practice field. Trainer Doc White was quoted by *PIC* Magazine as describing some of Justice's habits thusly: "The kid is first on the field every afternoon. There's absolutely no ki-yi or snob in him. Some teams might put up with a prima donna but not our outfit. Too much talent. Temperamentally I imagine he's gaited like Army's Glenn Davis was. They say he was easy to handle."

Many of the players on that 1946 team, a squad of healthy, rugged-looking men, were those who had played at Chapel Hill before or during the war and had returned to finish their education either on football scholarship or the G.I. Bill. There were not too many fresh recruits like Charlie. Joel Wright was a walkon, but he, too, had played before the war. The son of a wealthy Asheville oil man and bus executive, Joe did not bother with either a scholarship or the G.I. Bill. His father paid his way, and he never asked the football staff for favors, either on the field or off.

Gradually, as spring practice wound on toward its end, Charlie began to realize how deep in talent the Tar Heels were. They didn't have great size, but at most positions they were three or four deep, and most of the guys were talented and smart. Snavely and his recruiters had done their jobs well.

They had come up with a bumper crop of ends: Art Weiner, Joe Romano, Kenny Powell, and John Tandy at left end; George Sparger, Bob Cox, Mike Rubish, and Dan Logue at right end. Ernie Williamson, the biggest man on the team, and Len Szafaryn were to be the starting tackles. Both were standouts later in professional football. The guards, kcys to the success of the single-wing, were Emmett Cheek, later an assistant under Jim Tatum at Chapel Hill; Sid Varney, who coached Elon's unbeaten team in 1957; and Bob Mitten and Ralph Strayhorn, both outstanding players. Strayhorn was an older fellow from Durham who captained the 1946 team. Minton and Varney were recruited by Snavely and Russ Murphy in the Ohio-Pennsylvania area.

Later Justice said of Minton: "He was one of the greatest guards I ever played behind. He could hit! Unfortunately, he died young a few years later while coaching at a small college in Pennsylvania."

Highsmith was capable of playing for anyone. He had been recruited by Tom Young, the chief recruiter, and Jim Tatum and had played at Carolina two seasons before the war.

The blocking backs, like the guards, were essential to blocking in the single-wing, and Joe Wright and Don Hartig divided those chores. Both were crushing blockers. Jim Camp, Jack Fitch, and B. K. Grow were good runners who would handle the wingback position. There were other fine runners like Johnny Clements, Bill Maceyko, and Billy Myers who would have to wait their turns as tailbacks in the backfield, owing to the fact that Justice was a foregone conclusion to start at tailback. Maceyko had been a quarterback at Cornell for Snavely before the war.

Fullback was commanded by Walt Pupa and Hosea Rodgers, rugged 190-pounders with experience. They were equally good with fake charges up the middle, but in addition they were a different kind of threat: fullbacks who could pass, and Snavely's system took full advantage of that.

All of this worked to Carolina's advantage. Either Rodgers or Pupa might spin and hit the line. Or spin and pass. Or spin and hand off to Justice, who might run or pass. Carolina's offense never allowed the defense any breathing room.

Snavely's single-wing made use of all of Charlie Justice's great talents.

One of Justice's specialties, the quick kick, became a tremendous weapon for the Tar Heels.

Art Weiner, recruited by Murphy, became a bright star. He had never been a high school football standout, but had joined the navy at fifteen and played football in the Pearl Harbor games with Justice. The other end was Bob Cox, who laughingly claimed that the only reason he got to play was because his father courted Snavely's daughter every weekend. John Tandy was Cox's substitute. On any other team Tandy could have been number one; he was as good a receiver as Weiner except that Weiner was bigger and had better hands.

"Instead of having Tandy back up Weiner," Justice said later, "they should have put him at the other end for Cox, because Cox was our extra point kicker." Kenny Powell was probably the best defensive end on the team. He reached his peak as a defensive end in and after 1948 when college football allowed two-platooning.

There were three other players from Asheville on the team: Wright, Max Spurlin, and Billy Britt. "Britt enrolled at Carolina," Justice said, "thinking I was going to Duke. When I didn't, I think he was deeply disappointed, and he stayed on the squad a year or two, playing little, then quit and went back to Asheville to go into the glass business."

Wright, who played on the 1940 freshman team and on the varsity in 1941, was not a favorite of Snavely's. Good-hearted Joe took care of two or three hard drinkers on the team. This was not an unusual trait then, so many college students had gone through the hell of World War II. (It really isn't that unusual a trait today, when students have no war to blame it on.) Joe went around with them and cared for them every way he could. He was their chauffeur. Snavely began to think Wright was one of the drinkers, and all but removed him from his mind.

Justice, of course, was the prized recruit. He was the one the coaches looked to when they needed someone to accomplish the impossible on the field.

"Folks claim we were good because we were so big that year," Justice said, "but we weren't that big at all. Williamson was heavy, maybe 250 or more. Pupa weighed 185 or 190. I weighed 165. I guess Weiner was the biggest man on the team at 220 after Williamson left."

Even after half of pre-season practice was over, Charlie still thought the Carolina team lacked something. "I didn't think we had equal talent with Duke," he said. "They had a half-dozen All-Americans and had been to the Rose Bowl twice, the latest in the transplanted Rose Bowl of 1942, played in Durham because of fear of the Japanese bombing California. But what I failed to see developing, even though I was a part of it, was the feeling we all developed about our team. We began to believe in each other!"

Charlie's doubts, of course, were groundless, but he didn't realize that

Charlie with one of his coaches at Chapel Hill in 1946, George "Snuffy" Stirnweiss, who also played second base for the New York Yankees.

until the football season was four weeks old that fall.

Contrasted to the football equipment of today, the gear issued to the Carolina team would seem rather primitive – leather helmets and small pads, no face guards, canvas pants, high-topped shoes, and heavy pigskin footballs. But it was top grade for the day.

"They could slug us in the face while we concentrated on our running, if they wanted to," Charlie said, "and there wasn't much we could do about it. The helmet only protected our heads, not our faces.

"We couldn't run a hundred yards in an hour, it seemed," he said, "but the game was different in one respect. We ran the fake punts and quick kicks, and pulled trick plays like the Statue of Liberty, where the tailback took the ball and stood up as if to pass, holding the ball a bit behind his head, and the end coming around would take the ball and sweep the other end.

"I think football has changed more in these last fifty years than any other sport. Players are so big and fast today, it's a different game. I saw a halfback at Chapel Hill the other day who weighs 245 pounds and he can fly. I tried to play at 175 in 1948 and could hardly run; I had to get down to 165 or 170 before I could even maneuver. I don't understand it; I guess they feed 'em more vitamins and better food, and we have better medicine today. ..."

Charlie doesn't like all the changes he sees in football now.

"About half of our squad was married," he said. "Normally we would practice from four until six or six-thirty. We would eat dinner at the training table and go on home. We took the rest of our meals at home. I think the scholarships allowed about fifty dollars a month for that. Now football teams have their own dormitories and three-times-a-day training tables. Kinda like those square meals at Annapolis. Things are too regimented. The players would get a better education out among the students. They really should be a part of the student body when they come to school. I found a person got more education with people than with books – unless he was going into a profession like medicine or law."

Justice's presence gave North Carolina a beat in publicity. He became the most prized freshmen since 1941 when a big bruiser named Felix (Doc) Blanchard enrolled at Chapel Hill. The army took Blanchard away and sent him to West Point where he teamed with Glenn Davis to become a three-time All-American fullback.

Now the service had given Justice to Carolina in return, and before long folks began to think it had been an even swap.

After weeks of drills, sweating through the hot September sun, the Tar Heels finally opened the season against Virginia Polytechnical Institute at Chapel Hill, and, as far as Charlie was concerned, the first four games that fall charted Carolina's course for the four years he played there.

Justice showed flashes of brilliance in the first half against VPI, though he never burst into full bloom. He scored a touchdown on a 68-yard run and set up a second one. At halftime Carolina led, 14-0.

The world turned upside down, however, in the second half. A burly VPI tackle named John Maskas, a destroyer all afternoon, smashed through the Carolina line and blocked two Justice punts. VPI converted both for a 14-14 tie, and that's the way the game ended.

A disconsolate Justice sat in the dressing room staring at the floor. Teammates and writers tried to console him, but to no avail. That was the day he vowed never to have another punt blocked – and he didn't.

All was not right in Chapel Hill, even with Charlie's promise. The following week, with a game against the University of Miami coming up on Saturday, Russ Murphy, Snavely's offensive coach, suggested to Snavely that they start another tailback on Saturday.

"He's just a flash in the pan," Murphy said of Justice. "We ought to start Bill Maceyko Saturday." Murphy had recruited Maceyko in Ohio.

"No," Snavely said flatly. "Justice starts."

The Tar Heels beat Miami, 21-0. Justice gained 206 yards on the ground, highlighted by runs of 27 and 29 yards, and scored all three touchdowns.

The team had problems at blocking back that week, and Justice went to Crowell Little before the Miami game and suggested, "Coach, Joe Wright is a heck of a good blocking back. He could help us if he started."

Justice didn't know whether Little had told Snavely, but on Saturday when one of Snavely's assistants called for quiet and announced that Joe Wright would be the starting blocking back, Justice could see everyone applauding silently.

Wright started the Miami game and took charge immediately. Early in the game he called on Charlie to commit himself. Snavely liked to kick on third down if the situation was right. The Tar Heels ran two plays and had a third and five, and everyone expected Charlie to punt. The team circled in the huddle.

Wright looked at Justice. He called him Beaver. "Beaver," Wright said, "fake a punt. Eight-nine-one," and they broke the huddle.

Knowing about the two punts blocked by VPI, Miami came with a rush, figuring to block another. Justice stepped around the blitz and headed downfield. Wright took out two tacklers and Charlie faked the last one and scored on a 70-yard run.

He scored twice more, one from three yards out and the other from twenty-five, and the Tar Heels won, 21-0. Justice credited Wright with the win. He handled the team in the huddle like a true captain, an honor he attained in 1947. Occasionally he would make up his own plays. Once Justice remembers Wright saying, "Hosea, you get the ball and follow me. Beaver, you just fake." Justice attracted a bevy of tacklers with his fake, and Rodgers ran 40 yards behind solid blocking.

The next two games were meaningful to Justice and the team. A rather weak Maryland team came to Kenan Stadium first and Carolina beat the Terrapins, 33-0, in a pouring rain. Perhaps unwilling to risk an injury to Justice, or possibly to make a point, Snavely kept Choo Choo under wraps

Charlie, college freshman.

on the sideline. A pair of reserve halfbacks, Billy Myers and Jim Camp, scored two touchdowns each and B. K. Grow made another. Whatever Snavely's reasons for withholding Justice, things worked out all right, for newspapers the following morning carried the comment: "Carolina No One-Man Team."

Justice called signals that first season, but Snavely relieved him of that burden his sophomore year, and the blocking back called the plays the rest of Justice's career. One reason Snavely gave for the change was that Justice did not call his own number often enough.

The next game was with Navy in an icy Baltimore stadium. Justice scored on a two-yard run and Walt Pupa made two touchdowns. Carolina came from behind in the fourth quarter to win, 21-14. Justice, who had been slammed around by Navy's All-American center and linebacker, Dick Scott, was glowing with delight at the end of the game.

"This game was the making of our team," he explained later. "For the first time, I really felt we had that extra something – I suppose you'd call it greatness. Everyone realized I wasn't the entire show, that Walt and the line and real guts made us click. We barely got by Navy, but we had become a team."

This was the first meeting between Navy and North Carolina in forty years – since 1906 – and was the first time the Tar Heels had ever scored against Navy. Navy won 12-0 in 1899, 38-0 in 1905, and 40-0 in 1906.

The victory was so impressive that Choo Choo was mobbed by admirers outside the dressing room, and had difficulty tearing himself away to join his celebrating teammates inside.

Florida became Carolina's fourth straight victim in Chapel Hill the next week. With Carolina's old grads watching, Justice ran the second half kickoff 90 yards down the right sideline for a touchdown, and returned a punt 70 yards for another.

Charlie and his wife Sarah in a study session at Chapel Hill. Sarah attended the university on a football scholarship, but never ran a play.

The Associated Press reported that Choo Choo "exploded" with the second half kickoff. "Defenders were so scarce, owing to Justice's sudden explosion, that Charlie ran a one-way street 90 yards to the end zone."

With their record standing 4-0-1, the Tar Heels went to Knoxville on November 2 for their sixth game, and suffered their first defeat, 20-14.

After this game, fans sat in Shields-Watkins Field in awe over a 74-yard touchdown run Choo Choo made, but his thoughts ran to how Tennessee captain Walt Slater fooled him on a 78-yard punt return in the third quarter for the winning touchdown.

Knoxville newspapers the next morning reported that Justice ran 171 yards to cover the 74, so much did he switch back. One writer wrote that the run was "the finest broken field run seen in the South since Johnny Butler's memorable 56-yard run against Alabama on the same gridiron in 1939." Butler's run led Tennessee into the Rose Bowl. Justice side-slipped and outran the entire Vol defense. At least thirteen tacklers got their hands on him and couldn't bring him down, so elusive was his twisting, turning, and bursts of speed.

But Justice could only think of how he had let Slater outfox him. Charlie punted and the ball bounced along the sideline in fair territory. The Tar Heels, thinking Slater was going to let it roll, slowed up. At the

Both of Asheville's touchdown twins of 1942, Justice, left, and Billy Britt showed up to play football at North Carolina in 1946.

Charlie quenching a thirst in practice.

Photo: Hugh Morton

proper moment, Slater grabbed the ball at the 22 and came straight up the sideline. Charlie was the last man with a shot at him, but a big end, Jim Powell, running behind Slater, yelled, "Walt! Walt! Lateral! Lateral!"

Justice remembers thinking, "Oh, Lord, what'll I do?" and when Slater faked the lateral, Justice went for Powell. Slater raced by him and showed his heels all the way to the end zone.

Next morning the *Knoxville News-Sentinel* ran a picture of the end of the play that showed Slater turning and smiling at Justice, and for the next few years Tennessee used that picture on its game tickets.

Carolina didn't lose again, rolling over William & Mary, 21-7; Wake Forest, 26-14; Duke, 22-7; and Virginia, 49-14, ending the regular season at 8-1-1.

The Duke game gave North Carolina the Southern Conference championship. Justice threw a touchdown pass to John Tandy, and handled the ball with Pupa on a reverse pass that sent Jack Fitch to the second touchdown after Justice set it up with a 25-yard run to the two.

The Duke game was played on November 23 – Charlie and Sarah's third wedding anniversary.

It was following Carolina's victory over Virginia in Charlottesville that the Tar Heels received a bid to meet the Charlie Trippi-led University of Georgia in the Sugar Bowl on New Year's Day.

Justice had a fine day against Virginia, scoring on runs of 54, 45, and 19 yards. The Associated Press called him a "swivel-hipped, lightning-like running demon."

The bowl invitation was an answer to a Carolina dream: In 1935 Duke had beaten the Tar Heels 25-0 when it seemed certain that a bowl bid would be extended to Carl Snavely's team if it won the game.

On November 10, the day after UNC beat William & Mary, North Carolina newspapers carried a short item off the Associated Press wire that didn't make big news but carried as much portent as any story in the papers that day.

It read:

> The National Broadcasting Company estimated some 150,000 persons in New York, Philadelphia, and Washington saw the Saturday Army-Notre Dame game by television. These were in addition to the 74,000 who managed to get tickets for the game at Yankee Stadium.

Television that day began its drive toward domination of the game. A few years later it would bring it into the living rooms of America.

Following the 1946 season, Tar Heels dotted the ranks of the All-Southern Conference football team. Justice made first team; Ted Hazelwood and Chan Highsmith, the second team; Harry Varney, the third; and Art Weiner, Ralph Strayhorn, and Walt Pupa, honorable mention.

Justice thought often that season of how he had judged the team in pre-season to have a lack of interest, and of how wrong he had been once the season began. The intensity, the concentration, and the seriousness of the Tar Heel players was unsurpassed in Justice's years of playing football. He was proud of his teammates, and the feeling was mutual.

Justice almost made the All-America team, a rarity for a freshman, but settled for a consensus second-team berth behind one of history's most celebrated All-American backfields of Johnny Lujack, Charlie Trippi, Glenn Davis, and Doc Blanchard.

But the Tar Heels attained lofty heights for a team that had been on the down side for so long. They won the Southern Conference championship in the Duke game, and finished No. 9 in the Associated Press's national poll.

Justice ended with 943 yards in 131 carries from scrimmage and ran 344 yards on ten kickoff returns to rank third in the nation in each category. His twelve touchdowns led the Southern Conference scoring with 72 points, and seven of them were from 45 to 90 yards.

Among the spectators at the Carolina games that year were members of the Justice family. All, of course, could not attend every game, but there was always a Justice in the stands.

After Charlie ripped off spectacular runs, his brother Jack would point out his criticisms, always designed for a twofold purpose: to keep Charlie's feet on the ground, and to make sure he understood what he had done wrong, so he could improve on it the next time the occasion rose.

Jack wasn't the only one who chided Charlie on occasion. Snavely proved to be a stern taskmaster, and his weekly reviews of each man's play on Saturday spared no one. He would watch the game film over and over, writing criticisms of each man's play, figuring this would help his players remember what they had done wrong and do it right the next time.

One of his player critiques read like this:

> CLEMENTS: You were playing the receiver a little too closely when that interference was called. That proved to be very costly even though the ruling was quite questionable. Like CAMP you permitted a high short punt to drop at your feet, after which it rolled twenty-five yards, putting us in a hole on our own five yard line. You should have watched the ball and caught it instead of blocking on this one.
>
> WRIGHT: You were a little slow in reacting to passes to the flank. Moreover, you did not do a good job in warding off opponents who came through the line to block you. You stood too high; you did not use your forearms efficiently.
>
> JUSTICE: You got off-balance and made a very poor effort to tackle the runner who took the ball to the goal line to set up Georgia's touchdown. You made a bad mistake near the end of the game in leaving

your man to go after the quarterback when he faked a
run, after which he threw a forward pass which your
man caught for a long gain, and which gave them an
opportunity which might possibly enabled them to tie
the score.

Not any of this was to embarrass any player. It was simply Snavely's
methodical way of correcting even the slightest mistakes to prevent future errors on identical plays.

Charlie's dad, P.W., who was a great runner himself, always told his
sons that he could outrun them. His job with Southern Railway for the
depression years when scores of hobos rode the iron rails, was to dis-
courage them without injuring anyone. He worked with a partner, and
the two dug out a path from a favorite hobo heaven near the tracks down
to the Swannanoa River.

When P.W. spotted a group of vagrants there, he would approach
and strike up a conversation with them. In a few moments, his partner
would pop out of the brush and yell, "Look out! Look out!" and P.W.
would dart onto the trail, and the hobos, thinking a railroad dick was
approaching, would follow.

Down the trail P.W. would fly with the vagabonds making tracks behind him, throwing glances to the rear to see if pursuit was in sight.
P.W.'s partner, coming up behind, would give chase and the hobos would
increase their speed.

At the last second, P.W. would veer off the path, and the unsuspect-
ing hobos would run into the river.

"My dad could run like a scalded dog," Choo Choo said. "Any time I
got caught from behind and he was at the game, he'd come in the dressing room and say, 'Now, son, you can't get caught from behind. You
oughta run a little harder. I'd never been caught from behind like that.'

"And the truth was," Charlie concluded, "he probably wouldn't have."

A TASTE OF SUGAR

Thousands among the huge crowds that watched North Carolina play in Kenan Stadium during the 1946 season traveled to New Orleans for New Year's Day and the Tar Heels' Sugar Bowl game against the University of Georgia. Southern Railway ran a "Carolina Special" that carried an entire trainload of fans to the game.

Some of Carolina's home games in Kenan Stadium for the 1946 season had been sellouts, but others had not. Although the team played well on the field -- as good or better than any Tar Heel team in history – something was lacking when it came to drawing spectators into the stadium.

The team had played exciting football and had won eight of ten games.

That something apparently was the fact that it took the public longer to get over the war than it did the players, and it was only when they realized what they were missing that they began coming to Kenan Stadium in droves.

The Sugar Bowl's vaunted matchup of Justice and Trippi, and also of two evenly matched teams, drew 73,000 on this cold, damp, foggy day, filling every seat in Tulane Stadium. Undefeated Georgia was big and tough; Carolina was smaller but just as tough and determined. However, two of North Carolina's key players, Weiner and Highsmith, missed the game.

The athletic department cited "personal problems" for Weiner's absence. Highsmith had a good excuse. He had suffered a spinal injury and was in a body cast.

Weiner's personal problems were personal indeed. Choo Choo said the big end had walked into Snavely's office and made some "ridiculous demands."

Snavely said, "I'm sorry," and Weiner said, "Well, then, goodbye," quit the team, and went home to New Jersey.

He wound up driving a beer truck that winter in New Jersey's snow and ice, and one morning he said to himself, "You're crazy as hell. What are you doing up here when you could be down in Carolina enjoying yourself?"

He parked the truck, called the company and told them where the truck was, and added that they would have to come and get it because he had quit. He went back to Chapel Hill.

He told Snavely he wanted to rejoin the team, but Snavely wouldn't give his scholarship back until Weiner proved he really wanted to play.

That's why he missed the 1947 Sugar Bowl game.

But he became an All-American end.

The Tar Heels got a scare on the way to the stadium by chartered bus. Driving through the rain, their bus rammed another bus and Coach Snavely and End Joe Romano were slightly injured about the face. After a bit of first aid was applied, the team rode on to Tulane Stadium with no further incident and dressed for the game.

The Carolina Special disembarked most of its passengers to go out on the town before checking in at the stadium. "Most of its passengers" covers the situation well because at least one passenger failed to get off the train. He was a fan of Justice's from Asheville who celebrated so much on the way to New Orleans that he spent four days in a pie-eyed condition in his berth on the train, never setting foot on Louisiana soil. He dosed himself liberally with Jack Daniels during those four days, and when he returned to Asheville an ambulance met the train and took him home. He said later that he had had a great time, mostly because he laid a bundle on the gambling line, backing Carolina with 14 points.

The only thing the teams dosed themselves with was adrenalin. It dripped all over the field, so high were they pumped up. Georgia had a great football reputation already, but this was Carolina's first bowl game and the best football team it had ever had, and the Tar Heels wanted to prove to the world that they belonged in the class with the best of college teams.

In the Georgia dressing room before the game, Coach Wally Butts assigned a Georgia flankman, Joe Tereshinski, who liked his football rough, to hound Justice. "Stay with him," Butts said. "Don't let him get loose."

Tereshinski kept Charlie in check for most of the afternoon, using every tactic that came to mind, and Justice, usually calm in the face of such manhandling, came close to losing his cool on one play. Jake Wade, writing in *Sportfolio* Magazine, described the scenario this way:

On every play, Tereshinski roared through, drew a bead on Justice, and cut loose with both barrels. On every play Justice took the mauling in good grace, and, for the most part, kept his poise. But, after one superfluous entanglement, he gave vent to his pent-up feelings by giving a prone Tereshinski a gentle hoof. The officials missed that one, as they missed many other things in what has been called the worst officiated bigtime game in modern football history.

A few years later when Justice and Tereshinski were teammates on the Washington Redskins, the two hashed over the 1947 Sugar Bowl, and Charlie said, "I saw more than enough of you in the Sugar Bowl."

"That figures," Tereshinski said.

"What do you mean?"

"Simply that I had a job to do," Tereshinski replied. "My assignment on every play was to get to you and tackle you whether you had the ball or not."

Justice grinned. "You did a great job. I spent more time with you in New Orleans than I did with my wife."

History records that Georgia won this thirteenth annual Sugar Bowl game, 20-10, but the Tar Heels more than held their own. They threw more scares into the Bulldogs than any team had done in the regular season. So many, in fact, that Georgia had to come from behind twice to pull out the game.

As expected, Trippi, an All-American, had an edge on Justice in passing, but Choo Choo outrushed Trippi and outpunted the Georgia team, and at the end of the game their head-on competition was considered a standoff. Neither, however, had a good day. Judging by standards they had set for themselves, both played sub-par football.

Early in the second quarter, Bob Mitten put the Tar Heels in position to take the first lead by intercepting one of Trippi's passes at the Georgia 25. A few plays later fullback Walt Pupa bulled through the Georgia line to score from the four and Bob Cox kicked Carolina into a 7-0 lead.

Tar Heel fans rocked Tulane Stadium when the first half ended with Carolina ahead by that touchdown.

Georgia tied the score halfway through the third period. Tereshinski made an interception of a Pupa pass on the Georgia 24 and tossed to Dick McPhee, who raced down the right sideline to the Carolina 14 where Dan Steigman tackled him. Four plays later quarterback Johnny Rauch sneaked over from the one, and George Jernigan's kick tied the score at 7-7.

Carolina, showing great determination, drove right back and Cox kicked a 27-yard field goal to give the Tar Heels the lead again at 10-7. This was the first of only two field goals Cox kicked during the Justice Era. He booted one against Duke the following season.

Carolina All-Americans of the Justice Era, Charlie "Choo Choo," the passer, and Art Weiner, the receiver.

Before the third quarter ended, Trippi put Georgia into its first lead, throwing over the Carolina secondary to fleet Don Edwards, and although Jernigan missed the conversion kick, Edwards's touchdown gave Georgia all the points it needed at 13-10. Rauch made the final touchdown on a 13-yard run and Jernigan kicked the 20th point.

The game was not without controversy, which centered primarily around a Tereshinski lateral to McPhee to set up the first Georgia score.

Associated Press writer William Tucker described the play thusly:

> The ball game was decided on one play, wherein Joe Tereshinski of Georgia took a lateral from Charley Trippi and (1) passed it forward, or (2) threw it backward to Dick McPhee. Field Judge Gabe Hill of Wofford College was caught in the middle of the play. He threw down his handkerchief, then snatched it up, but his motion was a lot slower than Tereshinski's. Hill had to make a snap judgment and he looked bad in doing it, but in our book any player who can make the officials look bad is a good footballer.

Most Georgians saw Tereshinski's pass go distinctly in a lateral direction, but Carolinians swore it went forward, and for a split-second Field Judge Hill apparently agreed. But he changed his mind and the decision had direct bearing on the outcome of the game.

Actually, there were two controversial plays. The one called the "forward lateral incident" and another involving a touchdown pass thrown by Justice to Ken Powell, which was called back.

"There was no question but that the Tereshinski-to-McPhee pass was forward," Justice said. "It was not a lateral. I could have tackled McPhee, but Gabe Hill had thrown his flag, and I let McPhee go, sure that the play had been blown dead. But when Hill saw the play go for such long yardage, he snatched up his flag and shoved it back in his pocket."

The referee rushed to Hill and asked about the flag. "No, no, my mistake," Justice heard Hill say. "It wasn't a forward lateral."

Justice exploded. He called Hill every name he could think of. "You no-good, yellow blanketyblank," Charlie screamed. "You know the lateral was forward. You called the play!"

"Hill almost threw me out of the game," Justice said, "and he knew he was wrong or he would have thrown me out. He came up to me after the game and called my name, but I wheeled around and said, 'Don't speak to me. You know what you did.' I was really steamed. And we really won that ball game."

The second controversy came in the fourth quarter and was described by *Asheville Citizen* sportswriter Leroy Simerly, who was at the game:

The second decision that caused Carolina men to feel they were robbed came when Justice flipped a beautiful long pass into the end zone to end Ken Powell. The flankman and Rabbit Smith of Georgia both leaped high for the ball, Powell snagging it and falling just short of the last white stripe in pay dirt.

Head linesman George Gardner of Georgia Tech ruled Powell pushed Smith in going after the pass and Carolina's last desperate thrust failed.

Several sportswriters, including Fred Digby, a New Orleans sports editor who was in charge of arranging the reception for visiting scribes, cornered Gardner at the Sugar Bowl party the night after the game, trying to get a satisfactory explanation as to how Powell might have pushed Smith when he was in front of the Bulldog when he caught the ball, and how the head linesman could be close enough for a ruling on the play.

Gardner stuck by his assertion that Smith was pushed and countered the latter question with the argument he was much closer to the play than the writers.

This last contention could not be disputed. The press box was just about as high as a P-38 ceiling. Fog was closing in rapidly at the time the two plays in question were made and the field was about three city blocks from the press domain.

Carolina officials obviously were disturbed about the two rulings, some in greater degree than others, but none would make a statement.

This corner believes the whole thing should have been forgotten, because the score is still 20-10 in favor of Georgia and will stay that way in spite of all arguments. ...

Joe Wright was singled out by Snavely for his strong performance. He blocked magnificently for the ball carriers, played brilliantly backing the line, and at one point even took a pass for sixteen yards from Pupa.

The press thought Pupa, guard Harry Varney, wingback Jim Camp, tackle Ted Hazelwood, and co-captain guard Ralph Strayhorn all played exceptionally well.

The coaches were gracious in their post-game interviews. Butts said that "North Carolina made a great fight." He added, "They completely outplayed us in the first half, especially in the line. I'm proud of our team. It had enough stickability to win in the second half, and I guess that's what counts."

Snavely said how proud he was of his own team, which "played a great game of ball."

"With just a little better luck in the breaks," he said, "we could have upset the traditions and won the game. Anyway, I'm glad we played so well against a really fine Georgia team."

He offered no apologies, saying that Carolina had played the best game of its season, and then concluded with a smile, "The longer Trippi plays the better he gets."

The Tar Heels returned to Chapel Hill with the feeling that they had, indeed, implanted themselves among the most powerful football teams in the nation, and that feeling carried over through spring practice to the 1947 season.

But the incidents in the game were not forgotten. Ten days later, newspapers carried a United Press story bylined by Charles Nethaway, datelined New Orleans, that told the film story of the Sugar Bowl game. Nethaway discussed two films in the story, one a newsreel film and the other the official game film. His story read:

> Bing Crosby was getting a second billing to a football newsreel here today.
>
> The film that had shoved Der Bingle's latest hit aside and started a downtown movie reaching for SRO signs was the slow-motion story of the Georgia-North Carolina New Year's day game, or "the great Sugar Bowl robbery."
>
> Next week: "Back to the farm (for four football officials)."
>
> But the coming attraction will be shown only before clubs, schools, and other non-revenue audiences. It is the official Mid-Winter Sports Association movie of the Sugar Bowl classic.
>
> The official films will show that Ken Powell, North Carolina end, did not push Georgia's Rabbit Smith in an end zone play that would have been a Tar Heel touchdown.
>
> The newsreel didn't catch the Powell-Smith maneuver. It did record, however, the now famously-illegal forward pass which Georgia's Joe Tereshinski pitched to Dick McPhee to set up a third-period Bulldog touchdown.
>
> But it was the Powell-Smith play that promised to keep North Carolina's hot stove league bitter for at least a decade — maybe longer.
>
> The play came in the fourth period. With the ball on

Georgia's 20, Charlie Justice fired a pass through the fog to Powell in the end zone. The Tar Heel wingman hauled it down on a remarkable catch. He was in front, repeat front, of Rabbit Smith, and after making the catch turned and fell. Smith landed on top. Powell was knocked cold.

While North Carolina aides were helping Powell off the field, Referee Alvin Bell was stepping off a 15-yard penalty against the Tar Heels for what Head Linesman George Gardner said was pushing on Powell's part. That did it. On a clear night, you can still hear them howl, all the way from Chapel Hill.

Fred Digby, sports editor of the *The New Orleans Item,* member of the Mid-Winter Sports Association, and a quick man with a rule book, said that if Powell pushed Smith — the film, remember, shows he didn't — the rule called for giving the ball to Georgia on the Bulldog 20. Instead, North Carolina was penalized 15, given the ball on Georgia's 35, and subsequently lost it on downs.

The official films will get their first showing at the New Orleans Quarterback Club. Later they will travel the nation and most of the world. You can call this a prevue of an attraction which stars Referee Bell, Head Linesman Gardner, Field Judge Gabe Hill — who threw down the red flag on Tereshinski and then picked it up again — and Umpire H. W. Sholar, supported by two complete football teams and 73,000 extras.

No one in Georgia offered to forfeit the Sugar Bowl to North Carolina as Snavely had forfeited that Cornell victory over Dartmouth a few years previously.

LIFE ON CAMPUS

For many of the Tar Heel football players, the transition from dodging enemy riflefire to the more sedate campus life was a tremendous change, and no doubt there were those who exercised their warring instincts on the football field during the spring and fall of 1946. Between goal lines they got out of their systems the belligerence fostered by war, and campus life became fun.

About half of the Tar Heel players were married, and they settled into a routine filled with football, family life, and studies. They were serious about their studies because they were older and, without the interference of the war, would already have been out in the world, working and caring for their families.

When Tom Young drove Charlie and Sarah to Chapel Hill on the day that both he and the South Carolina recruiters waited outside the Justice home, someone came up with the excellent suggestion that the couple be housed in the famous old Carolina Inn, a hostelry that ranks with the best in the state.

"If it hadn't been for that," Charlie said later, "I guess we would have gone on to South Carolina where they already had us an apartment furnished and set up for living. Boy, that Carolina Inn was some place! It's the kind of inn that will spoil you."

Charlie and Sarah weren't the only ones who liked it. Tom Young would drop around every day to check on the Justices, see if there was anything he could do, like taking them places, and he would usually eat with them in the dining room at the athletic department's expense. When it was time to actually sign the contract that committed Charlie to Carolina and vice versa, Young jokingly said, "Charlie, can't you hold out a few more days. This is a pretty good life for me; I'm eating high on the hog."

Soon after the Justices were signed and set up, Young left the university for the head coaching job at Western Carolina Teachers College deep in the mountains of Western North Carolina. "I hated to see Tom leave Chapel Hill," Justice said. "He was a good friend and a likeable person. But he was the kind of person Western Carolina needed at that time. He did a good job over there." The field house at Western Carolina's football stadium was later named for Young.

The Justices lived in Carolina Inn four months, going to class from there. It was centrally located and they could walk anywhere they wanted to go.

Then the university arranged for the Justices to move into an efficiency apartment on Main Street – third floor, one room with a Murphy bed that pulled out of the wall. They lived there for a year and a half, and in early 1948 moved to Airport Road into a small four-room bungalow which had a living room, kitchen, and two bedrooms. From there they had a good uphill walk to class, but they liked the house and lived there until graduation. Airport Road was later renamed Justice Drive.

Sarah had graduated from Asheville High School in 1942, a year ahead of Charlie. She had gone to Appalachian State Teachers College in Boone and Charlie went to see her once and she came home once for a weekend and they dated. They reached the point that they committed themselves to each other, and when Sarah came home for Christmas she didn't go back. Her mother got mad at Charlie, worrying that Sarah would not get an education. Charlie quieted her fears. "Don't worry about it," he said. "I'll see that she gets an education."

Charlie was true to his word. When they enrolled at Carolina, Sarah went under the football scholarship and Charlie enrolled on the G.I. Bill of Rights.

"That's the only thing I ever asked the athletic department for," Charlie said. "Everybody would look at me and either think or say, 'Look at him, making all that money going to school. Everybody offered him cars and money and everything else to come to school.' But all I ever asked for was for my wife to have the football scholarship and I would take the G.I. Bill. I told them if they didn't agree to that, I would take the scholarship, and it would cost them the price of it anyway. The university agreed."

Sarah attended classes a couple of quarters and dropped out for two reasons: first, her eyes were hurting terribly from the strain of studying, and secondly, because she wanted to have a child.

In addition to free tuition, Charlie and Sarah drew a $50-a-month food allowance on the football scholarship and $50 more as an allotment for married couples. The Educational Foundation contributed this money. "That money is all donated by alumni," Charlie said. "It cost the university nothing. The university doesn't have to spend anything on athletic scholarships. Bowl money, basketball money, and other revenues generated by the athletic program go into the university and is not used for athletic scholarships."

When Charlie finally made up his mind to enroll at Chapel Hill, he took along his high school grades transcript. He suspected that someone might raise an objection, and sure enough, a Southern Conference school did, claiming that he could not be recruited because he hadn't finished high school.

When he went into the navy, he had not finished; he lacked one English credit. From Bainbridge, he had written to Asheville High, requesting that they send him the necessary work and he would complete it and send it back. He did, and was awarded his high school diploma by Asheville High.

Bill Plemmons, who had been Charlie's principal at Asheville High, was then dean of admissions at Carolina and he accepted Charlie's diploma without question. Some of the professors asked Plemmons about Charlie's grades. "What do you think," they asked, "can he do the work?" Plemmons replied, "If you make him, he can. You've got to keep pressure on him and tell him he can't play ball otherwise. I had to do that in high school."

He said, "You've got to tell him, 'Charlie, you're not going to play unless you get your grades.' "

"I'm glad he told them that," Charlie says today. "They required athletes to maintain a C average or they couldn't play. We had to have a 2.1 average in all our courses. If a person doesn't think enough of himself to do that, then he doesn't belong there. You can't play football all your life. You need to prepare to do something else when the day comes that you no longer play football. So we all found the time to study and keep our grades up.

"That may not be exactly the way I looked at it then," Charlie added. "The only interests I had were Sarah and football. I loved football so much I told her one day, 'I hope when I run the last play in my last game that I die as I go into the end zone.' I won't deny that football was my life. Had it not been for football, I don't know what I could have accomplished. I'd probably still be timid and shy and backward as the devil. I'd probably still be in Emma or Shiloh."

First year studies at Chapel Hill were the basics: English, math, science, history, and so on, and Charlie registered for all of them. Most of his professors were wary of him, probably because of all the publicity he was reaping. His first day in one of his classes, the professor made an introductory speech in which, without looking directly at Charlie, she said, "In this class, it makes no difference who you are, you'll have to come with the work."

Knowing the remark was for his benefit, Charlie stood up and answered, "Listen, please, I don't expect to get anything I don't earn. If I don't earn my grades in here, I don't expect you to give them to me." Turning, he walked to the back of the room and sat in an empty seat.

Charlie had no trouble in class once he established himself as willing to study. He made his professors understand that he was not a jock, that he was, indeed, willing to make his own grades, not only because he wanted to continue playing football, but he also recognized the fact that he was studying for life. What lay ahead of him twenty-five years down the road might be directly affected by his study habits for the next four years.

Most of the athletes came up with good grades in math and science, but had trouble with English and Spanish. Justice had to repeat both courses and go to summer school, but his eligibility survived.

A Spanish teacher who spoke fractured English usually greeted his students with something in Spanish.

Charlie walked into class one day, and the teacher addressed him with a Spanish phrase.

Charlie was puzzling over what he had said, and the teacher quickly switched to English and asked, "Do you not understand?"

"Hell," Charlie said, "I can't even understand your English, let alone your Spanish."

After an exam on which Charlie made a poor grade, the Spanish professor asked him in class how he could go on the field on Saturday afternoon and do so well with fifty thousand people looking, and he couldn't do the work in his Spanish class?

"I can understand it, prof," Charlie answered. "Out there I got ten guys helping me all the time, and in here I'm on my own."

The professor laughed and replied, "That's clear enough."

To say that life was carefree at Chapel Hill in 1946 and '47 would be stretching a point. So much time had to be spent studying, and so much on family life for the married players, and so much on football, that little time was left. Most of the married players didn't do much partying.

"We didn't go to parties and didn't give them," Justice said. "We were older and more settled than college guys today. Some of us were in our mid-twenties. Most had been in military service during the war and had grown up and matured more than the younger freshmen coming in. Our existence was more like good community life — except that few of us had any extra money, and we learned to get along on what we had."

What is it about Chapel Hill that keeps drawing people back?

"It's such a great community," Charlie said. "You can stay young for years there with all those students running along the streets. You can attend all the athletic events, go to plays at the playhouse."

"If you stay in Chapel Hill two months," Sarah said, "you don't ever want to leave."

Charlie added, "That aura of mystique that hangs over Chapel Hill is the best recruiter they've got. If a player comes down and stays a few days, he's hooked. He feels the difference. There is something there that makes you want to stay, and if you can't stay it keeps pulling you back again and again. One reason we got several players in '46 was that they had been in Chapel Hill on the pre-flight program. They get a lot of players today simply because there is something about Chapel Hill that they can't resist."

Charlie decided he would also play baseball and went out for the team in the spring of 1947. Not surprisingly, he made the team. Walter Rabb, the coach, told him that he would eventually be his second baseman. He liked Charlie's potential, how he played the position in general, how he went back on pop flies, and how he swung the bat.

"You're not ready now, Rabb told Charlie, "but you will be. Just be careful. If you got hurt and missed football, they'd shoot me if I was lucky and hang me if I wasn't."

Charlie practiced for several days and Rabb called him aside one afternoon. "Charlie, I've been thinking this thing over," he said, "and if you were to get hurt both of us would have to leave town. You have some potential but I don't think you should try it any longer because you're really not that good a baseball player.

"I could use you in certain spots," he continued, "but it wouldn't be worth the risk. So, since you're not going to be playing regularly, I think you ought not try it any longer."

Rabb didn't equivocate, which made Charlie believe he had been talking with Snavely. Spring football practice was going on, so Charlie checked out practice equipment and joined the football squad.

"I knew all along that I wouldn't be a starter in baseball," Charlie said, "and as I thought it over, two things came to me: First, if I was to get hurt, then the alumni and everybody else would say, 'Well, he shouldn't have been out for baseball in the first place,' and if I had a really bad year in football, they would have blamed it on baseball – so I gave it up."

Charlie didn't go out for the university team in basketball, but he couldn't resist playing. He could never resist playing any sport if he had the chance. There were others on the football team who felt the same way, who had played basketball before.

These players got together and organized a basketball team called the Carolina Clowns. They were joined by some basketball players who were not eligible, including a seven-foot center named Randy Burrough, of Hillsborough, who had flunked out of North Carolina State.

"We always had some ringers, too," Charlie said, "and we had a great time playing teams like Hanes Hosiery and McCrary. We were pretty good; we were undefeated for two years, and won the state amateur championship in 1948."

To show what life was like in Chapel Hill and the esteem in which Charlie was held, with everyone wanting to be near him, yet trying not to bother him, we must turn ahead to 1950.

Bill Stern, probably the best-known sportscaster of that era, had interviewed Charlie at length, and in appreciation sent him an eight-inch television set. At that time Charlie and Sarah were living in the Glenn Lennox apartment complex, which allowed nothing to be attached to the roof or the outside walls, so rigging up an antenna for the set became a problem. Finally, the complex manager had a large, tall telephone pole installed at the Justices' back door and the antenna was fixed to the top of the pole for better reception from the only television station broadcasting in the area. It was in Greensboro, and reception was as good as could be expected, but the picture was snowy and filled with ghost images and reflections.

The station had come on the air in August of that year, and its first telecast was of the College All-Star Game in Chicago's Soldier Field in which Justice led the college stars to a rollicking defeat of the NFL champion Philadelphia Eagles.

"It was an ordeal to watch anything on that television," Charlie said, "but because we had the only set around and television was new to the area, our neighbors and acquaintances came to see this marvelous thing. There was a football game on TV every Saturday, and more often than not it was the Notre Dame game. Remember, this was the season after I had completed my eligibility, and I was home during the season, and on Saturday our living room would begin filling up long before game time. When the kickoff came there would be twenty-five people watching that tiny TV that required a telephone pole to ensure reception from Greensboro. We'd sit staring at that little box, thinking it was the greatest thing in the world, happy as a roomful of larks. Later, I would look back on those days and laugh, thinking of a circus and a roomful of clowns."

GREATNESS IN '47

Today, if Carolina had a football team like the one of the Justice Era, the practice field would be swamped by media every day, but in 1947 the press – writers and an occasional radio man – came and watched practice but were no bother.

"They were never a problem," Charlie said, "never bothered us at practice. Our practices were always open and they were free to come. So were spectators. But no one ever became a problem. Reporters would come out once or twice a week and sometimes pick a quiet moment and ask a few questions. But no one ever got under our skin."

It was a different story when representatives of national magazines showed up from *The Saturday Evening Post, Collier's, LIFE, Pic, Argosy,* and others. They would come in, usually in early fall, and stay until they had the story they wanted.

"I guess I spent three or four weeks with *LIFE* Magazine," Charlie said, "and that wasn't a bother, because it meant national publicity and no football player in his right mind will resist that. If we had had television at that time we probably would have been besieged every day by media. Some of the teams are that way today, but they learn to handle it, and I'm sure we would have, too.

"We never looked on the media as a nuisance but as a huge help and a boost to our program. The press was necessary. It was simple as that."

Snavely may have envisioned the greatness of the 1947 team from the start of the year. He liked the idea that he had nine married veterans on the team. He had found that in a coeducational university such as North Carolina, which had 6,000 men and 1,000 women in 1947, that married men tended to settle down to their responsibilities better than the single bucks who stepped out to feel their oats once in a while. Among the nine wives, Sarah was the only coed.

Charlie himself may have seen himself as a leading candidate that year for All-American honors. Davis, Blanchard, and Trippi were gone, and Charlie's star was as bright as any along the horizon.

And certainly the fans thought something special was up. By early July, the four home games against Georgia, Wake Forest, Tennessee, and Virginia were sellouts, which was all the more significant because the seating capacity of Kenan Stadium had been enlarged from the 23,936 seats of 1946 to 43,000.

Opening day of the 1947 season was a big one for the ringtailed Carolina squad. The Tar Heels' September 27 opponent in Chapel Hill was the University of Georgia, which had beaten them in the Sugar Bowl after the last season.

A battery of sixty newspaper reporters, all five major newsreels, and five major radio networks gave the game by far the most comprehensive coverage any opening day game had ever received at North Carolina.

The Tar Heel team was basically the same unit that played the season before. There were a handful of new faces, but by and large Snavely depended on his veterans.

All except one. Ernie Williamson, a 6-foot-4, 245-pound tackle from Crewe, Virginia, resigned from school in the summer of 1947 – before his sophomore season – and signed a professional contract with the Washington Redskins. Williamson never had any trouble on the field. He could handle a tackle smash as well as anyone in football, but his textbooks knocked him galley west. Snavely said Ernie was "decidedly ineligible."

Earthquake Smith at 250 pounds was then the biggest man on the team.

Georgia came into the game without a defeat in its last seventeen games and for the first half and most of the third quarter it appeared that the Bulldogs would leave Chapel Hill with eighteen in a row.

The Bulldogs concentrated on Justice, shackling him on every play, and at the end of the game he had gained only 22 yards on 19 carries. But in concentrating so much of the defense on Justice, the Bulldogs had to lighten up on others – and that was their undoing.

Johnny Donaldson scored for Georgia in the second period on a one-yard plunge, after a pass interference penalty set it up, and at halftime the teams left the field with Georgia ahead 7-0.

With so much of the Georgia defense keying on him, Justice began to exaggerate his fakes in the third quarter, drawing the defense farther and farther away, and Walt Pupa took advantage of the lightened defense to throw two touchdown passes. The first went to Bob Cox to tie the game, and the second to Art Weiner to win it by a 14-7 score.

From Georgia's 39, late in the third period, Pupa threw over the short-handed Georgia secondary (remember, they were chasing Justice) and Cox caught the ball at the 20 and ran it into the end zone. He also kicked the point to tie the game.

Twice in the fourth period Carolina came within a few feet of scoring, but fumbled both opportunities away. Then the Tar Heels drove to the Georgia 17 late in the game and Pupa hit Weiner at the four and two steps later Weiner was in the end zone with the winner. Cox also kicked that point for the final 14-7 score.

"This game was for revenge," Charlie said. "We all remembered the Sugar Bowl and the two bad calls that we felt cost us the game, and we were determined to show the nation that we were as good as Georgia and in a class with the best teams in the nation."

But after that tremendous start, the roof caved in on the Tar Heels. They lost their next two games and undoubtedly began to wonder what had happened.

Following the Georgia victory, they went into Austin, Texas, the next Saturday to take on the Texas Longhorns, quarterbacked by Bobby Layne who quite often handed off to a fullback named Tom Landry. Layne passed for a touchdown and Landry scored one, and at the end of the first half Carolina had reached the Texas three, but time ran out, and in the second half the team never recovered that lost momentum. Texas made it an absolute blowout in the second half as the entire Carolina team suffered the effects of severe air sickness from the bumpy flight to Texas.

Even so, Charlie never took football any way but with the utmost seriousness. And he sought out all the help he could get.

Before the Texas game, an alumnus, Claude W. Rankin of Fayetteville, sent good luck pennies to Charlie and Sarah both.

Rankin sent Charlie an 1817 penny and asked him to carry it as a lucky piece throughout the football season. He sent Sarah a penny with the Lord's Prayer on it and told her to carry it to each game and clutch in in her hand "as a prayer that Charlie will make another touchdown and win for Carolina."

The first time Charlie carried the penny, Texas beat the Tar Heels, 34-0.

Still licking wounds from that game, the Tar Heels met Wake Forest in Kenan Stadium a week later, and the Deacons passed Carolina silly, winning 19-7. Tom Fetzer and his understudy, Bud Lail, completed 14 of 22 Wake Forest passes for 230 yards and two touchdowns. Wake's runners added 101 yards for a total offense of 331 yards to Carolina's 104. The game was more of a runaway than the score indicated, for North Carolina stopped Wake Forest twice on the five-yard line.

Carolina had to regroup the following week. Coaches burned gallons of midnight oil trying to figure what had gone wrong and how it could be corrected. The consensus was that a knee injury Justice suffered in the Duke game the previous season had flared up, slowing him enough to affect the team's performance, but Justice claims that discord and dissention had broken out among a few players who apparently resented Charlie for the lion's share of the spotlight his play demanded.

Justice told Snavely of the tension and volunteered to be demoted, but Snavely could find no way to question Charlie's worth to the team.

The dissension drifted by the wayside as the Tar Heels scored seven victories in a row the rest of the season.

Their opponent that week was William & Mary, which played Carolina as tough as any conference team during the Justice Era.

Coaches must have been holding their breath at halftime when neither team had scored. In the third period, Justice threw a four-yard touchdown pass to Jim Camp for a 7-0 lead, and then William & Mary came back before the quarter ended and Jack (Flying) Cloud bulled over from the one to tie the score at 7-7.

Only five minutes remained in the fourth quarter when Camp fell on Buddy Lex's fumble at the W&M 20 and the Carolina fans came to life. Alternating, Justice and Pupa bulled to the one-yard line in six plays, and Pupa crashed through center for the touchdown and the victory.

Even considering the two losses so far, the Tar Heels suffered their greatest fright of the season — perhaps of the era — just before the start of the game when the Southern Conference executive committee met in a two-hour, closed session to debate Justice's eligibility.

A Richmond lawyer, John J. Wicker, representing Vernon T. Morgan of the University of Richmond, who had been ruled ineligible for conference football because he had signed a professional baseball contract with the New York Giants at the age of 15, brought up the question of Justice's eligibility as a parallel case, claiming that Justice had signed a professional football contract with the Philadelphia Eagles while in the navy. Indeed, he had signed such a contract, and Wicker had read of the Justice contract in *PIC* Magazine.

After two hours of consideration, conference president Col. William Couper of VPI told waiting reporters that no conference member had questioned Justice's eligibility, and explained the circumstances under which Wicker had brought up the question. And then Couper announced that Justice had been declared eligible to continue playing since it was the committee's feeling that he had never really been under contract, so quickly was the matter handled by Coach Maniaci and NFL commissioner Elmer

Layden. The committee also voted that Morgan's eligibility would not be restored since his contract with the Giants was valid, and in those days professionalism in any sport constituted a complete separation from amateur status in all sports.

Justice was cleared only minutes before kickoff, and he did not start the game. Jack Fitch started in his place.

Now the Tar Heels were back on track, and they rolled over the last six opponents in good order, 35-7 over Florida, 20-6 over Tennessee, 41-6 over North Carolina State, 19-0 over Maryland, 21-0 over Duke, and 40-7 over Virginia, finishing with a strong 8-2 record.

Against Florida in Gainesville, the Tar Heels scored three touchdowns in the first eleven minutes and added two more in the fourth. Hosea Rodgers stole the show, accounting for North Carolina's first four scores. He passed 52 yards to Weiner for the first, made the second on a 76-yard run, threw a lateral to Justice on the 29 for the third, and passed to John Tandy for 15. Hosea had 238 of Carolina's 389 total yards.

The Tar Heel victory put a damper on Florida's homecoming.

The Tennessee game at Chapel Hill was a game of retribution for the loss inflicted on the Tar Heels in Knoxville in 1946. Justice and Rodgers rushed and passed almost at will. Justice ran 10 yards for a touchdown and passed for the other two, seven yards to Cox and 15 to Tandy.

Snavely had employed a bit of psychology in his preparation for Tennessee, telling his players, "I've never been beaten by a coach three times in a row and General Neyland trimmed me our last two meetings (20-6 in 1945 and 20-14 in 1946). I'd like to pay him back."

(It was ironic two years later that Neyland used the same tactics against Carolina, pointing out that no coach had ever beaten him three times in a row, and that Carolina had won 20-6 in 1947 and 14-7 in 1948. The strategy worked that time, too. Tennessee won, 35-6.)

The Carolina line tore Tennessee's forward wall to shreds in that 1947 game. Statistics showed the completeness of the rout: Carolina 19 first downs to Tennessee's three, and Carolina 395 total yards to 99.

The Associated Press reported that "Carolina clicked today like its pre-season buildup said it would, and it was a thing of beauty to see."

In Washington's Griffith Stadium, the victory over Maryland was not easy. The game was a battle of fumbles and punts in a driving rain, and neither team managed a score for three quarters. In the fourth, the wall caved in on Maryland. Justice, Pupa, and Fred Sherman scored touchdowns.

As momentum built and Justice played with All-Conference if not All-American accomplishments, press and fans alike rang accolades down on him.

The mayor of Chapel Hill remarked, "There are in this world several kinds of justice – tardy, poetic, speedy, terrible – and Charlie."

Wilton Garrison, sports editor of *The Charlotte Observer*, wrote in *SPORT*:

> Justice is not overly fast. Any second-file sprinter on Carolina's fine track team could outleg him on the cinders. It is his baffling elusiveness, his almost unbelievably fast reactions, which enable him to pick pin-point holes between converging tacklers, his slippery change of pace, that make him great. ...
>
> Charlie is as smart as they come on the football field. He knows every play by heart, can run it with his eyes shut. He can even dream up good ones in a tight spot and never loses his poise or courage. ...
>
> Every opposing team keeps "Stop Justice" signs in their dressing rooms weeks before they play Carolina. But he keeps delivering. Being put on the spot doesn't worry him; he loves it. He delivers when the chips are down.

The Duke game the following Saturday was also played in a drizzle which dampened 56,000 fans, announced as the largest crowd ever to see a football game between Baltimore and New Orleans. Justice scored twice and Cox once, and Cox missed all three extra point kicks but made up for them with a 14-yard field goal, the second and last field goal of the Justice Era.

Newspapers contained interesting wordage the following morning. The AP called Justice an "eel-hipped triple threat," whatever that is, and the *Asheville Citizen-Times* ran a long sidebar under an eight-column banner that read: "The North Carolina-Duke football game at Durham yesterday attracted a large number of Asheville people. They made the trip by automobile, train, and airplane." The remainder of the long story was a list of names of all Ashevilleans who attended, with the owner and executives of the *Citizen-Times* listed first, followed by the names of 130 other prominent Asheville folks.

Finally, Virginia felt Carolina's wrath in the season-ender. On a cold Saturday in Chapel Hill, Justice scored twice and Pupa, Johnny Clements, Camp, and Kenny Powell scored as Carolina totaled 506 yards in offense.

On Sunday, November 30, the day after season's end, the Tar Heels, finishing with such an exciting rush, were invited to play in nine different bowl games, but the faculty refused all offers without giving a reason. Justice has always thought it was because the players wanted to play Notre Dame in the Legion Bowl in Los Angeles on December 20.

Eight victories were enough to land the Tar Heels ninth in the AP national poll for the second straight year.

But because of the faculty's ruling on bowl games, the football equipment was packed away and players turned their attention to catching up on studies.

TOP OF THE HEAP

Many observers, Justice included, thought the Tar Heels in the last six games of 1947 were as good as any team Carolina ever produced, and that may have been true, but the year 1948 went the '47 team one better. Carolina finally achieved the undefeated season it had anticipated with the arrival of the Justice Era. It was marred only by a 7-7 tie with pesky William & Mary. Carolina reached the top of the Associated Press poll, rated No. 1 in the nation by midseason ahead of Notre Dame, Northwestern, Michigan, and Army in that order. Carolina held top ranking until the tie. The two-platoon system had been adopted and was used in 1948, which made things easier by taking a lot of pressure off great offensive players like Justice.

And on top of all this, Charlie and Sarah finally achieved one of their dreams: They became parents of a beautiful baby boy they named Ronnie.

The team, which had been rather static in personnel the first two years, began to change. Pupa graduated and Hosea Rodgers became a fulltime fullback. Joe Wright was gone and Don Hartig succeeded him at blocking back. Johnny Clements became the wingback with the departure of Jim Camp, and Justice was healthy and raring to go under the new two-platoon system. Weiner became a pass-catching fixture at left end.

Actually, the system did not completely relieve Charlie of his defensive duties. On occasion, when Snavely thought Justice was the man of the moment, he would insert Choo Choo at safety, which he played very well.

Veterans Chan Highsmith, Ted Hazelwood, Weiner, and Len Szafaryn anchored a murderous Tar Heel line. Weiner and Szafaryn made second team All-American, and Justice in his greatest season was a consensus first team All-American. Kenan Stadium's beautiful turf was filled with star players that season.

Justice and Rodgers formed a tremendous inside-outside punch, reminiscent of Davis and Blanchard at Army a couple of seasons earlier.

And the Tar Heels rose six notches in the final AP national rankings, from ninth position in both 1946 and 1947 to a solid third place behind Michigan and Notre Dame. All in all, it was one of those seasons that most coaches dream of but only a handful attain.

No one gave all of this to North Carolina; it was achieved through the hard work, blood, sweat, and tears of the talented players and an equally talented coaching staff.

The Southern Conference adopted the freshmen team system under which freshmen teams from each conference school played each other and the players were not eligible for varsity play until their sophomore seasons.

Nineteen forty-eight was a year of retribution for the Tar Heels. In the opening game, Carolina smashed Texas, which had beaten the Tar Heels in the 1947 opener. Played in Chapel Hill, the game's score was 34-7. Carolina scored three touchdowns the first four times it got the ball, and after five minutes the score was 21-0. Justice returned a punt 38 yards to the Texas 21 and passed from there to Weiner for the first touchdown. Tom Landry fumbled the return kickoff and Carolina recovered on the five, from where Justice scored standing up. Two minutes later Justice passed from the two to Cox for the third touchdown and Texas was already thoroughly whipped. Justice ran two more touchdowns in the second half and Billy Hayes added another.

The game produced a 61-point turnaround by Carolina from 0-34 a year before to 34-7, and the nation took immediate notice.

Still harboring the normal athlete's superstitions – and, of course, to leave no stone unturned – before the Texas game Charlie had a rabbit's foot sewn inside the lining of his game pants. It must have worked.

On the following Saturday, North Carolina proved its win over Texas was not a fluke. The Tar Heels went into Athens, Georgia, and played brilliantly to score a 21-14 victory over the University of Georgia.

Justice scored all three touchdowns, from 14 yards on an off-tackle buck, on a nine-yard end sweep, and on a spectacular 85-yard punt return.

The Tar Heels won the victory in dramatic fashion. Georgia led 7-0 at the half, but Carolina exploded in the second half. In addition to the three Justice touchdowns, the Tar Heels had two touchdowns called back and two other Carolina drives were stopped by Georgia near the goal line.

Charlie was at his best in this game. He ran and passed for 304 yards to set an early-season one game total offense high for the nation. In addition to that, he returned three punts for 125 yards and a kickoff for 20 to account for an amazing total of 449 yards, a national high for the season.

Charlie runs behind brusing blockers.

So, now the last eight Carolina opponents knew what to expect. Writers around the state were calling the Tar Heels a juggernaut, and indeed they were. They were still not monstrous in size, but were fast, agile, and hard-hitting. Justice himself marveled at the sharpness of the blocking, and avowed that the coaches could pick up someone off the street who could run as well behind such blocking.

During the entire month of October, which had five Saturdays, the Tar Heels were brilliant. After the Georgia game on the 2nd, they cut down Wake Forest, 28-6; North Carolina State, 14-0; Louisiana State, 34-7; and Tennessee, 14-9, and went into November ranked third in the nation, but after the Wake Forest game on November 9, the Tar Heels gained the top, rated No. 1 among all college teams.

The victory over Wake Forest was the Tar Heels' 10th in a row, stretching over the last seven games of 1947. Justice, Maceyko, Kennedy, and Rodgers scored touchdowns against Wake as the Tar Heels showed their depth.

Billy Britt, Charlie's old Asheville High running mate, played briefly in the Wake Forest game, his last for UNC. He left school soon afterward.

"I got mad at him for not staying," Justice said. "I tried every way in the world to get him to stay. They could have moved him to wingback to take advantage of his speed, but he didn't want to block, and wingbacks had to block.

"He laid back one year," Charlie continued. "If he'd gone anywhere else he could have played. He went to Chapel Hill thinking I was going to Duke, and when I showed up, he didn't get the playing time he thought he deserved. He was on the team for the first three games of 1948, and then left for home. He got into the glass business and was quite successful at it."

The week of Carolina's game with North Carolina State, the Wolfpack was rated the best defensive team in the nation — and proved it against the Tar Heels. Carolina went into the game ranked No. 1 in the nation, but those in attendance wouldn't have known it if they hadn't read the papers.

Carolina didn't cross the 50 in the first half, and had to stop State drives at the one and the 13. But the second half produced a Tar Heel turnaround. A minute and a half before the end of the third quarter, Justice ripped off a 50-yard run to the State eight, and Rodgers went over from there. No one scored then until three minutes remained in the game and Justice hit Weiner with a 49-yard touchdown pass to forge the final score of 14-0. Justice was held in check most of the way. He netted only 35 yards on 13 carries.

The Tar Heels cranked up against Louisiana State the following Saturday, winning 34-7. Entering the game third in the nation on defense, the Tar Heels hit LSU with a rockhard line and kept the Tigers at bay all afternoon.

The AP referred to Hosea Rodgers as "a berserk bulldozer," and called Weiner and Cox "sticky-fingered ends." Weiner made a one-handed catch with his left hand that United Press wrote would have done credit to Joe DiMaggio. "Justice was at his top form as a broken-field runner," AP reported. "When the 165-pound Justice wasn't dazzling the boys from the Bayous, his big buddy, Hosea Rodgers, was ramming center like a berserk bulldozer."

Justice dodged tacklers by stopping sharply and jumping back as they fell at his feet, and then moving on with a burst of speed. He skirted right end "behind a phalanx of blockers," for the first touchdown from the seven, and after Rodgers scored from the four, Justice passed to Cox and Kenny Powell for third period touchdowns. Rodgers made the last one to complete the rout.

In one of his best performances that season, Justice completed seven of 10 passes for 138 yards, and carried 17 times for 71 yards. He also averaged 48 yards on six punts. Rodgers, the heavy-duty fullback, ran for 90 yards on 18 carries, and Weiner caught five passes for 69 yards and gained 19 more on an end-around.

Tennessee fell the following Saturday, 14-9. Carolina scored the first time it had the ball with Justice throwing into the end zone to Bill Flamis from the three. A few moments later Hal Littleford's only bad punt of the game set North Carolina going from the Tennessee 27, and Justice hit Weiner, charging through the end zone, with a 12-yard touchdown pass.

Justice punted beautifully, including one quick kick that traveled 74 yards, but he was guarded so closely by Tennessee defenders that he gained only 47 yards in 13 running tries. General Neyland, who remembered that 74-yard run in 1946, concentrated his defense on stopping the choo choo.

At that point, the Tar Heels were 6-0 for the season, and had a 13-game winning streak going back to 1947. William & Mary came into Chapel Hill for the next game on a muddy, slippery field that all but nullified North Carolina's sharp running game, and played the Tar Heels to a 7-7 tie. Actually, North Carolina overpowered the Indians, racking up 17 first downs to W&M's one, and it came on a penalty, but Carolina couldn't put points on the board. William & Mary intercepted four passes and recovered three Tar Heel fumbles in a tough day of slipping and sliding.

Now, Maryland, Duke, and Virginia stood between Carolina and an undefeated, once-tied season and a major bowl bid, and the Tar Heels turned up the aerial throttle a notch. Carolina had passed for eight touchdowns in its first seven games, but against the last three opponents threw seven scoring strikes.

In Washington's Griffith Stadium, Jim Tatum's Maryland Terps went down, 49-20. Justice passed for two touchdowns, caught a pass for another and got off an 84-yard punt. His punting average of 44 yards kept Maryland in a constant hole, and Bill Maceyko, playing his senior season, intercepted two passes and returned them 60 yards for a touchdown and 68 yards to set up another.

"From the start of the Maryland game," Justice said, "we were as determined a bunch of football players as I've ever seen – and as talented, too. We were determined that no one else would get a chance, like William & Mary, to spoil our best season."

At the end of this game, Tatum entered the Carolina dressing room and said to Justice, "Charlie, we wanted to see if you were a man today – and we're convinced."

Carolina whipped Duke, 20-0, and steamrolled Virginia, 34-12. Against Duke, Weiner scored twice on passes, once from Justice and again from Rodgers, and Justice broke away for 43 yards for a touchdown that Snavely called the best run he ever saw. Before a sellout crowd of 44,500 in Chapel Hill, Justice went through the line behind crisp blocking, almost fell on a cutback but saved himself by putting a hand to the ground to regain his footing, and then used his blocking beautifully, slicing through the crowded secondary to cut back to the left sideline from where his teammates opened a lane to the end zone. He switched his field so many times on that run that he had his blockers looking back to see where he was going.

That was the run that Justice also called his best, even more satisfying and executed through more difficulty than the 74-yard run against Tennessee two years before.

The mounting pressure on Justice, created by several things, including the widespread publicity and the expectations of the fans, became a subject in the press. The week following the Duke game, Herbert Foster, a writer for United Press, sent out a story that included these paragraphs:

> Seven rugged teams had singled out the little North Carolina halfback for special attention this year, and it left him a little battered. But if the Duke Blue Devils thought they had corked up Charlie Justice, they were wronger than a presidential poll.
>
> The pressure mounts on a great individual star as the season wears on. The weight of his publicity is enough to bow his back. The fans expect miracles every game. The opposition watches him hawklike to stop those miracles before they start. So it's sometimes tougher for a gridiron genius to do his stuff than if he were some guy named Joe, fresh from the bench.

On November 27th in Charlottesville, Virginia, Justice ran and passed Carolina into the Sugar Bowl, throwing for two touchdowns and running two more. He rushed for 159 yards in 15 carries and passed for another 87.

Knowing the bowl bid was forthcoming, the Tar Heels put on an offensive show, and almost everyone got in the act. The game was six minutes old when Rodgers slammed into the end zone from the five. Thirty-five seconds had elapsed in the second quarter when Justice whipped a 40-yard TD strike to Weiner, and five minutes later Justice streaked 80 yards to score on a scrimmage run.

Virginia passed for two touchdowns, making the halftime score 21-12, and the Tar Heels had to soak up more determination at the half. No one scored in the third, and early in the fourth Choo Choo hit Bob Cox for a 31-yard score. A minute later wingback Bob Kennedy handed Dick Michel's punt to Justice on the Cavalier 47 and watched Charlie flee down the west sideline to the goal.

So it was Justice at his best, and the Tar Heel team working like a well-oiled machine that ended the first undefeated season for North Carolina since a 9-0-0 record in 1898. After the Virginia game the Tar Heel record for the last 18 games was 17-0-1.

The Tar Heels immediately accepted the Sugar Bowl's invitation and began to prepare to meet Bud Wilkinson's first great post-war Oklahoma football machine in New Orleans on New Year's Day.

One of the great lines of that season came from the pen of Jake Wade, North Carolina sports publicist, who slipped a one-paragraph description of Choo Choo into a press release which read,

> He dresses according to the college tradition. He belongs to the Beta Theta Phi social fraternity, but some of his best friends are non-fraternity men or belong to other groups. He has a cheerful disposition. He neither smokes nor drinks, cusses mildly.

After three seasons Justice's value to the Tar Heel team was still under debate by fans who crowded Kenan Stadium for all home games. Ray Howe, sports editor of *The Charlotte News*, wrote:

> There is one question for which there will never be a definite answer in Chapel Hill. How good would North Carolina have been in football this season without Charlie Justice? Some think that the ball club would have been just about as good if Billy Hayes or Bill Maceyko had been able to pile up as much time at that position, others say that Charlie is the difference between a good team and a great team. Others just shudder. But the young man who faced a tremendous psychological handicap when he first reported to the University of North Carolina as a boy wonder is now the country's top candidate for the Heisman Trophy. ...

It was inevitable, with Justice making the headlines like he was, and with his name on the tip of every tongue in North Carolina, that the poets would begin putting words together about him. He was balladized about as much as anyone had ever been in the Tar Heel state.

Two poems worth reading came out following the 1948 season, both of which could be set to music.

The first came from John Wightman:

> Having lost some cash on Dewey
> (And last week on Penn State)
> You'd think that I'd have sense enough
> To just sit back and wait,
> And only say, "I told you so,"
> With nothing to take back,
> But – the Carolina Choo Choo
> Is a'coming down the track.

> Of course, there always is a chance
> That there could be a wreck.
> (Like good "Old Ninety-Seven"
> That got it in the neck).
> But may I say to Wah-Hoo-Wah,
> Watch out! Alas! Alack!
> For the Carolina Choo Choo
> Is a'coming down the track.
>
> And you Tandy and you Stirnweiss
> And you elder Folger, too.
> And all of you other Tarheel great
> Who wore the White and Blue,
> Please re-arrange your Hall of Fame,
> Make room for one more plaque –
> For the Carolina Choo Choo
> Is a'coming down the track.

Marvin Wilson of Edenton wrote the following to the tune of Carolina's traditional song, "Hark the Sound":

> Hark the sound of Charlie's footsteps,
> Pounding down the field;
> Demon Deacons howl in anguish,
> As he victory steals!
>
> Hail to the brightest star of all,
> Justice is his name;
> When he's in the Tarheel lineup,
> They can't lose a game!
> So it's rah rah for Justice — Justice,
> Rah rah for Justice — Justice,
> Rah rah for Choo Choo,
> Rah, rah, rah!

Accolades for Justice following that great 1948 season ran knee deep in the press. One of the best came from the typewriter of Furman Bisher, then columnist for *The Charlotte News* who later became sports editor of *The Atlanta Journal* where he gained national acclaim for his penmanship. Bisher wrote this column at the end of the Virginia game, which brought Justice's third collegiate season to an end:

> CHARLOTTESVILLE, Va. – As to all great men of his sort, the millenium must come some day to Charlie Justice. Many a Saturday these past three falls students of football have nodded their heads in unison. "This was it," they have said. "He can never improve on this day."

I felt that way, loosely speaking, after the Georgia game, when he got off on the longest run of his college life – 84 yards – and when Wally Butts accused him of single-handedly beating his team. Ray Howe came back from the Duke game with stars in his eyes and gorgeous quotes on his tongue. "You'd live another lifetime to see something else like that 43-yard run," he said.

Each successive week-end, as the feats have multiplied, so have the adjectives. It became a question of just how good can a man get, and when do we hit ceiling in dealing with Justice? Against Virginia Saturday, in that 24-12 finale to the greatest football season in all University of North Carolina history, another high-water mark was reached. Justice can improve on that day's work only by going or throwing for a touchdown every time he gets his stubby hands on the ball. What we have all been waiting to hear, or to write, was said for us by Art Guepe, the Virginia coach who was a great backfield man himself at Marquette some twelve or thirteen years back. He was also backfield coach here when Bullet Bill Dudley was becoming the only All-American Virginia ever had.

"Justice was better today than Dudley in that 1941 game," said Guepe in retrospect. Dudley considers the '41 game against Carolina the game of his career. "Justice was the greatest football player I ever saw."

That leaves nothing unsaid. Guepe knows better than any of us just how great Justice was Saturday. Whether by order or happenstance, his young men went onto the field in the third quarter to knock Justice's block off. He had wrecked them in the first half. Only because of him were they behind, 21-6. (Add to that, Art Weiner, Hosea Rodgers, Bob Kennedy, and a supporting cast of magnificent blockers.) On into the fourth quarter the not-so-cavalierish Cavaliers did their job well. They added a second touchdown, again by a pass. The first was a sixteen-yard job from Whitey Michels to Mike Mausteller. The second covered eight yards from Joe McCary to Barney Gill. By this time, the Virginians among the record 26,000 house were being teased by a mirage of what would have been the South's amazer of the football year.

Justice, however, was still up and about, in spite of the mob treatment he'd been getting. It had been touch-and-go until less than five minutes were left on the clock. Then Justice faded to his right, appeared to be trapped, but flipped a rushed pass to Bob Cox on the goal line for a 31-yard touchdown and the pressure was off. Justice further punctured Virginia morale four plays later, took a punt handoff from Kennedy about the 50-yard line, knifed through three bewildered Cavaliers and rushed down the sidelines for the final touchdown. But these were climactic plays. Justice had delivered his major thriller in the second quarter on Carolina's third touchdown. The ball on the Carolina 20 after a Virginia punt, Justice cut to his right as if sweeping the end, then pivoted hard to his left, off tackle, positively exploded into the Virginia backfield. Four Virginia backs were between him and the other end zone. You've heard that Justice actually isn't fast. Don't believe it. He outran those Virginia backs, though it appeared all four had a chance at him, Johnny Papit first, Steve Osisek last, both swift on their dogs.

Just for a sample of his work in less glamorous moments, look at Justice's figures prior to the 80-yard run. He had gone for 22, 9, 5, 8, and 13 yards on the ground, and passed for 15 and 40 yards. The 40-yard pass connected with Weiner for the second touchdown, on which Weiner demonstrated his artistry. The pass was a tall one and Weiner leaped for it over McCary's head about Virginia's fifteen. Weiner came down with the ball, outshifted McCary and scored while McCary, the Virginia captain playing his last game, knelt, bent double, and beat the earth in frustration.

By the statistics, too, it was Justice's finest day of the season. His fifteen rushes got him 171 yards, his four pass completions 88 yards. For the day: 259 yards. That was enough to win him the No. 2 position to Stan Heath of Nevada in total offense. He went into the game in third place, eleven yards behind Lindy Berry of Texas Christian, but Berry was not so outlandish in that SMU tilt. For the year, Justice will show 1,633 yards, 778 rushing, 855 passing. No Carolina man has ever reached such a peak. That could be considered Heisman Trophy business. ...

Among his many feats of the day and year, it was almost overlooked that Justice had set a new national punting record. He went into the game with a 44.3 average. He got off three boots Saturday for a 40.8 average. On 57 boots for the season, he has an even 44-yard average.

FAMOUS BELLYACHE

T he last week of December, 1948, was festive in New Orleans. The Justice-led Tar Heels came to town to prepare for the Oklahoma Sooners in the Sugar Bowl on Saturday, January 1.

The biggest damper on Carolina's spirits was a stomach problem Justice suffered early in the week at the Tar Heels' training camp in Hammond, Louisiana, and Choo Choo was forced to live on liquids that week. It persisted until the day of the game. He spent Friday, the day before the bowl game, in bed, trying to recover.

On the morning of game day, Justice's tummy ache had taken on the proportions of that suffered by Babe Ruth on Monday, April 26, 1925, in Asheville, Choo Choo's hometown. It kept the Bambino out of action with the Yankees until the first of June.

Charlie's bellyache didn't keep him from playing in the Sugar Bowl, but it weakened him in the second half so that he misfired on passes and was not as swift and sure on cutbacks when he ran the ball.

Oklahoma won the game, 14-6, but the story might have been different had Choo Choo been at full strength for the entire game.

But that's crying over spilt milk.

The truth was that Oklahoma's exploding split-T formation heralded things to come for the whole of college football, and Quarterback Jack Mitchell ran it to perfection.

A crowd of 82,000, again said to be the largest ever to see a football game in the South, filled the stadium and saw the Big Seven champion Sooners strike swiftly in the first and third periods and hold the favored Tar Heels in check most of the afternoon, especially in the second half.

At the start, Justice appeared to be none the worse for wear, getting off several nice runs. He and Hosea Rodgers ran like demons as Carolina drove the opening kickoff from its own 37 to the Sooner 15. Justice also completed passes to Bob Kennedy and Art Weiner in the drive.

But Myrle Greathouse, an Oklahoma linebacker who had lived through the hell of Guam and Okinawa, intercepted an errant Justice pass at the 14 and ran 72 yards before Eddie Knox hauled him down on the Tar Heel 13. Moments later, from the one-yard-line, Mitchell rammed off tackle for the game's first touchdown. Leslie (Bingo) Ming converted from placement for a 7-0 lead.

Later in that opening period, Carolina's Joe Romano recovered a fumble at the Oklahoma 30. Rodgers hit Kennedy with a pass on the 15, and Justice ran to the two. Rodgers powered over from there, but Bob Cox missed the kick for extra point and Oklahoma still led, 7-6.

The Sooners ran the split-T so explosively on the ground that Wilkinson saw no need to pass. Thus, in the third quarter, Oklahoma caught North Carolina unaware and Darrell Royal, who went on to greatness as a coach at the University of Texas, threw the Sooners' only pass completion of the day, a 43-yard strike to Frankie Anderson caught on the Tar Heel 10. Lindell Pearson went over on second down and Ming converted again for a 14-6 lead, and scoring was finished for the day.

The remainder of the game was a punting duel between Justice and Royal, and Justice got the best of it because of Royal's erratic kicks. Charlie got off punts of 65, 65, 57, and 53 yards. Royal punted out of bounds once, just missing the coffin corner. Again, however, late in the game, he booted short and Carolina took over at midfield, starting goalward with determination.

Unfortunately, Justice's physical weakness had caught up with him by this time and he threw an interception to Bobby Goad to kill the drive. When the game ended, Oklahoma was on the march deep in Carolina territory.

Charlie punted seven times and averaged 43 yards. Four times his kicks traveled more than 50 yards.

After the game, as dusk settled over Tulane Stadium, Justice trudged with bent shoulders into the Carolina dressing room, and sat on a bench, his head covered with a blanket, and cried.

A newsman spoke to him four times before he pulled the blanket back and looked up with tear-dampened eyes. "I lost it," he said harshly. "You can say that."

Snavely wasn't saying anything like that. "Without taking anything from Oklahoma," he said, forming his words carefully, "I would say that we beat ourselves. We didn't capitalize on our breaks and didn't play our best game."

Justice, right, and tackle Len Szafaryn watch action from the sidelines.

Asked about Justice's physical condition, Snavely made no excuses. "He was not bothered by the stomach ache," Snavely said, "which kept him out of heavy practice all week, but he wasn't in top shape because he missed so much work."

Carolina took nothing away from Oklahoma, however. Hosea Rodgers said, "I never got rushed so fast and so hard."

Ill all week, and playing behind a line that was consistently outcharged, Justice got away for more rushing yardage than anyone else on the field. He gained 81 yards in 15 carries for an average of 5.1, only a tenth of a yard below his season's average. He hit six of 15 passes for 53 yards, but his passing game was sub-par at the end when his tosses wavered. Four of his last five passes were wild, and the fifth was intercepted.

He had enough steam left to negotiate the game's best play. Going through right tackle on the 50-yard line, he cut quickly back to the left to gain 22 yards to the Oklahoma 28, and as he was tackled he tossed a lateral to Chan Highsmith who ran on to the Sooner 16, a thrilling 34-yard gain. But Justice was stopped at the Oklahoma seven on fourth down to end the drive.

Post season accolades were plentiful for the Tar Heels after the 1948 season. The most prized trophy eluded Charlie Justice – the Heisman Trophy went to Southern Methodist's Doak Walker, who also had a great season, but Justice won the Walter Camp Memorial Trophy as player of the year, and received this award from House Speaker Sam Rayburn. He also won the Teague Award as the outstanding athlete in North Carolina for 1948. "I've been following the Teague Award three years now," he said, "each time hoping I'd get it. Now that it's mine, all I can say is it's one of the greatest honors that can come to a fellow."

Charlie led the nation in punting with a 44-yard average for 62 kicks. He was second in total offense with 1,620 yards to Nevada's passing specialist Stan Heath. Justice and Heath tied for first in touchdown responsibility with 23 each. Charlie scored 11 himself and passed for 12 more.

Justice, Weiner, and Len Szafaryn made All-America teams that year. Justice was named to the first team of 20 All-American teams (almost everyone in the business picked his own); Weiner made two first teams, two second teams, and two third teams; and Szafaryn, a second team.

JUSTICE
(First Team)
The Associated Press, United Press, NEA, Football Coaches, *Sports Week*, International News Service, Central Press, All-America Board, Williamson's, All-Players Team, *The Sporting News*, Paramount, Bill Stern Team, *Police Gazette, Football Digest, Boston Record, College Football Illustrated, New York News, Complete Football*, Deke Houlgate Team.
(Second Team)
Football Writers of America.

WEINER
(First Team)
Football Writers of America, *New York Sun*.
(Second Team)
The Sporting News, All-Players Team.
(Third Team)
Central Press, NEA.

SZAFARYN
(Second Team)
Football Writers of America.

The All-America lists containing North Carolina names were considerably longer than those of the previous two seasons.

In 1946 Justice made no first teams, was a second team-choice by United Press, NEA, *Gridiron Weekly*, and *PIC* Scouts, and a third-team pick by the Football Coaches and *Sports Weekly*.

Fewer accolades came in 1947 when Justice made second team for the Associated Press and NEA, and third team for INS and Central Press. Walt Pupa was a third team choice on the All-Players team that year.

Justice was disappointed in not winning the Heisman Trophy in 1948, but since he didn't win he was happy that his friend, Doak Walker, did. He doubled his determination to win the Heisman the following year.

FAMILY LIFE

Ronnie, the Justices' son, was born August 23, 1949, just a month before the September 25 football opener with the University of Texas. The hospital staff was concerned about the entire Justice family, of course, but showed its concern more for Charlie than for mother and son.

"It was comical," Justice said. "Doctors and nurses would come by and check on the three of us, and then say, 'Are you sure you're all right, Charlie?' I assured them that I was, and somehow I lived through the stress of becoming a first-time father."

Suddenly the Justice house became the place to be. More often than not, it was filled with people. "It was hard to find a time when someone wasn't there," Charlie said. "It seems there was always a crowd in the house, especially on weekends."

Folks would drop by and say they wanted to see the baby, but Charlie felt many just wanted to rub elbows with celebrity. So many came by on weekends that Charlie had to spend Friday nights before Saturday home games at Orville Campbell's house in order to get sufficient rest. Campbell was the Chapel Hill newspaperman and one of Charlie's champions.

People would come in and get Ronnie up at all hours, bounce him around and stay awhile. The Justices, both of whom are gregarious people, were generous in giving their time to others and were patient even when they thought the crowds were getting out of hand.

Annie Mae Mason, whose husband, Morris, was equipment manager for the football team, practically raised Ronnie. She even sat with him at all football games. She also worked for Snavely.

"We came home after the Texas game," Sarah said, "and the living room was full of people, passing Ronnie around and having a good time. We didn't know a third of them."

Charlie's main interest was football, of course, but he discovered that he was suddenly wearing another hat. In addition to those of husband, student, and athlete, he now had a headdress called "father." He tried to be as good a daddy for Ronnie as possible, sandwiching that time between the others.

The Justices were good parents. However, duty called and they had to respond. When they went to the 1949 Sugar Bowl and Ronnie was four months old, they left him with their mothers in Asheville. While they were gone, Ronnie began to run a fever. His grandparents treated him and took him to the doctor but his fever hovered around 104 and 105 for a day or so until Charlie and Sarah returned.

They took him immediately back to the doctor, who checked him over and rushed him to Asheville's Memorial Mission Hospital. Ronnie remained in the hospital ten days and when he was released the doctors told Sarah and Charlie that they didn't think any damage had been done.

Later, however, Charlie and Sarah discovered that Ronnie was a bit slow for a boy of his age and that he had poor hand-eye coordination. The damage was such that doctors couldn't put their fingers on the exact cause or identify the problem.

"I'm sure he was dyslexic," Sarah said. "He had a bad reading problem. Intellectually, he seemed to be all right, and when you talked to him you didn't realize he had a problem at first."

Charlie said, "He couldn't turn his hands over palms-up to take anything. As he grew for a few years he became very sensitive about his condition."

When he reached six or seven, folks would say when they saw the three Justices, "Oh, is that your son? Is he going to be a ballplayer like his father?" Ronnie became so sensitive that when someone said, "Oh," he would turn and run.

Charlie tried to protect him by saying, "Oh, no, he's smarter than that. He's not going to be a dumb football player."

At that time Charlie had no inkling that Ronnie already harbored a desire to be like his daddy. He really wanted to play ball but couldn't. Soon Charlie and Sarah began to feel that trying to protect him was hurting him.

His learning capacity diminished but as far as being able to think, he was all right; he just couldn't cope with everything.

He didn't do well in school. Doctors finally said that the motor part in his brain had been burned by that high fever. He couldn't write, and he found it hard to use his hands. Then other children began picking on him. They tried to make him play football but he couldn't turn his hands

Ronnie

to catch the ball. His eyes revealed that he badly wanted to catch the ball, but he couldn't get his muscles to function at the proper time.

"I coached a midget football team one time," Charlie said, "and Ronnie tried to play, and when he realized he couldn't, it hurt him badly."

Ronnie lived to the age of forty-four, always dependent on his parents. At lunch one day in 1992, he fell over in the kitchen and died of a massive heart attack.

"His coordination was so bad," Charlie said, "I thought he had just stumbled, but when I tried to help him up, he was gone. I tried to revive him but couldn't, and the doctor said he was probably gone as soon as he fell.

"He was an unusual son," Charlie added, "and we loved him very much."

The notoriety that surrounded Charlie affected Ronnie. "Notoriety is good," Charlie said, "and I won't say I didn't enjoy it, but it's a handicap in a lot of ways, especially for children. Ronnie couldn't understand why he wasn't the center of attention instead of his father."

That was another hill Charlie had to climb. The adoration of his fans was excessive at times. At home in North Carolina and sometimes in South Carolina and Georgia, the Justices found it hard to eat out and enjoy their time together. People would come to their table to tell Charlie how much they enjoyed watching him play football, or how much he meant as a role model to the young people, or simply to ask for an autograph and shake his hand.

"Sometimes I couldn't eat," Charlie said, "but you know, as Kay Kiser said to me once, "Charlie, don't ever be rude to people. Remember, they're who made you. It's when they don't come up that you're going to start worrying about it."

Kiser, who made his home in Chapel Hill, knew from personal experience what he was talking about. He was one of the country's most famous big band leaders, and a movie actor at the same time

Charlie's oldest brother, Jack, was perhaps his most steadying influence. Jack would say to Charlie, "Know you're good, believe you're good, but don't tell everybody how good you are. They'll find out and let you know."

"I was very, very fortunate," Charlie said, "to be at Chapel Hill when I was, and at Bainbridge, too. Those guys in service kept telling me, 'If we ever hear of you getting the big-head, we'll come and look you up.' We were undefeated for two years, and the number one service team in the nation in 1944. 'Remember,' they kept saying to me, 'you're only as good as those seven men in front of you and the other three in the backfield with you.'"

Charlie managed notoriety as well as anyone ever. "Twenty-five years from now," he said, "mention my name and they'll say 'Who?' It's the greatest honor for me today, when I'm walking down the street and somebody comes up and says, 'Say, aren't you Choo Choo Justice?' And its been fifty years! I'd say, 'How did you recognize me?' and they would answer, 'Oh, it wasn't hard. We recognized you.' Anybody who says they don't like that is lying through his teeth."

He continued, "I know I got every break in the world, but I didn't glory in it. After a game, I wouldn't stop outside the dressing room and bask in the limelight. I'd go charging in and get out of the way. I was usually the first one dressed, and I got out of there. I didn't hang around for anyone to pat me on the back.

"I'd rather have my teammates say what they say about me today than all the publicity in the world. They give me credit for not getting my head too big. All the sports writers were awfully good to me. Only one, Jack Horner at Durham, ever gave me any real bad press. He was a Duke fan, and I knew it, but he and I became good friends, and once I said to him, 'Well, Jack, you had all the right to write what you did about me.' I didn't get mad and cuss him out, or go see him. I said maybe he's right."

"The press and the fans make you," he said. "If it weren't for the fans coming in there paying their money to see you play, and the sportswriters putting your name up there on the board, you wouldn't be there.

"I could have gotten a bad press," he said, "when it looked like I was shopping around in 1946 for a place to go to school, but I was lucky that the press accepted me and understood that I was not shopping for the highest bidder, but simply trying to find the school where I ought to go — and it appears that I made the right decision."

Dave Bristol of Andrews, North Carolina, who managed four major league baseball clubs — the Reds, Giants, Braves, and Brewers — said once when asked how he kept his feet on the ground, "I always thought about having to meet those same people on the way back down that I met coming up."

"I didn't pay much attention to what others said of me, even in the press," Charlie said, "because my teammates were who I worried about. As long as I got along with them and they with me, that's all I really cared about."

So Charlie tried hard to keep his notoriety from interfering with his family life — but he could only do so much.

MIRACLES HAPPEN

As September 1949 rolled around, there was little hope in the Tar Heel football camp that the team would be as strong as in the last three years. Justice and Weiner were still there, and everyone hoped that the rest of the team would mold quickly around them, but the players would not be nearly as experienced as even the 1946 team.

That was part of the rub. So many of the 1946 team had been at Chapel Hill before the war that the graduation classes of 1948 and 1949 had stripped the Tar Heels of much of their experience.

Snavely was scratching his head over personnel. He planned to use many combinations of players on the practice field to build his starting lineup.

He knew he was going to be short in personnel. Most of his players were sophomores, and this had come on him before he realized it was happening, Justice believes, that most of those he had recruited and started with in 1946 were no longer around. Snavely and his staff were not well prepared for this shortcoming.

The offensive unit had experience in Justice, ends Weiner and Kenny Powell, blocking back Eddie Knox, and wingback Johnny Clements, but the others, center Joe Neikirk, tackles Julian King and Jim Hendrick, guards Dick McDonald and Peter Hywak, and fullback Billy Hayes, had little playing time coming into the season. Some had been around Chapel Hill for a while, but mostly as bench warmers.

The Justice Era was drawing to a close on a little less than optimistic note. Still, Justice was Justice, and Weiner was Weiner, and newspapers and fans touted that fact and said, in effect, that the two All-Americans could pull the Tar Heels through a lot of early rough spots while the others gained experience.

Snavely's thinking was that the experience he had, especially that of Justice and Weiner, would win some games, and that the season could develop the sophomores into leaders for the early-1950s Tar Heel teams.

But the fans and much of the press still had faith in Choo Choo, figuring he alone would pull the Tar Heels through some games. Shirley Povich, sports columnist for *The Washington Post*, wrote of Justice's importance on Sunday, September 18, just before the season began.

> If there has been a more important citizen than Charlie Justice in Carolina the past three years, his fame has not come to light. Carolina is a state gone daft over the 165-pound Justice, the boy from Asheville, home-grown tailback of the Tar Heels. ...
>
> At the end of last season, Justice's fame as a national football figure was secure. By whopping margins in the voting, he was selected on the All-American teams announced by both the Associated Press and United Press.
>
> But Grantland Rice kicked up a storm in North Carolina, the equal of any that had ever assaulted Cape Hatteras. In his All-American selections for *Collier's*, Rice conceded Justice a berth only on the second team. Carolina citizens questioned Rice's sanity. Calmer heads were all for hailing him before the Un-American Activities Committee on clear-cut evidence of treason.
>
> Small wonder Carolina is nuts about Justice. Over a three-year span Choo Choo has averaged a touchdown every thirteenth time he got his hands on the ball. Last season he shattered all known collegiate kicking records with his average of 44 yards flat on his punts, measured from the scrimmage line. ...

Few people, especially those in the know, envisioned the Tar Heels of 1949 as a bowl team – especially after an illness befell Justice on the opening day of practice.

The entire squad reported for the morning drill on September 1 and went through the paces with eagerness. Near the end of the session, Justice began feeling woozy and left the field to sit on the sidelines. By noon he was running a high fever and was swiftly dispatched to the hospital.

Doctors administered to him but couldn't lower his temperature, and nurses gave him injections – he has no idea what – every three hours. For several days the fever persisted, though it never got near life-threatening degrees, and the physicians were baffled over what caused it. They could not diagnose the illness.

In fact, the problem was never diagnosed. Charlie has no idea to this day what his ailment was, but he suspects mononucleosis, which weakens the victim. Probably it was more than that or a diagnosis could have been made.

After conferring with doctors, Snavely insisted that Charlie remain sidelined at least until the week of the opener with North Carolina State.

Until the ailment popped up, Charlie thought he might be able to have a good season, despite the team's inexperience. But as the opener approached, he was suddenly riddled with doubts. He did not feel well, but couldn't pinpoint the nature or source of his sickness. Regardless, he came back to practice five days before the State game and by game day felt physically well enough to play.

"They didn't want to let me out of the hospital," Charlie said, "but Snavely insisted and they did. The doctors told me I should take the entire season off.

By that time, he did not hold strong hope for a good season, either for himself or for the team.

But miracles happen. ...

Looking back in retrospect, Justice admires the accomplishments the team made in 1949, although he is quick to say that the Tar Heels were not of world-beating strength.

"The Southern Conference limited varsity rosters to forty-five players," he said. "That was four teams of players to do it all, and if a coach couldn't find the proper combinations among forty-five men, he went without.

"Today they have a hundred and some players on the squad. I'm still trying to figure out why they need so many. That's enough personnel for ten football teams, and if a coach hasn't found a man for a certain position, he doesn't have far to look for a replacement.

"A lot of players spend four years practicing and never get to play. They are cannon fodder for the first teams to beat up on through the week. They would be better off studying chemistry or science. The professional teams, which are the best football teams in the world, capable of doing everything, don't have half as many players as colleges do. College football has reached ridiculous proportions. They can only play eleven players at a time.

"Today colleges play eleven men on offense and eleven on defense, and usually eleven more on suicide squads to return kicks and such. Then they have second and third, and sometimes fourth, offensive and defensive units. Every team has all these specialists – long and short kickers, certain players to put in on offense and defense when they're in a certain position on the field.

"Things were different with us and football was a lot easier for the fans to keep up with. I did all the punting and most of the passing, returned punts and kickoffs, and ran the ball. The first two years I played defense and even in my last two seasons, when Coach Snavely thought we needed two safeties on the field, I played defense.

"The thing that hurts most universities now is that football costs too much money. That's why you see certain teams always at the top of the rankings. They're the ones that can afford to play the game. Now and then you'll find a team that rises out of the ashes of the previous season to make a good mark, but those exceptions are rare. A primary reason there are so many bowl games today is because teams – even the big ones – need the money to continue their programs on such an upscale grade. Teams with 6-5 records go to bowls, and that's ridiculous. It takes away from the purpose of bowl games.

"During my four years at North Carolina, we put more than a half-million dollars into the university through the three bowl games we played.

"Something needs to be done to give college football more parity. But no one seems to know the answers. I certainly don't."

Charlie knew the answers to his own questions of how to get in good physical condition for a football season and how to maintain that condition. Bob Deindorfer wrote about this in the *Atlanta Journal's THIS WEEK* Magazine, September 11, 1949:

> Charlie points his weekly schedule toward one 60-minute period on Saturday afternoon, when he carries, kicks, or throws the ball 28 or 30 times for Carolina. He sleeps eight to 10 hours a night, passes up pastries and all rich foods, and practices two hours a day. When an arm or a leg is muscle-sore, he carefully soaks it in the whirlpool bath (a tub of hot, swirling water) or warms it under a heat lamp. From Thursday until Saturday night Charlie even gives up one of his favorite treats – malted milks.
>
> Right now, with his million-dollar legs in perfect shape, Justice can perform tricks few other college ball-carriers are permitted to try. He is one of no more than six who can successfully reverse fields without a loss, swinging laterally back and forth across the gridiron until blocks are set up or a path opens up. Then he skitters toward the goal, picking his way through opponents with blinding speed combined with deceivingly abrupt stops and starts. He reversed his field three times against Texas in 1948 before he bolted 38 yards down the sidelines to score without being touched. ...
>
> One lesson Charlie learned from the professionals appears to be of only marginal value, but he isn't sure that it hasn't won games for the Tarheels, too. Profes-

sional athletes are notoriously superstitious and Charlie became aware of hexes and charms while he was at Bainbridge. That explains why he wears No. 43 on his helmet. After the Tarheels lost two 1947 games, Justice changed to 43 for the William & Mary game. Carolina won, which meant Justice had a good day. He's worn it ever since.

Charlie's wife, Sarah, thought part of Charlie's superstition might have been attributable to the fact that he was nervous before a game. "Charlie does get nervous before games," she said. "I guess that's only natural. He wants to win so badly. Naturally, he makes me nervous, too, and I get right shaky before the kickoff. Then I'm all right – unless Charlie drops the ball!"

So the Justices had a good time being nervous together.

After three weeks of practice for the team and five days for Justice, the 1949 season began on September 24 against North Carolina State in Chapel Hill. A crowd of 44,000 watched on a warm, sunny day.

Everyone wondered how Charlie's illness would affect his play.

UNC faltered and bumped along with a 7-6 lead for three quarters before calling up its old dazzle and dash to finally crush the Wolfpack, 26-6. State drove the opening kickoff to the North Carolina four-yard line, but the Tar Heels stiffened and held for downs. With Billy Hayes and Skeet Hesmer hitting Weiner regularly with short pitches, Carolina moved the ball to the State 10 and Justice came in to throw a strike to Kenny Powell in the end zone for the touchdown. Egbert Williams kicked the extra point and Carolina had a 7-0 lead that held till halftime.

State scored in the third and the Tar Heels led 7-6 going into the fourth period. That's when Carolina cut loose its tiger, and it was Justice's old magic that opened the gates. Feeling better, with adrenalin shooting through his veins in the excitement of battle, he took a punt on his own 37 and slipped the ball to Hesmer. Justice went to the right sideline and set sail down the field with the State team in hot pursuit. Around the 20, Justice showed both his hands and the startled Wolfpack looked around quickly to see Hesmer running the ball all alone down the other sideline and across the goal for a 63-yard touchdown. Williams kicked this point, too.

Carolina kicked off and State had to punt, and Carolina moved the ball 94 yards in seven plays with Justice circling left end behind good blocking for the final 10 yards. That put the margin at 20-6.

The same handoff magic worked on the next State punt, but this time it was a fake. Justice took the ball, faked a handoff to Billy Hayes, and hiding the ball behind his leg, paused to watch Hayes tear off empty-handed, inches ahead of the State team. Then Choo Choo snaked 35 yards to State's 26. Carolina lost the ball deep in State territory, but minutes later fullback George Verchick intercepted an Ogden Smith pass on the 10 and ran it in for the last touchdown.

That forged a 26-6 finish and the crowd – and the Tar Heels – went home happy.

State Coach Beattie Feathers summed up his team's loss by saying it was "too much Justice and Weiner."

"The only consolation I can find," Feathers added, "is that we never have to face those two again."

Jake Wade, who had left his position as sports editor of *The Charlotte Observer* to become sports publicist at North Carolina, covered the game for several smaller papers, and, always one who had a way with words and analogies, wrote:

"Charlie (Choo Choo) Justice, the Asheville Express, was a locomotive as entrancing as any Thomas Wolfe ever wrote about. Charlie was never in a bigger hurry, never shook his hips more tantalizingly or curved his direction more astutely."

Turning his pen toward others, Wade added: "George Verchick may turn out to be a key man on the defense which was more completely remodeled than the offense. He backs up the line as a pal to Irv Holdash. The two teamed on Carolina's brilliant goal line defenses which thwarted State twice."

As a rule, the defensive backs were Dick Bunting and Eddie Knox, with Hesmer at safety. When it was double safety, Justice was there.

So... perhaps, just perhaps, thought the people going home, the Tar Heels may have more power than was originally thought – especially if Justice can completely regain his health. They knew that the Tar Heels' strength would be taxed to the utmost the following Saturday when the University of Georgia came to Chapel Hill.

It was, indeed.

Carolina stopped two Georgia threats in the second quarter, one at the four and another at the 12, and then cranked up its own offensive machine to take a 14-0 lead into halftime. Weiner scored the first touchdown on an eight-yard pass from Justice, and Choo Choo made the other from the 13.

The second half became a turnaround as Georgia scored twice to tie the game, its second touchdown coming with 2:20 to play when fullback Eli Maracich went 88 yards on a punt return.

Weiner then supplied the finishing blow for the Tar Heels. They took the kickoff and passed their way downfield to the 33 from where Hayes shot a pass to Weiner who took the ball at the 20, wiggled away from Maracich, and breezed over the goal with 1:20 left – a one-minute drive.

That capped a 21-14 Tar Heel victory.

Justice hit nine of 14 passes for 115 yards, throwing for one touchdown

Photo: Hugh Morton

Justice agonized when things went wrong.

and scoring another himself. He carried 21 times for 65 yards, and punted 11 times for a 45.9-yard average. On North Carolina's first touchdown march Justice handled the ball on five of the six plays, and on the second march he handled it 10 of 13 plays.

Weiner caught six passes for 103 yards and two touchdowns, and stamped himself as a very real candidate for the All-America teams.

Georgia Coach Wally Butts, like Beattie Feathers a week before, was happy that his Bulldogs wouldn't have to face Justice and Weiner again. "Carolina had two individuals better than anybody we had," Butts said. "I mean Justice and Weiner, especially Weiner. He is the finest pass receiver I've ever seen."

Snavely was elated. "It was a great ball game," he said. "I've seen lots of fine games in my time, and that one was the best. I don't suppose we'll ever have another game like that."

Some credited assistant coach Russ Murphy with a huge assist in winning this game. Frank Spencer of the *Winston-Salem Journal* described it:

> The eagle eyes of Russ Murphy, the Carolina coach, who perched quietly on top of the press box with a telephone connected with the bench, probably was the deciding factor in Carolina's victory over Georgia Saturday.
>
> Things were a bit confused after Eli Maricich had taken a handoff on a punt return from Ken McCall on a Justice kick and raced 88 yards down the north sideline to tie the score with less than three minutes remaining. ...
>
> Coach Carl Snavely called his two brilliant ends, Art Weiner and Ken Powell, to the sidelines to determine if they were physically able to play the last three minutes.
>
> Both ends urged Snavely to leave them in the game. At that moment the telephone rang. It was Murphy.
>
> He told Snavely to send Weiner out wide for a pass, the same fadeaway pass Art had snagged in the final second of the first half to score. Russ called that pass play, too.
>
> "Maracich, the defensive halfback, is drawing to the center. Throw Weiner wide and pass," was what Murphy told King Snavely. So Snavely rushed to the sidelines and gave Weiner the instructions. On the next play Weiner went out to the sideline, took Billy Hayes' pass and raced 33 yards to score the winning touchdown.
>
> Incidentally, Weiner told me Saturday that he wasn't over three or four inches from the sideline when he was bumped by Georgia's Maracich. Fans had crowded to the lines and an unidentified spectator in a yellow sweater gave Art an assist by giving Maricich a shoulder as he made the vain tackle.

Hugo Germino of the *Durham Sun* saw Maricich as the goat of the game:

> Weiner faked him out of position when he caught the first
> touchdown pass, Justice sidestepped him on his touchdown
> sprint, and finally Weiner caught the winning touchdown
> pass in Maricich's territory, shaking the Bulldog off his
> shoulders at the 10-yard stripe and going over untouched.
>
> Of course, Maricich almost was the hero. His long
> touchdown run which tied the score in the fourth quarter
> was a beautiful thing to see.

Jake Wade offered more praise, writing:

> Some folks have remarked that Carolina has one of the
> greatest passing attacks ever launched on a football field.
> Some were afraid that Justice's picture on the cover of
> *LIFE* Magazine, which came out yesterday, might have
> put the whammy on him. He has run and passed better
> than he did today, but he was always in there, the guy to
> be watched. His touchdown run was about the best thing
> that has happened in Kenan Stadium for a long time. He
> had the old Asheville High School touch on that one,
> sidestepping, swivel-hipping, moving along.

The magazine to which Wade referred was the October 3, 1949, issue of
LIFE, a 118-page supermagazine that sold for twenty cents. Charlie's photo
filled the 14-by-10.5-inch cover. The story was headed "CHOO CHOO"
SPELLS FOOTBALL IN 1949," and was sub-titled "North Carolina's Justice stands out as college teams begin new season." Inside the magazine was
a roundup story of college football for 1949 bearing four photos of Justice,
including one drawn with lights of the "Celestial Choo Choo" from inside
Carolina's Morehead Planetarium.

The story read in part:

> A resident of Chapel Hill recently described Halfback
> Charlie ("Choo Choo") Justice as the greatest Southerner
> since Robert E. Lee.
>
> Part of this adulation, which also has been expressed
> in song and even in the stars (a reference to the celestial
> Justice), results from Choo Choo's undoubted technical
> talents on the gridiron, but part of it also can be attrib-
> uted to the sense of drama he brings to the game. When
> Justice goes back to receive a punt he somehow looks
> like a man who is going to run 60 or 70 yards for a touch-
> down. He often does. In 1948 Justice averaged 5.2 yards
> by rushing, completed over 50% of his passes and led
> the nation in punting with an average of 44 yards. Al-

though he is not phenomenally fast, he is extremely adept
at sidestepping would-be tacklers.

The *LIFE* treatment had no effect on Charlie's attitude toward the
game and toward his friends and fans. Publicity had never affected him.

But he began to feel that the time he spent working with *LIFE*'s writer
and photographers might have contributed to his illness.

"*LIFE* called and came to Chapel Hill," he said, "and I spent three
weeks posing for all kinds of pictures. The photographers shot hundreds
of photos. This was from the middle of July through the first week of
August, and on several days I would swear that the temperature reached
105. The photographers insisted I wear winter-weight clothing since the
story would not run until October. I lost several pounds very quickly,
and maybe that had something to do with the sickness.

"The worst part was that even though they were shooting up many
rolls of film each day, they told me they didn't even know if they were
going to feature me in the magazine. They must have been photograph-
ing other players around the country at the same time. Just in case I was
used, they said, they wanted to be ready. So they photographed everything I did, sometimes in uniform, sometimes in street clothes.

"They went away after attending the first North Carolina East-West
High School All-Star football game in Greensboro in early August. I threw
out the first ball and they wanted to photograph that."

Charlie was going through his sickness when *LIFE* decided it was
going to use him, because they felt (and wrote in the story) that he "looked
like Rudolph Valentino made up as Superman," and sent another photographer to Chapel Hill to shoot the cover picture.

"It was a terrible picture," Charlie said. "Boy, did I look awful. But
the magazine's editors liked it and ran it.

"I didn't fully recover from the illness the whole season," Charlie
added, "and after a fast start, it became a long season."

They were still in that fast start when on Saturday, October 8, without scoring a point, Charlie led the Tar Heels to a 28-13 victory over
South Carolina at Columbia.

On a wet field with slippery footing, Justice's running, passing, and
kicking was outstanding as usual. His deadly accurate passes to Weiner
led to the first three North Carolina touchdowns; and Weiner's receiving
was nothing short of sensational. He caught eight passes from Justice
and Billy Hayes for 118 yards and barely missed several others.

After North Carolina took the opening kickoff 81 yards, highlighted
by Charlie's passing, Fred Sherman scored on a six-yard reverse, and
after South Carolina tied the game 7-7 at the half, the Tar Heels went
back to work with a vengeance in the second half.

The New York press watches Justice practice in Yankee Stadium.

North Carolina scored twice in the third. Justice passed the way downfield and Sherman took a reverse the final 12 yards, and a few minutes later Justice threw a down-the-middle pass to Weiner on a 40-yard play to the two, and Hayes smashed over. Fullback Dick Weiss went eight yards through center for the last touchdown.

One of the South Carolina scores was a 70-yard aerial strike from Boyle to Jim Pinkerton. Remember Pinkerton? He was one of the stars on the Asheville High School teams with Justice. He went to South Carolina because he thought Charlie was going there.

As usual, when the smoke of battle cleared away, Justice was on the long end of the statistics. He had gained 57 yards on 17 carries on a wet field, passed 20 times for eight completions and 144 yards, and his kicking average was 44 yards on five punts.

Weiner, third in the nation in pass receiving, caught eight for 137 yards. His total for three games was 21 catches.

The Tar Heels' record was 3 and 0 and the Choo Choo was building steam.

On Monday following the Saturday game at Columbia, North Carolina found itself ranked sixth in the nation, a position not surprising at the time, but if anyone had suggested it before the season began, he would have been laughed at.

Wake Forest was next on the Tar Heel schedule, and Chapel Hill knew the Demon Deacons would be tough. They usually were. The Tar Heels subdued them, 28-14, in Kenan Stadium, but not before Wake threw a good scare into Carolina fans with a first quarter burst of uncommonly good football.

Two Wake Forest quick kicks by fullback Bobby Stutts dominated that quarter. The first traveled 58 yards and the second 64. They kept the Tar Heels bottled up until Wake could mount a drive that culminated with 1:15 remaining in the period when quarterback Carroll Blackerby sneaked over from the one for his first ever collegiate touchdown.

The Tar Heels tied the score early in the second with Justice scoring the first of his three touchdowns. From the five-yard-line, he raced around left end and scored standing up.

Dick Bunting, who had been understudying Justice, playing his first game at right defensive end, intercepted a pass and ran it back 31 yards for a 14-7 halftime lead, but Wake wasn't finished yet. The Deacons turned a third-quarter interception into a touchdown with Bill Miller scoring from the one, and the game was tied again, 14-14.

Now Justice took over. In one of his busiest games, he scored twice in the fourth and the Tar Heels won their fourth straight game. Choo Choo carried the ball 23 times for 102 yards and hit six of 12 passes for 52. He was not spectacular, but methodical and businesslike. Jake Wade recalled that Charlie had never scored three touchdowns with more ease.

Weiner, too, was outstanding. He caught seven more passes for 72 yards to bring his four-game total to 28 catches for 404 yards.

After this game, Red Miller, sports editor of *The Asheville Citizen*, Charlie's hometown newspaper, perhaps summed up Justice's intentness on the field as well as anyone had to date:

> Justice sets the pace in everything (a real leader). He is the first man on the field and the first man to go into his warming-up exercises. He is the first man to head out on the field when Coach Carl Snavely's team goes out to do battle. When he comes out of a game, he goes down on one knee as near the sideline as permissable and never takes his eye off the team on the field.
> He is an intense young man.

So, now, with their record 4-0 and a national ranking supporting them, the Tar Heels felt like flexing their muscles again against the Southeastern Conference. They had two chances in a row, with their next game against Louisiana State in Baton Rouge and a game the following week against Tennessee in Chapel Hill.

But when the dust cleared from those two games, the Tar Heels were no longer unbeaten, they had a 4-2 record, and their national ranking had fallen by the wayside.

In a night game, LSU slowed Justice to a crawl and whipped the Tar Heels, 13-7. The loss to LSU was Carolina's first defeat since early 1947 – the Tar Heels' first loss in 22 regular season games.

The Tiger defense was effective against Justice and Weiner both. Charlie carried 11 times and picked up 48 yards. His punting was up to par. He kicked eight times for a 47-yard average. And Weiner was well covered for most of the game.

North Carolina was ahead 7-0 at the half, thanks to a 97-yard drive which culminated when Billy Hayes threw four yards to Weiner for a touchdown. LSU scored six in the third, and pushed over the winning score in the fourth on a one-foot plunge by Zollie Toth.

The Tennessee game was a blowout, 35-6. During the week leading to the game, General Neyland reversed the psychology Snavely had used on him in 1947, telling his players that no team had ever beaten him three times in a row "and I don't intend for it to happen now." His players responded just as Carolina had responded to Snavely's plea two years earlier.

The press called the game a "major upset" because Carolina had been a two-touchdown favorite. A great part of the credit went to the Tennessee defense which hammered Justice unmercifully and finally knocked him out of the game early in the third quarter with a hairline-fractured rib. Tightly bound, he was able to come back into the game only to punt.

Remembering all the fireworks Justice had set off in Carolina's victories the previous two years, General Neyland set his defenses for Charlie and the only big noise Choo Choo made was a 55-yard return with Bert Rechichar's game-opening kickoff.

General Neyland, carried off the field by his players after the game, had called the shots and his players responded beautifully.

Justice miscued more than ever before. Starting the second period he caught triple-threater Hal Littleford's punt on his goal line and slipped and was downed on the spot. He kicked out feebly and Tennessee marched to a touchdown. A few moments later, Justice fumbled on his three-yard line and Tennessee recovered in the end zone for a two-point safety. Following the return kickoff, Charlie threw an errant pass that Gordon Polofsky intercepted at the North Carolina 22, and halfback Hank Lauricella promptly pitched to Rechichar for a touchdown.

Jake Wade credited the Tennessee pass defense with the victory. J. W. Sherrill, Bill Jasper, Bud Sherrod, and Polofsky made up the Tennessee secondary, and they slowed the Carolina aerial game almost to a standstill. The Tar Heels gained only 25 yards on four completions, and Tennessee intercepted five times, all of which led either directly or indirectly to Volunteer touchdowns.

After the game, Tennessee rooters chanted:

> This is what happened to Tennessee,
> Or at least it's the way it was told to me.
> Due to the strike of the CIO
> There wasn't any coal to make Choo Choo go!

Now the rigors of so many years of football began to catch up. Justice missed every day of practice except one the next week when pleurisy developed in his side near the broken rib.

Hard on the heels of Tennessee came troublesome William & Mary. The Tar Heels scored a 20-14 victory to run their record to 5-2, and Justice played well, although late in the game he was given a more severe injury than the cracked rib, and for the second time — the first was against Tennessee the previous Saturday — a derailed Choo Choo had to be carried off the field.

Before that, however, William & Mary led 7-0 at the half, but the Tar Heels scored twice in the first three minutes of the third quarter. End Ed Bilpuch recovered a W&M fumble at the 19, and after a penalty, Justice passed to George Verchick 21 yards for the first touchdown. Choo Choo scored the second himself on the longest Tar Heel run of the 1949 season, 75 yards on a punt return. Fielding the ball on his 25, Charlie went down the right sideline, sifting through a mass of Indians, and Kenny Powell knocked punter Buddy Lex out of the play on the W&M 30, giving Justice clear sailing on in. The score stood 13-7 after those two touchdowns.

Things began to look dark for Carolina when with eight minutes to go in the fourth, Lex hurled a fourth-down pass to Ed Magdziak for a three-yard touchdown that put the Indians back in front, 14-13.

Now came the trial for the Tar Heels. Less than six minutes remained when the Indians punted for the last time. Carolina started the drive 59 yards from the goal and ended it with three minutes to play when Hayes fired a pass over defender Don Howren to Weiner crossing in the end zone.

Before the game, Snavely gave Justice strict orders to step out of bounds when any William & Mary tackler approached him near the sideline. Snavely was looking ahead to the Notre Dame game the following Saturday in New York's Yankee Stadium.

Near the sideline in the fourth quarter, Lou Creekmur, William & Mary's All-American tackle, bore down on Charlie, who stepped out of bounds, planted his right foot, and stopped. Creekmur didn't stop. He barreled into Justice with a late hit, and knocked Charlie hard into the sideline crowd. Choo Choo came up limping with severe shooting pain in his ankle, and couldn't walk back to the bench.

"I would have been all right," Justice said, "except that when I set my foot and stopped, my cleats dug into the turf, and when he hit me, it was like my foot was pegged to the ground and since something had to give, it was the ankle. I didn't let them know he had hurt me; I kept on playing."

When Charlie got up the next morning, he couldn't put his weight on the ankle and couldn't walk.

"I had the ankle taped pretty well," Charlie said, "so I tore off the tape and the trainers started working with me. Snavely got mad at them. He thought they should have been treating me overnight. I didn't tell him they both got drunk celebrating. But that morning they slapped me into the training room and went to work."

This injury was diagnosed as a chipped bone in the right ankle. For the remainder of his life, the ankle would give Charlie trouble, swelling and paining.

In the fall of 1950 Justice and Creekmur played together on the College All-Star team against the National Football League champion Philadelphia Eagles.

One day after practice, Charlie said to Creekmur, "Damn you, Lou, I was all the way out of bounds when you hit me."

Creekmur replied in good nature, "You little son of a bitch, I had been shooting at you for four years and when I had a chance to hit you I did."

Charlie believes that late hit by Creekmur cost him the Heisman Trophy he so desperately sought.

For a week, with Justice limping around like Chester, Snavely pondered a problem. What to do with Charlie? He wanted him to play against Notre Dame because he knew it would be the most important game of Justice's collegiate career.

He also knew that Charlie could play, if his ankle were deadened and he wore enough protective bracing. But the Duke game was coming up in Durham on the Saturday following the Notre Dame game, and Duke hadn't beaten Carolina since Justice came to play. If he withheld Charlie from the Notre Dame game, he might be whole for Duke, and beating Duke was the making of a season for Carolina. If the Tar Heels finished 1-9 and beat Duke, many alumni would judge the season successful.

There was one other consideration. Charlie wanted to novocaine the ankle and play, but Snavely feared deadening it and allowing him to play against Notre Dame might cause permanent damage − and that settled the issue in the coach's mind.

He would have Justice sit out the Notre Dame game and play against Duke!

He broke the news to Justice who went away with tears in his eyes. Charlie feels he could have overruled Snavely, because that's the way the coach worked, but he didn't.

Charlie—not yet a Redskin, just another Indian in the outdoor drama, "The Lost Colony," in Manteo, North Carolina.

"Now I wish I had," Charlie said. "I might have been able to play in both games, Notre Dame and Duke, but when Snavely said to me, 'Charlie, we can't beat Notre Dame with you or without you,' I almost dropped my teeth, and said no more about it. That statement floored me. I think we could have beaten them."

On Saturday a capacity crowd of 67,000 filled Yankee Stadium, even though the people didn't expect to see a titanic struggle since Notre Dame was favored by 30 points with Justice out.

In the opening minutes, Dick Bunting scored the Tar Heel touchdown on a five-yard carry and Carolina led 6-0. Notre Dame tied the score in the second period, and AP writer Gayle Talbot wrote that "there probably never was a more astonished set of athletes than the Irish" when they left the field for halftime tied 6-6.

Justice entered the game only twice, once to hold on an aborted conversion attempt, and later in his capacity as captain to protest the awarding of a safety to Notre Dame. Aided by the safety and a third period touchdown, the Irish led 15-6 going into the fourth quarter.

In the fourth, Notre Dame piled up the score with four touchdowns and went away with a 42-6 victory.

The teams got into a bench-clearing brawl in the fourth when an unidentified North Carolina player threw a punch at Notre Dame guard Paul Burns as the teams walked off the field following an Irish touchdown.

"We played them a good ball game," Charlie said, "and this was the game in which I learned I didn't know much about coaching. Coach came to me and said, 'Charlie, we can have a moral victory if we can hold the score here.' It was 15-6. I said, 'Coach, we don't want a moral victory. Let's go for it.' We did, stressing the offense – and Notre Dame scored twenty-seven points in that last quarter."

Before Notre Dame took the lead, Carolina protested two plays, one a supposed lateral from Leon Hart to Bill Barrett which Barrett carried over for a touchdown, and then the safety, which the Tar Heels claimed should have been a touchback.

Snavely thought the lateral was forward and said so after the game.

And Talbot wrote: "Whether the Tar Heels would have continued to battle Frank Leahy's monsters on even terms will never be known. Certainly they had up to that point."

Joe Reichler of the AP wrote at game's end: "A battered, bruised, and beaten North Carolina football squad trudged into its dressing room still breathing fire after giving mighty Notre Dame the scare of its life for more than 30 minutes."

Quiet, stoical Snavely, a disappointed man, commented: "Without attempting to take away any credit from Notre Dame, I believe three mistaken decisions hurt us badly. Now, understand, please, I'm not saying those breaks beat us. We probably would have lost anyway, but they certainly hurt us. I thought Bunting might have made that touchdown early in the second period, but the officials ruled he hit the ground on the half-yard line. My boys swear that Dick was over. So, instead of us leading 12-0, Notre Dame scored and tied us 6-6. I, myself, didn't see it. However, I did see that forward handoff that Hart gave to Barrett which gave Notre Dame its second touchdown. That definitely is illegal. However, the officials ruled it a lateral. The third miscall came in the third period. The referee called a safety against us, although one of the Notre Dame players knocked the ball into the end zone before we recovered it. It should have been called a touchback."

Joe Neikirk, the Tar Heel reserve center, who recovered the fumble in the end zone, claimed afterward that two linesmen officials called the play a touchback, but were overruled by Referee Bill Blake.

So Justice did not get exposure to the influential New York press, and Leon Hart, the Notre Dame end, won the Heisman Trophy.

"He won it with no reason to," Justice said almost a half-century later. "Even Doak Walker, who won the trophy in 1948, said I should have won it the year he did, and he should have won it the year Hart did. But Hart played for Notre Dame, and he played in Yankee Stadium. That was apparently enough. Anybody else and I wouldn't complain, but Hart didn't deserve it."

During the week following the Notre Dame game, Justice received the first pressing of the recording of the song, "All the Way, Choo Choo," which was inspired by his great football career. Johnny Long, a band leader and a graduate of Duke, recorded the song and presented the first copy to Justice.

Orville Campbell wrote the lyrics and Hank Beebe the music, basing each verse on real incidents and accomplishments by Justice. The lyrics went like this:

> Talk about your football heroes old
> Talk about your great ones, brave and bold
> Just hark the sound of Tar Heel voices
> Singing the same old tune:
>
> All the Way Choo Choo, all the Way
> A-chug chug chugga with a Hip Hooray
> Bing, bat, boot that ball around
> Open that throttle and cover ground
>
> A two-ton tackle got his man
> Across him laid his two-ton span,
> "Don't move," Two-Ton said to him,
> "Choo Choo may come by again."
>
> A touchdown pass would break a tie
> The end said, "Hit me in the eye."
> While thousands roared, the coach looked glum,
> Choo Choo merely said, "Which one?"

Punt formation once was called,
Choo Choo waited for the ball.
Why, it ought to be against the law,
They found that ball in Arkansas.

At the football game he does all the stunts,
He runs, he passes, fakes, or punts;
Between the halves he leads the band,
Then sells peanuts in the stands.
A football field is a hundred yards long,
Check these figures, they ain't wrong;
He took the ball, poured on the coal,
Ran a thousand yards from goal to goal.

He took the kickoff on the ten,
The crowd yelled, "Man, he's off again."
Zigging through tackles, zagging through guards,
He razzle dazzled for ninety yards.

Campbell and Beebe campaigned for more than five months before their song was put on wax and released by Long's band. The record came out on a ten-inch disc with vocals by Janet Brace, the Johnny Long Glee Club, and the Longshots.

On the reverse side was an instrumental medley of the Carolina Victory March, "Here Comes Carolina-lina," "Tar Heels on Hand," and "Hark the Sound."

Johnny Murphy, a North Carolina alumnus of the late 1930s, who had arranged the famous "Shanty in Old Shanty Town," handled arranging of the Carolina melodies.

Actually, Benny Goodman made the first recording of the tune on a Capitol record, but Capitol never released it.

Long felt that the song would become a standard football tune, which it did for a long time. Justice modestly thought that it was a joke that anyone would want to write a song about him, but at the same time he felt honored.

Those who bought the record said the Choo Choo number was "a perfect shag beat," and that even the "Carolina fight songs could be jitterbugged to."

On Saturday, November 19, the big day arrived, and no one wearing Carolina blue in Duke Stadium was sorry Snavely had held Justice out of the Notre Dame game so he could play against Duke. With a conference record 57,500 fans screaming their lungs out, North Carolina scored its fourth straight victory over the Blue Devils, 21-20, in a game that produced as wild and breathtaking a finish as any ever played.

Justice passed to Weiner for two touchdowns and scored a third for a 21-6 lead. Duke scored in the third period and again with three minutes to play, but missed a try for a game-winning field goal on the last play of the game.

The Tar Heels won the Southern Conference championship for the fourth time in a row.

From the first play to the last, this game was spectacular. Duke's Billy Cox raced 75 yards through the Carolina defense to score a touchdown on the game's first scrimmage play.

In a game in which every point was vital, Kenny Powell blocked Mike Souchak's kick for extra point and Duke led 6-0.

In the second period, Justice threw 40 yards to Weiner who stretched high in the air to pull in the ball on the goal line. Abie Williams kicked the point and the Tar Heels led at the half, 7-6.

Early in the third period, North Carolina made one of the game's crucial plays. Tackle Dave Wiley broke through the line and blocked a punt by Duke's Billy Cox on the 13 and the ball rolled into the end zone where Carolina covered it for a two-point safety, making the score 9-6 for Carolina.

As the game progressed and the Tar Heels scored two successive touchdowns for a 21-6 lead, the safety seemed to be incidental, but it produced the points that eventually won the game.

After the safety, still in the third quarter, Bob Gantt returned a Duke punt 37 yards to the Duke 19, and five plays later fullback Billy Hayes hit Justice in the end zone from the three for a touchdown. The score then stood 15-6 for Carolina.

The last Tar Heel touchdown also came in the third period. A 68-yard quick kick by Justice that rolled out of bounds on the Duke one-foot line put the ball where Carolina wanted it. Cox had to punt for Duke and got off a short one that died on the Duke 33. Four plays later from the 13, Justice hit Weiner just across the line of scrimmage and the big end was hit by three Blue Devils at the five. Weiner dragged two of them the last five yards into the end zone for a 21-6 lead and Carolina's last points.

From there on, no one sat on his laurels and the huge crowd hardly breathed as lightning scorched the field, bolt after bolt.

After the last Carolina touchdown, Duke halfback Tom Powers ran the kickoff back 93 yards for a touchdown and Souchak kicked the point to pull Duke within eight at 21-13, and put the Blue Devils back in the ball game with the entire fourth quarter to play.

The break Duke sought came when Carolina's George Verchick fumbled the ball away in the fourth quarter and Duke recovered on the

Carolina nine. Cox scored on a fourth down play from the two and Souchak kicked the Blue Devils within a point of Carolina at 21-20. At that moment, the value of that safety looked as big as the Rock of Gibraltar.

Duke had the momentum and moved the ball rapidly downfield during the last minute, arriving at the 10-yard line from where Souchak was setting up a 27-yard field goal try when Referee J. D. Rogers signalled something that appeared to be a game-ending motion, and a thousand fans poured onto the field to pound the victorious Tar Heels on their backs.

However, time had not expired, and several minutes were required to quiet the crowd and make order out of pandemonium.

Souchak, later to become a successful professional golfer, hovered over the ball for a headon try for field goal and at the snap Weiner charged through the line like a wild horse and blocked the kick with his chest. As time expired he lay on the ground, grinning like an idiot.

Later it came to light that the referee's mistake in those final few seconds might have cost Duke the victory. The Blue Devils had planned a fake field goal attempt and pass, and the first time they lined up, Glenn Wild, a good passer, was in to hold the ball for Souchak. The strategy was for Wild to take the pass from center as if he were going to hold for Souchak's kick, and rise quickly to his feet and pass to Billy Cox.

But when the referee halted the play and then allowed it to be played over, Duke changed its mind and decided to kick the field goal. Fred Schoonmaker went in to hold the ball for Souchak that time, in place of Wild, and Weiner blocked the attempt.

The game produced other humorous sidelights. Smith Barrier wrote in the *Greensboro Daily News*:

> Freddie Folger, Duke's fearless one, might wonder today how in the world a punting average is figured.
> Take his first kick. He stood on his 25 and punted six yards into the end zone on the fly (with the wind). It was 81 yards in the air. Officially for the records, the kick was good for only 45 yards — from his 35 (the line of scrimmage) to the Carolina 20. Two kicks later he punted 78 yards to the Carolina seven — and this time he got credit for 70 yards from the line of scrimmage.

Justice's ankle pained him so much that for the first time in his career he netted minus yardage on the ground, running the ball only five times for a net loss of 15 yards. Most of the losses, however, came on smeared passing attempts. He threw the ball well, gaining 93 yards on seven completions.

Weiner entered the game tied for the national lead with 41 pass receptions and added seven to that total for 105 yards and two touchdowns.

Duke's Billy Cox had the biggest day, rushing for 149 yards in 22 carries, and adding 27 more on a 4-for-13 passing day.

In his four games against Duke, Justice either scored, passed for, or had a direct hand in 11 of North Carolina's 12 touchdowns.

It was after the Duke game that Charlie received an accolade that he cherishes. Ken Alyta of the Associated Press wrote an "open letter" which he addressed to C. Justice, Chapel Hill, N. C. Many newspapers around the nation carried the letter, which read:

Dear Charlie:

Since I won't be making the Virginia game this week, the Duke-Carolina game last Saturday marked for me, at least, the last chance to see you play college football.

I just thought I ought to tell you how much I've enjoyed watching you this year and last and thank you for the thrilling afternoons of football you've given me.

You see, being a Connecticut carpetbagger I could watch you play in a more or less detached manner without the emotional stress and strain of an old grad trying hard to be impartial.

I saw you and Carolina in action eight times beginning with that breathtaking Texas game last fall. You always won – I escaped those things with William & Mary last year and Tennessee this season.

I've admired the way in which you've stood up under pressure. It was terrific for three years, but this fall it must have been all but unbearable. You were expected to combine the better features of Frank Merriwell and Superman week after week. Usually you did.

You've been given the full treatment a la Hollywood the past three months. Magazine covers, All-America reputation, featured articles, even Orville Campbell's song, have all told the nation about you and, of course, led it to expect you to deliver more than ever before.

I think you'll be the first to admit that going into the Duke game, this season had not been a howling success either for you or for the team.

There was honest doubt in some quarters that you had merited a repeat All-America berth, in the strictest sense, going on this year's record alone.

But that three-touchdown job fashioned last Saturday clinched it in my book.

You've kept your head, refused to cry over the bad breaks and kept pitching. You've been All-America off the field as well as on.

Just thought I ought to let you know. So long, Charlie. It's been wonderful watching you.

From that point on, the season was anticlimactic for the Tar Heels. The conference title was wrapped up and only Virginia remained on the schedule. The game was played in Kenan Stadium on Saturday, November 26 – the last regular collegiate game for Justice and Weiner and the remnants of the team Snavely built in 1946.

In a storybook finish to a season that was better than it was expected to be, and to two great careers, Justice and Weiner each scored a touchdown in the second quarter, Justice running 14 yards for his and passing 63 yards to Weiner for the other. Abie Williams converted both.

Then the Tar Heels had to hang on for dear life as Virginia quarterback Whitey Michels sneaked over from the one-foot line in the fourth, and, after recovering the ball on an onsides kick, smashed to the North Carolina seven before the Tar Heels found the stopper and won the game, 14-7.

Virginia had been one of Justice's favorite opponents. In 1946, he streaked for touchdowns on runs of 54, 45, and 18 yards, gaining 169 yards in a 49-14 win. In 1947 he scored twice in a 40-7 victory, gaining 141 yards rushing, 30 more on two pass receptions, and 78 on a pair of kickoff returns. The 1948 game, a 34-12 win, found Charlie having a hand in four of the five touchdowns. He ran for two, going 80 yards from scrimmage and 50 on a punt return, and passed for two more. His total offense figure for that game was 246, 159 by rushing and 87 passing, plus 66 on punt returns. His figures fell off in 1949, his year of injury, but he still gained 26 rushing and threw for 99 more on four completions. He punted six times for a shade over a 37-yard average. He was sorry to see the last Virginia game end. He scored eight touchdowns in four games against Virginia.

But when it was over, the Tar Heels received and voted to accept a bid to play Rice in the Cotton Bowl in Dallas on January 2, 1950. Justice was against accepting the bid, of the opinion that the Tar Heel season of seven wins and three defeats had not been good enough to put the team in a major bowl game.

"We didn't deserve the bowl trip," Justice said almost a half-century later. "The Cotton Bowl invited us so my playing could be measured against Doak Walker, who had a great season for SMU. Texans had seen Doak play all season but hadn't seen me, so this gave them the opportunity."

Photo: Hugh Morton

All-American running backs, Charlie Justice and Doak Walker ride in the Cotton Bowl parade with their wives, Sarah Justice and Norma Walker.

Justice signs autographs in Greensboro, North Carolina, after the Cotton Bowl game.

HONORS

onors stacked up for Justice in November. He received more votes from coaches and writers than any other player for the All-Southern Conference Team, beating out Art Weiner by a few votes, and thus was named captain of the team. Center Irv Holdash also made the All-Conference team.

A day after the All-Conference team was announced, Justice was given the Southern Conference Player of the Year award, voted by the writers, and again Weiner was runnerup.

In nine games in 1949 – remember that he missed the Notre Dame game – Justice completed 50 of 99 passes for 731 yards and ran for 377 in 123 carries, so his ground game was well under his standards of years past. He kicked 1,777 yards on 63 punts for a 44-yard average.

Weiner had a tremendous year. His catch total of 52 passes for 762 yards was just one pass short of the national record. In his four-year career, Weiner caught 108 passes for 2,402 yards and scored 16 touchdowns.

Justice's career figures were phenomenal: 536 rushes for 2,634 yards and a 4.91-yard average. He threw 321 passes, completing 159 for 2,307 yards, putting his total yardage record at 5,176.

According to NCAA statistics, he punted the ball 5.9 miles in four years – 10,376 yards – on 245 kicks for an average of 42.6 yards. He scored 39 touchdowns on the ground – rushing and returning kicks – and passed for 25 more, an accountability per season of 16 touchdowns running and passing.

And when the All-American selections came out, Justice was voted

Photo: Hugh Morton

Grimy-faced Justice during a tight game.

first team on 12 different teams. Weiner made first team on five and second team on six others. Kenny Powell, whose play at end improved every year, was mentioned on one.

JUSTICE
First Team
AP, UP, Football Coaches, INS, All-America Board, Williamson, All-Players Team, The Sporting News, Paramount, Police Gazette, Football Digest, College Football Illustrated.
Second Team
Central Press.
Third Team
Football Writers of America.

WEINER
First Team
UP, The Sporting News, New York News, Sports Review, St. Louis Globe Democrat, Deke Houlgate.
Second Team
Football Writers of America, All-Players, Central Press, INS, Football Digest, Police Gazette.

POWELL
Second Team
NEA.

Notice that Justice was again named to the All-Players team, which was chosen for the Chicago Tribune by college players themselves. Norman L. Sper, a widely-known football analyst, supervised the All-Players selections, and in Chapel Hill to visit his son, Norman, Jr., Carolina's head cheerleader, Sper said that of the 127 players who played against Justice and voted, the Choo Choo received 110 votes as the best backfield man they had played against all year.

DISAPPOINTMENT IN DALLAS

L ed by quarterback, Adrian Burke, Rice defeated Carolina in the Cotton Bowl, 27-13, and Justice had what he termed a bad day.

Rice used ground power to build a 21-0 lead, then Carolina finally got it cranked up and threatened to sweep the Texans off the field at the finish. Choo Choo pulled his teammates together for the rally. On the running of battering Billy Hayes and the running and passing of Justice, Carolina scored two touchdowns in nine minutes. Until then the Tar Heels had not advanced farther than the Rice 37.

Justice, Hayes, and Paul Rizzo smashed the Rice line to bits with Rizzo scoring both touchdowns, on a six-yard pass from Justice and an eight-yard lateral from the Choo Choo. Hayes was the game's leading ground gainer with 107.

Burke led the Rice team, and in the air he was in a class by himself, connecting on nine of 20 for 140 yards and two touchdowns.

Justice had no excuse for what he considered a poor showing. "My ankle didn't hurt," he said. "I was in perfect shape. I have no excuses for my game. I just didn't do well."

Snavely felt similar sentiments for the Tar Heel team. "We just didn't have a bowl team this year," he said.

Thus, heralding the Blue and White's resurgence to gridiron glory, was born the "Justice Era." During those four years huge throngs were drawn to Kenan Stadium by the magnetic excitement of the Carolina Choo Choo and his famed number 22. The Tar Heels became a national powerhouse with a four-year record of 32-6-2, fifth best in the nation behind only Notre Dame 30-0-2, Army 31-2-4, Michigan 30-4-2, and Oklahoma 32-6-1.

While the Tar Heels were in Dallas for the Cotton Bowl, Charlie and Sarah spent much of their spare time with Doak Walker and his wife. Doak, the All-American from SMU, did not go to a bowl game that year and had the time to take in the Cotton Bowl festivities.

After the Cotton Bowl, Justice and Walker went to Jacksonville together for the first Senior Bowl. Others to represent the Southern Conference in the Senior Bowl were Art Weiner and Kenny Powell of North Carolina, and Red O'Quinn of Wake Forest.

The squads were divided into North and South units and a payoff was mapped out in which the winning team would receive 60 percent of the payoff and the losing team 40 percent, all monies to be divided among the players.

Justice and Walker, however, were offered a better deal, $1,500 each to captain the two teams, Walker the North and Justice the South.

Ten thousand North Carolinians went to Jacksonville for the game, and without them, Justice said, "they wouldn't have had anybody in the stands."

Bowl officials asked Justice and Walker after the game to take less money, but Walker said, "No. We agreed on $1,500 and I want it."

Justice said, "Well, since the crowd was all North Carolinians, and since Doak wants all of his money, I want all of mine, too."

So the payoff was made.

Justice's South team won the game, 21-14. Travis Tidwell of Auburn was declared the most valuable player, and Weiner was the most valuable lineman.

Justice played more on defense than on offense. The South's offense was clicking well, but the defense was porous against passes, so Justice went in to try to shore up the defense, and it worked well enough to win the game.

"I didn't score," Justice said, "but I intercepted a couple of passes."

The game didn't take hold in Jacksonville and was soon moved to Montgomery, Alabama, where it continues to be popular today.

Thus, Charlie Justice finished his collegiate career at North Carolina and his eleventh season of football. He was beaten almost to a pulp from the injuries he received in 1949 and the battering he took playing the single-wing. He didn't care if he never saw another football.

But when all was said and done, Justice had had a brilliant collegiate career and the pleasure of leading the Tar Heel team that put the University of North Carolina into big-time college athletics. Basketball was a few years behind. Frank McGuire moved it into the upper echelon when he built the Tar Heels into an undefeated national champion in 1957.

ACHIEVERS

A fter graduation exercises in 1950, the Tar Heels who had played together so magnificently for four years scattered to be on with their life's work. Jim Camp, Bob Cox, Ted Hazelwood, and Walt Pupa remained at Chapel Hill on Snavely's coaching staff. Weiner went to pro football as an end with the New York Bulldogs but his promising career was cut short by a severe knee injury. The others went their ways, and as the years passed many remained in contact with each other, and all seemed to do well in private life.

In 1993, a story appeared in the business sections of most North Carolina newspapers, announcing that a former dean of the business school of the University of North Carolina at Chapel Hill, Paul Rizzo, had been recalled as an adviser to IBM chairman John Akers in an attempt to shore up IBM's slump as one of the world's leading computer manufacturers.

Paul Rizzo had come off a New Jersey farm to enroll at UNC in 1946 and study business. To finance his education, like so many others, he became a member of the Tar Heel football team under Coach Snavely and served admirably as blocking back for Charlie Choo Choo during those magnificent years of Tar Heel dominance on the gridiron.

"Well, well," some said, "a football player who made good in another field! He must not have gotten all his brains knocked out." Actually, he didn't, and he played in the days before face masks. However, he was smart enough – and tough enough – to provide his own physical protection for his face.

He was a plucky guy who played with a trick shoulder. He wore a strap which prevented him from raising his arm above his head to keep the shoulder from flying out of joint. He never let it interfere with his football, though.

Another story revealed that a former Duke player, Ken Younger, whose college career paralleled that of Rizzo and Justice, had been called out of retirement to help bail a major freight company out of trouble. Younger had played high school football for Coach Price Leeper at Asheville High in 1936.

"It's about time," Charlie Justice said, "to give athletics credit for making men out of boys."

In those days, football players went to college to prepare themselves to face the world – not to face an opposing lineup of professional footballers. No one majored in football in those days. Playing in the pros was the last thing in the minds of most of the collegiate players of the late 1940s. They used college football as a means to pay for their education, and in return they learned skills with which they could make a decent living after graduation. This was a kind of bartering system.

Pro football was not a popular pastime with many college football graduates because the pay was so poor. Many a hard-nosed lineman played pro football in the late 1940s and early 1950s for a salary of $300 to $500 a game, which amounted to about $3,600 to $6,000 a year. Justice was offered one of those $500 contracts but wound up waiting a while and signing with the Redskins for $1,500 a game – $18,000 a year.

"Paul Rizzo was very smart," Justice said. "He finished with high grades in business school and after a successful career with IBM he headed the university's school of business for five years. This was what athletic scholarships were all about in those days."

The Carolina teams of the Justice Era were loaded with people like that. They were not just big, beefy athletes; they were also scholars who cracked books with regularity and drained them of all the knowledge they could.

"Besides Paul Rizzo," Justice said, "we had Joe Neikirk, who became vice chairman of Norfolk Southern Railway; Art Weiner, vice president of Burlington Industries; Hosea Rodgers, vice president of Container Corporation of America; Bob Cox, national Jaycee president in 1958 and a vice president of Pepsi-Cola; Ted Hazelwood, vice president of Remington Arms Company; John Tandy, vice president of Hanes Hosiery and mayor of Winston-Salem; Sid Varney, now a dean at the University of South Carolina; Ed Washington, a judge in Greensboro; Joe Wright, owner of his own oil company in Hendersonville.

"I could go on," Charlie said. "Our football team produced six doctors and dentists, eight lawyers, and several high school coaches and

Justice, left, and Weiner, right, show Coach Snavely a scrapbook at a team reunion in Chapel Hill in Snavely's later years.

teachers – all successful people. Probably the least successful among them was old Charlie who got all the credit and the biggest press."

Actually, that isn't really so. Charlie was also a successful businessman as a partner with his son-in-law, Billy Crews, in Justice-Crews Insurance Agency in Cherryville, North Carolina. He also had a fine pro football career and was television's first football color man, doing Redskins telecasts and paving the way for the John Maddens, Pat Summeralls, Lynn Swanns, Terry Bradshaws, et cetera, who were to follow him.

"This is the reason I like to talk about this group," Charlie said. "I've always said the way to success is surrounding yourself with successful people, and that's what happened to me at Chapel Hill. This wasn't just a bunch of athletes; they were first-class people in every way. They put UNC athletics in the mainstream for the first time, playing in three bowl games, and put Chapel Hill on the map."

Much of the success in the UNC athletic program today can be traced to that Justice Era football team.

"I just wanted to make it clear," Charlie said. "These were great people, as all athletes should be."

As an example of how sharp these men were, Charlie points to an incident with John Tandy, who played in 1946 and 1947, graduated in 1948 and applied for a couple of jobs.

Orville Campbell, the Chapel Hill newsman, and Justice went around getting ads for the football program, and the principal of Reynolds High in Winston-Salem asked Justice who he would recommend from the football team at Carolina to be football coach at Reynolds.

Justice recommended Tandy, who took the job. Since football practice began in high schools before colleges, Tandy asked Justice, Bob Cox, and Hosea Rodgers to come to his early practices and help him with the single-wing.

The three worked with Tandy and the Reynolds players a week or ten days, and on the way back to Chapel Hill after their last coaching session, the three shook their heads sadly, and Rodgers put what they were thinking in words.

"Poor old John. We've got him in trouble."

Justice said, "Oh, Lord, it doesn't look like he can do the job."

But Tandy fooled them. He won his conference championship, then added state championships to that. He moved on up to principal at Reynolds and then left education to work at Hanes Hosiery and became vice president there.

"That's the way athletics should be," Justice said. "Today, they have a different perspective. Everyone wants to study pro football or basketball. I didn't take advantage of the free education I received. I should have paid more attention to my studies. Looking back, the only reason I got any education was because of football. Otherwise, I wouldn't have gone to school at all.

"But every man I played with at Chapel Hill became a credit to his community. We all got more out of college than football.

"I think those early post-war years of the late 1940s produced the best college football ever. Players were more mature, and many had played service ball or college football just before the war. I wasn't the only one who felt he had a professional career behind him before he went to college.

"When you went back to school after the war, you didn't have to return to your original school. All slates were wiped clean and players could be recruited by anyone and could play wherever they chose.

"We were accused of being overpaid to play college football, but nothing could be farther from the truth. The money just wasn't there. The deciding factor usually was which campus appealed to you, or which college offered what you wanted to study.

"Most of our players were very serious about education."

Justice wanted to clarify one thing. "It was written that I was the fastest man on the Carolina team," he said, "but that just wasn't true. There were about three on the team who were faster. I could run the hundred in 10.1 or 10.2, which was fast enough, but Billy Britt could run 9.9 or better, and a couple of others could, too."

With a chuckle, he added, going back to his high school days and those taillights on the seat of Clint Castleberry's pants: "Castleberry must've run the hundred in about nine seconds. I don't believe anybody could catch him."

He thought a moment more, and then turned his attention to individual players and their attitude toward the game.

"One thing I know is that players today don't have the affinity with fans that we had," he said. "Some of them seem to think that they're the only ones who can do what they're doing. They have struck out any relationship with the fans who pay their way through the turnstiles to watch them play, and in that way they help these athletes maintain their careers.

"Many athletes today don't realize what good relationships with fans will mean to them on down the road. Here it has been fifty years for me, and I still cherish all those people who came up to speak, or asked for my autograph. I didn't mind that a bit; in fact, I relished it. When today's players get older and nobody pays them any attention, it'll make them think."

Charlie said this in an interview in the Biltmore Dairy Bar in Asheville, and as he had come into the room, a tableful of men – the board of directors of the Asheville branch of the American Red Cross – recognized him and came to their feet collectively to shake his hand and clap him on the back.

Charlie has never failed to sign an autograph when he could. He will sign only one for each person now, however, since autograph-seeking has become a business.

People send him blank cards by the bunches in the mail and ask him to sign them. He signs one card and mails all the cards back with a note that usually reads, "I don't charge for my autograph, and I don't want anybody else charging for it."

It disturbs him when people approach him with pen and pad and ask, "How much do you charge for autographs?"

"That's what has happened to sports today," he said. "I can understand how the top athletes are hounded for multiple autographs and that's possibly the reason they dodge autograph-signings. But I'll sign one for anybody, especially for a kid. To me, it's an honor to be asked for an autograph, and it was an honor in my playing days. I think we were more respectful and appreciative of fans. We knew they were the ones who paid their way into games and made playing possible for us. We didn't have benefit of all the television money that is poured into games today. Unfortunately, too many athletes today are more interested in money than in relations with fans."

It is no wonder people hound Justice for multiple autographs. Charlie's signature sells for $35, according to one price guide, and make it $100 if it's a signed photo. Pictures of Charlie in a Redskins uniform are rarer and with his autograph will bring more than a hundred dollars!

"My brother Jack," Charlie said, "once told me: 'If I ever hear of you refusing to sign a kid's autograph, I'll stomp hell out of you!' He never had to. Signing autographs is the least I could do for those people who followed my career."

Charlie has few regrets from his career, but he can always single out one in particular. "One of my regrets," he said, "is that they didn't let blacks play when I was in college. There were many great black athletes then, and we missed something by keeping them suppressed. In Asheville, Stephens-Lee High School, our black school, had great teams under Coach C. L. Moore. They won state championships in all sports, and Coach Moore had to coach them all and be athletic director at the same time.

"Blacks and whites played together on the streets and sandlots of Asheville long before integration came along, and we never had any problems. Let me tell you, there were some black athletes in Asheville who could whip your tail on a football field."

At an oldtimers' meeting in 1995, members of the UNC-Justice Era teams included, left to right: front row—Ralph Strayhorn, Charlie Justice, Dick Bunting, Eddie Knox; second row—Fred Brauer, John Culbreth, Joe Neikerk, Max Cook; third row—Jim Camp, Bob Cox, Ed Washington, and Art Weiner.

A GAME TO REMEMBER

A lthough tired of playing football, Charlie did not divorce himself from the game. In July, 1950, he was scheduled to go to Europe with coaches Jim Tatum of Maryland, Wally Butts of Georgia, and Frank Leahy of Notre Dame to hold football coaching clinics for the Armed Forces in Germany, but the trip was cancelled due to the outbreak of the Korean War.

Then he signed to play one more game. He could not resist the opportunity to play with the College All-Stars against the two-time National Football League champion Philadelphia Eagles in Chicago's Soldier Field on the 11th of August. This was the big charity football spectacular that usually filled the huge stadium and poured tens of thousands of dollars into charity.

Charlie's mind held a troubling thought that over the years he had played in two bowl games – the Orange Bowl and Milk Bowl – with Asheville High School, and in the Sugar Bowl twice and Cotton Bowl once in college, and the Senior Bowl, and had not scored a touchdown in any of them. He knew the College All-Star Game would be his last chance, and his decision to play and his performance against the Eagles eventually set the seal on his fame.

He couldn't resist adding his talents to such a galaxy of college stars that included his friend, Doak Walker of Southern Methodist. Also on the All-Star roster were Lynn Chandnois of Michigan State; Fred Morrison, Ohio State's star of the 1950 Rose Bowl; Dick Kempthorn of Michigan; Larry Coutre of Notre Dame; George Thomas of Oklahoma; Hall Haynes of Santa Clara; and Travis Tidwell of Auburn.

The Eagles, led by the great Steve Van Buren, former LSU star, were rated as one of the best professional teams of modern times and were immediately made a 14 1/2-point favorite. This was virtually the same Eagle squad that had slaughtered the All-Stars 38-0 a year before.

The Philadelphia line was rugged and fast and intended to spend the 1950 professional season shoving opposing lines around like they had before, protecting the passing artist Tommy Thompson (Tulsa) who had few peers in pro football and whose best target was Pete Pihos, one-time Indiana end.

The All-Stars, also big and fast, bristling with college might, and some, like Justice, with service experience, were a 50-man squad, reduced from the unwieldy number of 70 the previous season. Coached by Dr. Eddie Anderson of Holy Cross, they chose to forego the social diversions of training camp at suburban Northwestern University, and went instead to the isolated town of Delafield, Wisconsin.

During practice they were all business, knowing the size of the task cut out for them but feeling up to the job.

There might have been another reason for training in a remote place: to keep practice sessions hidden while the All-Stars installed the belly series from T-formation, and this would be the first time it had been seen east of the Mississippi River. They had quarterback Eddie LeBaron to introduce the series, which he had run to perfection that season at College of Pacific.

Justice, of course, was no stranger to the T. He had played it at Bainbridge. The formation wasn't Charlie's concern; his weight was. He was more than 10 pounds overweight at nearly 180. But in practice he showed the same magic he generated during his college career.

Charlie had been chosen for the team only to return kickoffs, and thus, when Anderson announced his starting offensive lineup, Justice was not included. Anderson listed Weiner of North Carolina and Jim Martin of Notre Dame at ends; Don Campora, College of Pacific, and Leon Manley, Oklahoma, at tackles; Porter Payne, Georgia, and George Hughes, William & Mary, at guards; and Clayton Tonnemaker, Minnesota, at center. The backfield included quarterback Travis Tidwell of Auburn, halfbacks Doak Walker, Southern Methodist, and Hall Haynes, Santa Clara, and fullback Fred Morrison, Ohio State.

Justice knew he felt right when the game began. He figured he would play well, but there was no way he could have guessed how well. He was magnificent, leading the All-Stars to a stunning 17-7 victory before 88,885 fans.

Before the game, something had changed Anderson's mind about using Justice only on kickoff returns, and when Choo Choo returned the first kick-

Choo Choo laces up for a big run.

off, Anderson instructed LeBaron and Justice to stay in the game. He wanted them to test the Philadelphia defense.

The coach's decision proved to be wise. LeBaron engineered a brilliant first-quarter march of 54 yards in seven plays, with Justice running for 31 yards and then again for 12 to the five-yard line. Villanova's Ralph Pasquariello barreled over from the one for the touchdown. Minnesota end Gordy Soltau kicked the extra point and the All-Stars were ahead 7-0.

The shock had begun to wear off the crowd in the second quarter, and it began to realize the All-Stars might indeed pull off an upset. The All-Stars went up 14-0 in that period on a brilliant coup by Justice and LeBaron on a broken play. From the All-Stars' 40-yard line, LeBaron dropped back to pass and finding all receivers covered appeared to be set up for a 20-yard loss, but Justice, who had gone out in the pass pattern, quickly came back upfield 15 yards to the Eagles' 45 and LeBaron hit him with a quick strike. Charlie wheeled and exploded down the sideline for the second touchdown on a 60-yard play.

His drought was over! He had finally scored a touchdown in a post-season bowl game — and it was to be the game's deciding points. Soltau kicked the point and the All-Stars led by 14-0.

Soltau buttoned up the victory with a 24-yard field goal in the fourth quarter just after Philadelphia's Steve Van Buren, who had a miserable night, scored the Eagles' only touchdown on a one-yard smash. Cliff Patton kicked the point, and the Eagles were finished.

It was runs by Justice that set up the first touchdown and Soltau's field goal and Charlie broke an All-Star record by gaining 133 yards in nine carries. He streaked downfield on runs of 47, 31, 28, and 12 yards. He also caught five passes from LeBaron, opening up new horizons as a receiver when he finally turned pro later that year. At Chapel Hill he had been the passer, seldom a receiver, and this game proved he could catch the ball. He often caught passes in the pros.

The superiority of the All-Stars' ground attack showed in the game statistics. The Stars gained 221 yards rushing and held the heralded Eagle runners to a mere 25.

Tommy Thompson's passing in a 15-for-28 night netted 131 for the Eagles who never seriously threatened the alert collegians' defense.

The Associated Press reported that the 57-yard touchdown drive by the Eagles in the final period resulted more from the All-Stars relaxing than Philadelphia's power. Van Buren, the NFL's ground-gaining champion for the last two seasons, was held to 32 yards in 13 tries. This was primarily the result of bruising defensive work by Minnesota's Clayton Tonnemaker and Leo Nomellini, College of the Pacific's Don Campora, Nebraska's Tom Novak, and Notre Dame's Leon Hart.

When the game's highest individual prize was announced, the most valuable player award, Justice was an overwhelming choice over second-place LeBaron.

Wilfred Smith of the *Chicago Tribune* wrote of Justice the day after Justice's selection:

> Charles Justice, North Carolina half back, yesterday was named the most valuable All-Star player in the collegians spectacular 17 to 7 triumph over the Philadelphia Eagles. Justice was chosen in a poll of newspaper men who covered the game in Soldier field on Friday night and as a result he will receive the coveted Chicago Tribune silver trophy at the 1951 game.
>
> In winning the approbation of the reporters, Justice outpointed Eddie LeBaron, College of Pacific quarter back, whose brilliant generalship and forward passing also were major contributions to the All-Stars' sixth victory in the series with the champions of the National Football League. Never since this award was established in 1938 has the voting been so concentrated.
>
> It may be unfortunate, as one writer indicated when he cast a ballot for both Justice and LeBaron, that the honor cannot be divided. The choice centered on whether Justice's running or LeBaron's passing was more important. The combination of these talents subdued the Eagles as the All-Stars' rugged defense encompassed the professionals' attack.
>
> There was little doubt in the vote, however, Justice had a 2 to 1 majority over the 20 year old California star who now reports to the United States marines for training. Six other All-Stars, all linemen, received a total of seven votes in the tabulation.
>
> Justice's running Friday night was exceptional. No half back has done better against the pro champions. In nine attempts he gained 133 yards. He also caught a touchdown pass from LeBaron. ...

What a way for Justice to end a fantastic college football career!

As a marine, LeBaron distinguished himself in Korea, and on his way home, in Hawaii, he was asked to play service football there, for the entertainment of returning, war-weary veterans, the same as Justice had done seven years earlier. "No thanks," LeBaron answered, "if I play football, I'm going to be paid for it."

He then rewrote much of the Redskins' record book.

Band leader and movie actor Kay Kyser, a resident of Chapel Hill, explains football to the Choo Choo.

But wait! There was more to come!

Charlie's nationwide fame reached such proportions after the All-Star Game that many felt he could name his own price in the pros. George Preston Marshall, owner of the Washington Redskins, apparently felt so, too.

In an unprecedented move, Marshall offered Justice a blank five-year contract and told him to write in his salary figure – and this is where Charlie made a major mistake, although he felt he was doing the right thing at the time.

He refused Marshall's offer, but by a stroke of fate he was playing with the Redskins by late October for a figure far less than he could have written. Charlie's statements of having no real desire to play pro football were made in all sincerity. He wanted to spend his time at home with his family, living a normal life, working like any other 9-to-5 man, and he refused to sign.

Thus, Charlie, who often made light of his tremendous potential in order to boost his teammates, turned down the most fantastic offer ever made to a young man by a NFL team.

A JOB HE COULDN'T DO

In the summer of 1950, before the All-Star Game, Charlie had taken a job with the Medical Foundation in Chapel Hill to work as a fund-raiser for the university's new hospital and four-year medical school. Deep down, he wanted to be a coach and had majored in physical education with that in mind, but no one offered him a coaching job and the pay was going to be good with the Medical Foundation, so he accepted that.

He took time away from his job to play in the College All-Star game but even after returning home in the full bloom of gridiron glory he was still adamant about quitting the game.

Charlie worked directly under Billy Carmichael, comptroller of the university and chief fund-raiser for the medical projects.

"Mr. Carmichael was one of the smartest men I ever knew," Charlie said. "He gave up a seat on Wall Street to come to work for the university. He loved Chapel Hill. His father was chairman of the board of Liggett & Myers Tobacco Company, so he didn't need money. But he sure knew how to raise it.

"He was one of my greatest boosters. I was like a son to him. He went everywhere we played in 1949, to New York and Dallas, and everywhere else. When he came up to Virginia, he and his wife brought Sarah with them and they waited after the game so I could ride back with them.

"I feel I let him down, but I hadn't been working for the Foundation long when I knew I was out of my league. The hardest thing for me was to ask someone for money. I found it hard to ask people for anything, really, but for money in particular. So I should have turned him down when he made the offer of a job to me, but I was so beat up from the football season that I didn't care if I ever saw another football. My condition was that bad. An illness that lasted the season, keeping me tired all the time, and two fractured bones were punishment enough. With all the pounding I took, that made me want to forget football."

Charlie and Sarah were the first to take an apartment in a new Chapel Hill complex called Glenn Lennox. It was there that their son Ronnie went skinny dipping with the two young daughters of a Duke couple who lived next door. Returning, Ronnie, with a puzzled look on his face, said, "You know, Daddy, those Duke people are different."

On Charlie's first day with the Foundation, Carmichael took him calling on clients to show him the ropes.

"As long as he was with me," Charlie said, "I did all right, but when he was not with me, I couldn't do the job. He was the greatest fund-raiser I ever saw. I don't know how he could get so much money out of people, and, of course, they thought I would be able to do the same because of my name and reputation."

They called first on Mr. Coble of Coble Dairies. When they walked in, Coble saw who it was and threw up his hands. "Oh, Lord," he said, grabbing both hip pockets, "I know it's going to cost me. What do you want now?"

Carmichael greeted Coble and then started his spiel. "Well, Mr. Coble, this is Charlie's first day and his first call and blah! blah! blah! We're going to let you off light, make it easy on you. We're going to give you the privilege of being the first to contribute to the Medical Foundation."

"How much?"

"All we want is $25,000. ..." Carmichael said, and Coble whipped out his checkbook and began to write the check before Carmichael changed his mind and upped the ante.

"That was in 1950," Charlie said, "and $25,000 was a lot of money. We raised $120,000 that first day and I thought, 'Boy, there's nothing to this!' And then I found out. When Mr. Carmichael left me alone, I couldn't do it. It was like pulling my own teeth for me to ask people for money."

So Charlie went to Carmichael and confessed his shortcomings. Carmichael saw how serious he was.

Charlie told him, "Mr. Carmichael, I should have told you that I couldn't do this job, but maybe I had to find out for myself. I was so beaten up from playing football that I would have grabbed at anything to keep away from the football field this fall. I really didn't want to play football, but I have found out that trying to ask people for money is worse, so I'm going to leave you and let you find a man who can do the job."

"What are you going to do, Charlie?" Carmichael asked.

"I'm going to play pro."

"Well, Charlie," Carmichael said, rubbing his chin, "if you're going to leave, I think the best thing to say to the Foundation is simply that you've decided to go pro and play with the Redskins."

Choo Choo heeded Carmichael's advice and left the Foundation with no ill feelings.

He signed with the Redskins on Saturday before the fifth game of the 1950 NFL season.

Charlie, who took up golf after football, tees off at the Country Club of Asheville.

A publicity photo of Justice when he joined the Washington Redskins.

ON THE FIELD AGAIN

J ustice's joining the Redskins culminated machinations by NFL teams to sign him that were as entangled as any ever faced by Nero Wolfe.

The Chapel Hill All-American had been drafted originally by the Eagles, who had signed him to that aborted contract in Hawaii when he was in the navy, but when the Eagles realized he was not interested in a professional career they traded the rights to sign him to the Pittsburgh Steelers for their No. 1 draft choice in 1950. The Steelers wanted Justice desperately to run at tailback in their single-wing offense. But Charlie's continued non-interest in pro football caused the Steelers to toss him back in the NFL hopper to be redrafted.

The night before the draft in January of 1950, the Browns phoned Charlie, hoping he had changed his mind, but he had not. The New York Giants, coached by Steve Owen, who had coached Justice's Rebel Senior Bowl team, also wanted him badly, as did the Steelers and Chicago Bears, but he told all of them, "You're gonna waste one if you draft me because I'm not going to play."

Finally in the 16th round of the 1950 draft, after all the players were gone in whom the Redskins had special interest, Marshall took a chance and drafted Justice.

Marshall figured if Charlie didn't play he wouldn't be out anything because he had no one else to draft, but if for any remote reason, Charlie changed his mind and decided to play, then the Redskins would have the right to sign him.

"That's how I eventually came to be with the Redskins," Charlie said, "the most valuable player in the College All-Star Game, runner up for the Heisman Trophy, but the 200th draftee among 390 players in the original draft pool."

Charlie signed a three-year contract with the Redskins and announced it in the Kenan Stadium press box at halftime of the Tar Heel-Wake Forest game on October 14, 1950. The press greeted the announcement with applause, happy that Charlie Justice would soon be back in uniform.

Charlie joined the Redskins on Monday following their fifth game in 1950. He skipped the 1951 season to be Snavely's backfield coach at North Carolina, and after a season he left that job because coaching was not nearly as much fun as playing, and he did not like the way Snavely was being treated. It appeared that the university wanted Snavely out, and, indeed, he was fired after the 1952 season. Charlie was dismayed at this treatment of a man who had done so much for the university.

Snavely's firing prompted Charlie to abandon any idea of becoming a football coach. "After what they did to him," Choo Choo said, "I didn't want any part of coaching anywhere."

Unofficial reports and reliable sources had Charlie's salary with the Redskins at astronomical figures for the time, but he said he got a thousand dollars for signing the contract and $1,500 a game, which gave him an income of $18,000 for a 12-game season. That was more than the $1,000 a game some "insiders" reported that Charlie was making. Either way, it was not a small salary for 1950, and especially not bad considering that the season only covered three months, leaving nine free months a year to work elsewhere for additional income.

As he signed the Redskins' contract, Justice thought back to the blank check George Preston Marshall had laid before him after the College All-Star Game, and said to Marshall, "This isn't the check you gave me the first time."

Marshall chuckled. "No," he said, "this is the real one."

Justice's presence had an instant impact on the Redskins' fortunes. The team's faltering gate was suddenly bolstered, as Marshall figured it would be, and sometimes Griffith Stadium, where they played, rocked to the cheers of sellout crowds.

"The pros," Justice confided later, "were altogether different from colleges. They think faster and don't fake as easily. I found that out in my first game."

Indeed, the Redskins played the Chicago Cardinals in Washington in their first game after Choo Choo's arrival. The Cardinals ran up a 26-0 lead in the first half against the inept Redskins.

Washington staged a second-half rally and the final score was 37-27 for the Cardinals.

Justice went into the air to catch a pass from Redskins quarterback Slingin' Sammy Baugh and came down on the four-yard line. A solitary safety stood between him and the goal line. Justice wiggled his hips this way and that way, and the defender simply smiled and put his fists on his hips in a gesture of impatience. Charlie faked him once more and started around him, and the safety smeared him all over the four-yard line.

"They knew that the first three fakes were false," Charlie said, "and if you didn't make good on the fourth, you'd had it."

There were other things about the pro game that Charlie learned that day. In the huddle, Baugh would make up pass patterns. He would tell his ends and halfbacks where he wanted them to go.

Once he said to Justice, "Hook around the goal posts and I'll hit you."

Charlie hooked around and looked up to see if Sammy had thrown the ball and almost got it in the mouth. "When I looked up, the ball was right there in my face," Charlie said. "I had to catch it or it would have knocked out every tooth in my head. The ball was thrown so hard it knocked me down, but I hung on."

Charlie enjoyed pro football. He had no more trouble running in the pros than he had had in college.

One thing he didn't like was the money involved. "I had always played for the love of the game," Charlie said, "but when I started getting paid for playing it seemed too much like a business."

At halftime in that first game Justice played, with the score 26-0 against the Redskins, Justice said the dressing room door flew open and Marshall steamed in.

"He was an earlier personification of George Steinbrenner," Justice said.

For a few moments Marshall paced back and forth and the room was utterly quiet. Then he exploded: "You're the sorriest bunch of sons-a-bitches I ever saw on a football field!"

Marshall fired five players on the spot, Justice recalls. "Go on," Marshall told them, indicating the door. "I don't need you!"

"One of the guys he fired grabbed him by the collar," Choo Choo said, "and was gonna hit him, but some of the other players persuaded him not to."

Marshall's outburst worked wonders. The Redskins outscored the Cardinals 27-11 in the second half.

"Marshall was like that," Charlie said. "If he liked you you didn't have to worry, but if he didn't like you you'd better get out of town."

Baugh, the quarterback from Texas Christian, showed Justice what real cowboys were after the game.

"He took a shower," Charlie laughed, "and came out and put on his ten-gallon hat and high-heeled boots before he dressed the rest of himself."

Thousands of North Carolinians filled the highways every Sunday the Redskins played at home, driving to Washington to see the games. Special railroad trains ran out of Charlotte, up through Fayetteville and Rocky Mount, to Washington, carrying loaded cars of Carolinians who went to watch Justice.

When 10,000 Tar Heels showed up for Charlie's first game, Choo Choo joked with Marshall: "Aren't you gonna up my salary?"

"Oh, hell, no," Marshall shot back, seriously. "You've already signed your contract."

Marshall didn't really care whether the Redskins won or lost, Charlie thought, as long as he looked out in the stands and saw big crowds in Griffith Stadium. "The Redskins didn't draft particularly to fill certain vacancies on the team," Charlie said. "They drafted to draw people. Marshall always had two or three guys from the area that people would come to see. He had Dudley from Virginia, Scarbath from Maryland, and me from North Carolina. He figured that was enough, and he filled the stadium with us.

Linemen didn't matter. "People pay to see the runners and pass-catchers," Marshall would say. "They don't pay to see guards and tackles."

"Several linemen made only $300 a game," Justice said. "Most couldn't run the hundred in an hour and a half, and they'd have had trouble blocking their grandmothers. Those of us who ran the ball took our lives in our hands every Sunday afternoon.

"Everything was geared to money," Charlie added, "and everybody had to root for his own salary. Everybody didn't have an agent then. But when we got on the field, the players would say, 'Let's play as a team. Doesn't make any difference what you're making. If we don't play together we're not going to win.'"

Charlie missed a golden opportunity with the Redskins. There was only one sports business manager or agent, a man named Fred Cochran whose clients included Ted Williams, Stan Musial, and Babe Zaharias. "He wanted to be my manager for ten percent," Charlie said, "but I threw his offer in the trash can. I figured I didn't need an agent, but things might have turned out differently for me later if I had taken his offer."

Most made an effort to play together and to win, but certain individuals exerted their best effort only when they were involved in crowd-pleasing plays like running or receiving.

"Bones Taylor was a good receiver," Charlie said, "but he wasn't gonna block anybody."

Once Charlie cut across the field and had a good run going. He saw

Bones out to the left and thought he'd block for him, so Charlie cut that way and when he approached Bones he was smeared by three tacklers. Bones, Charlie noticed, had tried to get out of their way."

Back in the huddle, Baugh asked, "Charlie, what the hell did you cut back for?"

"Well, I saw Bones out there," Charlie said.

"Bones!" Baugh laughed. "Bones ain't gonna block anybody. You want to run away from him."

Despite the rigors of the Washington-style game, Justice came to like the pro game and many of the individual players. He thought a lot of players were simple thugs, and he often said he wouldn't associate with some of them in private life.

He was overweight and out of condition when he reported to Washington and Coach Curly Lambeau used him sparingly at first. But as the season progressed, Lambeau used him more and more, and Charlie's contribution to the team began to grow.

He made long runs of 71 and 59 yards, and several in the thirties, and gradually worked his way into the regular halfback slot. At season's end, despite the fact he had played only seven games, he had gained 286 yards rushing in 59 carries for a 4.8 average and was the Redskins' second leading rusher. He also had caught 19 passes for 180 yards.

However, he could not overcome his distaste for the innerworkings of pro football, and at the end of that 1950 rookie season, he resigned from the team and returned to Chapel Hill to coach the backfield for the Tar Heels. When he saw that Snavely was slowly but surely being moved out, Charlie returned to Washington and Marshall gladly gave him his old contract back.

He needed the gate revenue Justice generated.

Several other teams tried to trade for Justice, and some tried to buy him outright, but Marshall refused all offers. He told Justice, "You'll never play for anybody but me – and you can play as long as you like."

By this time the Redskins had broken into the Southern television market. They were about the only team telecasting to the Southeast, and Justice was the star. He was magic on the tube.

The 1952 season, everyone felt, would be a big one for Justice after a year's layoff. Working hard in training camp, he began to feel once more the full freedom of running on a football field.

The exhibition season opened and the Redskins appeared to have a solid team. On August 21 they went into Los Angeles to play the Rams in their annual charity game and 87,582 fans came to the mammouth Coliseum to see the game, and Justice came away with a broken arm.

The Rams won, 45-23.

There is something wrong with this picture. Shouldn't Justice be passing to Weiner?

A few years later, describing Justice's career in *The Asheville Citizen*, Dick Kaplan wrote of that game:

"Charlie ran wild. He gave perhaps the greatest display of running ever seen in the West in one of the epic performances of grid annals. He carried

11 times for an amazing 199 yards to set a new Coliseum record, keeping the huge crowd in a constant uproar as he reeled off long gallops of 49, 53, and 63 yards."

In that game, Charlie made a brilliant run. He thought it was the best he had ever run in professional football.

With the ball on the Redskins' 35, he went around end on a sweep and, dodging tacklers, raced across the field, sideline to sideline, three times before he found a channel cleared to the goal line by his blockers.

"Herb Rich, the Rams great cornerback who had played on my team in the first Senior Bowl, was the last man between me and the goal," Charlie said, "and I faked him and scored."

Rich, however, accidently got even later in the game. Charlie broke his arm trying to stiff-arm Rich.

"I shouldn't have straight-armed him," Charlie said, "and I wouldn't have except that one of our coaches kept telling me, 'Push him off! Push him off! Stiff-arm him!' so I finally tried to push him off and broke my arm." He had to be carried off the field on a stretcher and spent the first six weeks of the season with his arm in a cast.

At the end of the game, George Preston Marshall rushed into the dressing room, glaring all the way, and went straight to Justice, who sat holding his aching arm.

"I've told you a thousand times," Marshall railed, "if you see you're cornered, if you see you're gonna be hit, get out of bounds. Don't take the punishment. You're worth too much money to me."

Except for the pain in his arm, Charlie might have laughed. "He wasn't worried about me," Choo Choo said afterward. "He was worried about his money."

"Why didn't you get out of bounds?" Marshall screamed.

In deep pain and not thinking straight, Charlie answered without realizing he was getting someone in trouble, "Mr. Marshall, the backfield coach told me to stiff-arm him and push him off."

Marshall reacted quickly. "Who the hell pays your salary?"

"You do, Mr. Marshall."

"Well, by God, you listen to me."

Charlie held his broken wrist, hurting like crazy, while Marshall chewed him out like a wild-eyed expert.

Still, Charlie got off easy.

Marshall fired the backfield coach.

Charlie's arm was broken in the third quarter, and it is reasonable to assume that he would have exceeded the professional rushing record of 218 yards but for the tragedy.

"If I hadn't broken my arm," Charlie said, "I believe I would have gained 250 yards, maybe 300. It was fantastic the way everything I did that night seemed to be right. Everywhere I went with the ball, the way was opened for me."

As Marshall stewed, Charlie missed the first several games of the regular season, but Marshall didn't let him rest. To keep from paying Charlie's salary for nothing, Marshall put him in the broadcasting booth with his play-by-play man, Jim Gibbons, and told him to help Gibbons describe the games.

Charlie returned to the lineup in time for some late-season dramatics.

His magnificent running knocked both the Eagles and the Giants out of contention for the NFL's American Conference title. Justice's 26-yard run off tackle to within inches of the goal line, from where LeBaron crashed through for the winning touchdown in the last minute of the season-ending game, gave the Redskins a 27-21 victory over the Eagles and knocked them out of the running.

Determined to continue at his 1952 pace during the 1953 season,

Charlie opened the season with the prospect of having his best year ever and of playing a full season. He had played only parts of his first two seasons.

He did not disappoint anyone, gaining 616 yards in 115 carries for a 4.5 average to lead the Eastern Conference in rushing. Against the Cardinals in two games he gained 114 and 127 yards; he got 114 against the Giants and 115 against Baltimore. He was the No. 4 rusher in the entire NFL. Also, he caught 22 passes for 434 yards, and set a one-game Redskin record of 120 yards in 15 carries.

His year was indeed tremendous as he led Washington to third place in its division.

As good as his season was, he took a fearful beating, reminiscent of the threshing administered him at Chapel Hill in 1949.

"I thought about quitting right then," Charlie said. "I figured nothing was worth the beating I had taken, and I could see nothing down the road but more of the same."

He went to Marshall to ask for a raise in salary and told him he was going to quit if he didn't hire some big linemen to block for him.

"Don't quit, Charlie," Marshall begged. "I'll get some help for you. Instead of a raise, I'll take the money and find some big linemen who can block. Just don't quit."

"I'm going to hold you to your word," Charlie said, foregoing extra money to get some blocking.

He stayed, and when he saw no changes in the Redskins' line in 1954, he was dismayed. He even volunteered for partial duty on the defensive team. He was that good a safety, and he played a lot both ways that fall.

Choo Choo scored a touchdown in each of the Redskins' last three games. He made his touchdowns on a 51-yard run from fake punt formation, and 80 and 46 yards on pass catches, using his faking and good speed on each. He punted all season and had a 40.3-yard average on 61 kicks to finish as the eighth best punter in the NFL.

When he finished the 1954 season second to Billy Wells in team rushing yardage, he was the Redskins' third leading rusher of all time. But the 'Skins hadn't won more than four games in any season since 1948.

Justice sat pooped in the locker room after the final game in 1954 and Marshall came in and sat beside him.

"You're not thinking about quitting, are you?" Marshall asked.

"Yes, sir, Mr. Marshall, I am. I'm not just thinking about quitting," Charlie said. "I am quitting. I'm getting killed every Sunday because you didn't hire the blockers you said you would."

"Oh, no, you don't want to do that," Marshall said. "You know you can play for me as long as you want to. You don't have to worry about getting cut from the squad or anything like that."

"I'm not worried about getting cut," Charlie said. "I'm worried about getting killed."

Justice then reminded Marshall again of his promise to hire better linemen. "You didn't do it, Mr. Marshall," he said. "You lied to me, and I'm through."

"What's that?"

"I said you lied to me," Charlie was straightforward. "I'm not coming back to take this beating any more."

"Well, you come on back," Marshall said. "If you promise not to ask for a raise in salary, I'll get the linemen for you."

Charlie couldn't help but think that Marshall, right to the end, was still more interested in his money than his players' lives.

Choo Choo figured it was time to give it up anyway. He had played football sixteen years, and felt that he had taken as many punches as Joe Louis. The game had lost its glitter. Time to go, he said to himself.

Charlie never held any animosity toward Marshall, who was one of the great characters of the game.

"He helped make professional football what it is today," Charlie said, "him and George Halas of the Bears, Art Rooney of the Steelers, and Wellington Mara of the Giants. The game profited from having all of them."

When he left the Redskins, Charlie went to work for the American Oil Company in a public relations capacity. Amoco considered the hiring of Justice to be a coup of considerable proportion. The oil company knew the esteem in which Charlie was held by everyone in North Carolina. He was assigned to Eastern North Carolina where the Redskins' telecasts, sponsored by Amoco, were shown.

It was Charlie's job to travel around Eastern North Carolina, making speeches and attending events in Amoco's name, and then someone at Amoco, probably remembering the games Charlie helped telecast in 1952, got the idea of putting Charlie back in the broadcast booth with Jim Gibbons, and have him add color to Gibbons' play-by-play. Charlie would comment on plays and players and strategy, and generally give a sideline summation of the game.

Amoco agreed that it would be a good public relations gimmick, and Charlie found himself back in Washington for the 1955 season. He brought a knowledge of the game to the air that Gibbons didn't have, and those who watched the telecasts liked it. From the start, Charlie was a winner.

"I felt a little out of place," he said, "but I was with the team, and I liked that. I'd go up there every Saturday, go over the opposing team's roster and the scouting reports, and do the game on Sunday with Gibbons.

But Charlie needed polishing. Amoco arranged for him to take speech classes at the University of North Carolina after the season in an effort to improve his delivery on the air.

On weekdays, Charlie traveled the South, making talks and appearances for the American Oil Company. It was interesting work, but he soon grew tired of having Sarah meet him at the airport with a suitcase full of fresh clothing, so he could continue on his way, and he missed being with his family. He felt his family needed him at home more than he was able to be.

"The original deal was that I would cover Eastern North Carolina," Charlie said, "but when I went on TV, Amoco expanded my territory and I was traveling the South and occasionally other sections of the country. When things expanded like that and I found myself on the road seven days a week, I thought that this was no way for a married man and father to live."

So he gave it up. He withdrew from the speech classes in Chapel Hill, resigned from Amoco and moved to Hendersonville, near his hometown of Asheville, and went into the oil business.

He left a legacy behind him, however. The telecasts with Gibbons and Justice had been so exciting that other teams and the networks began to employ ex-players and later ex-coaches as color men, and Charlie's work in Washington opened the way for all the color men who make pro football telecasts so interesting today.

Justice accomplished one more thing for the University of North Carolina. He helped lure Jim Tatum away from Maryland and back to Carolina where Tatum wanted to be all the time. He had been a wartime head coach at Carolina in 1942, and his team posted a 5-2-2 season.

Tatum and Bud Wilkinson had been assistant coaches together at Oklahoma immediately after the war. Tatum left to take the Maryland job in 1947 and Wilkinson got the head coaching job at Oklahoma.

Tatum built the Terrapins into a national powerhouse that won a national championship. He was probably the best college recruiter in the nation.

But his heart lay in North Carolina, where he had played for Snavely during the mid-thirties and coached and recruited some before moving to Oklahoma.

By the mid-fifties Carolina was also interested in Tatum, and Justice became a sort of message bearer or go-between. Tatum came to the Redskins' games, and he and Justice would get together afterward and talk. Justice kept Tatum informed on what feelings were in Chapel Hill, and vice versa.

The night Tatum made up his mind to return to Chapel Hill, his wife, Edna, apparently tired of moving so much, told him she didn't want him to go.

He said, "Edna, I'm going. This is what I've worked for. That's where I've dreamed of coaching."

He accepted the job and moved to Chapel Hill to take over the Tar Heels' football fortunes in 1956, and immediately the team began to improve. In three seasons under Tatum the Tar Heels were successively 2-7-1, 6-4, and 6-4. Unfortunately, Tatum died of Rocky Mountain Spotted Fever in the summer of 1959. From that time until 1970, the Tar Heels had only one winning season.

Tatum was a winner in every way – on the field, off the field, recruiting, speaking and spreading good news about the university. One of his outspoken foes was J. O. (Buck) Buchanan, who owned one of the finest restaurants in the South in Asheville. Buck and Justice had been close friends for years.

Buck cussed when Tatum was hired at Carolina. "Oh, that damned Tatum," he said, "that damned Tatum, blah, blah, blah!"

Charlie brought Tatum to Asheville and made it a point to take him to eat at Bucks. He had told Tatum what the situation was with Buck.

During their meal, Charlie beckoned Buck over and introduced Tatum to him.

The two began to talk, and by the time Justice and Tatum left, Buck was charmed right down to his bootstraps. He joined the Educational Foundation and became a big supporter of North Carolina football. He gave Tatum a thousand dollars that night for athletics and when Charlie and Tatum left, Buck was patting Tatum on the back.

"You'd have thought they were long lost buddies," Charlie said. "Buck came to every Carolina game that year and went to Tatum's house after every home game."

Until his death in 1995, Buck was a loyal supporter and heavy contributor to North Carolina athletics, and an avid booster of Jim Tatum.

"If Tatum had lived," Justice said, "Carolina would really have been a powerhouse. It would rank today with Notre Dame, Nebraska, Texas, Southern Cal, and all those dynastic football schools."

So go the fortunes of football.

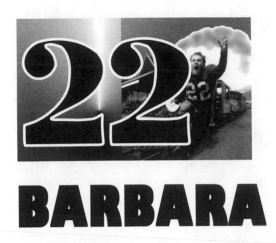

BARBARA

The Justices became parents of a healthy baby girl in 1952. They named her Barbara. Early in her life, Charlie and Sarah noticed that she could sing beautifully.

When Barbara was twelve and the Justices lived in Greensboro, Charlie and Sarah were told by those who knew music that Barbara could sing well enough to go as far as she wanted to go in music.

She majored in music at Greensboro College, and sang in college productions, and everyone marveled at her voice. She was small, only five-two, and weighed no more than a hundred pounds, but when she reached and got a high note, people couldn't believe that all that sound was coming from one little girl.

She forfeited a singing career for marriage at the age of eighteen. She and Billy Crews were married and now live in Cherryville where he manages the family insurance business.

Her singing for years has been in church and at weddings and other gatherings.

"She has had a better life," Charlie said. "In a professional singing career, with movies and television and all... well, if we thought football's notoriety was tough, hers would have been worse."

In the summer of 1968 Barbara and Billy were introduced on a blind date. From that time on, they dated steadily, and the day Barbara graduated from Grimsley High School in Greensboro in 1970 they became engaged. The wedding was held a little more than a year later, on Saturday, November 27, 1971, in St. Andrews Episcopal Church in Greensboro.

The Justice family, left to right: grandmother Sarah, granddaughter Sarah, granddaughter Emilie, daughter Barbara, and proud papa and grandfather Charlie Choo Choo.

Barbara was in her sophomore year at Greensboro College when she married. She was an outstanding member of the Glee Club.

Billy was handsome and redhaired, according to the Greensboro *Daily News*, and was a graduate of Page High. He had one year at Mitchell Junior College in Statesville, and had completed his sophomore credits at Guilford College. He stayed out of college in the fall of 1971, working as a salesman for an automobile company to support his wife, and from there on while he finished college he worked part-time for the firm.

The *Daily News* ran a picture of Barbara with her engagement announcement with an apologetic line in the story that read: "If you know Barbara Justice you know that she's a lot prettier than this picture. It doesn't do her justice.

Barbara and Billy have given Charlie and Sarah two granddaughters, Emilie, who has followed her grandmom and granddad to study at Chapel Hill, and Sarah, who broke ranks and went to Appalachian State University.

Barbara could have gone to Broadway," Charlie believes. "All her professors thought so. She can play the piano and sing, and she is a beautiful girl.

"She's a competitor, too. If she had been a boy she would have been a great ballplayer. She has great coordination, ran track in high school, and her competitive spirit would put a lot of athletes to shame."

Billy loves people. "That's the reason he's so good in the insurance business," Charlie said. "He goes to see the high officials in a business first, and this sometimes bothers him a little, but when he gets to talking to the troops, he's in his element. He does a great job servicing contracts."

NEW HORIZONS

O ut of football and away from the university, Charlie began to look for work. He attended an oil jobbers meeting in Pinehurst and the Phillips 66 people from Asheville asked why he didn't take over the Phillips distributorship in Hendersonville.

He worked out a deal with Phillips 66 and borrowed the money from A. E. Finley of Raleigh, a big booster of both North Carolina and North Carolina State.

You could have written on a pinhead what Charlie knew about the oil business, and he went belly up. Lost his money.

He talked to Joe Wright, who had been blocking back on the Tar Heels during Charlie's first two seasons at North Carolina, about taking the Pure Oil distributorship in Asheville. Joe was running his family's oil company in Hendersonville.

Charlie bought the distributorship and found that it was a tougher job than the one in Hendersonville. He went broke, belly up, flop, bankrupt! So he left Asheville again and moved to Greensboro in 1966. A couple of men from there had approached him when he was with the Redskins and offered him a partnership in an insurance agency.

"Insurance?" Justice had said. "Oh, no, no, hell, no, not the insurance business. I'm not going into insurance."

So he wound up in the insurance business.

"I was really strip broke," he said. "I had put too much faith in other people and other things. That's when I realized I should have stayed with Amoco and gone up the ladder but I would have had to be on the road seven days a week. I had a wife and two kids to feed and had to do something."

Insurance turned out to be the right business for Charlie. With his name, he could sell – and this time he was not just asking for money, as he had been with the Medical Foundation, he was selling something of value.

Suddenly he had ideas about selling insurance in bulk to industry, not just to individuals. He called on a trucking company and while there happened to encounter Buck Fraley, president of Carolina Freight Carriers in Cherryville. "I talked to him about payroll deduction for insurance," Charlie said, "and he invited me to come to his office and explain my ideas. When I did, he apparently liked it because he launched his company into an insurance plan with me. From there things went boom! Boom! BOOM!"

He then approached the Carolina Truckers' Association and got good business from them.

"Business was so good," Charlie said, "that after the first month I sent a check for $150,000 to the home office in Chicago for all the insurance I had sold. They telephoned and asked me to explain how I had sold so much in a month. They thought I was doing something wrong. Now, though, most insurance companies are selling payroll deduction."

Charlie and his family, who had lived in Hendersonville five years and in Asheville five, lived in Greensboro for sixteen years, and then moved to Cherryville in 1981 to be nearer the bulk of his business. Needing help in the business, Charlie took Billy in. Billy and Barbara also moved to Cherryville so Billy could directly service the Carolina Freight Carriers account.

Billy now runs the business from the office, and in November of 1991 in semi-retirement Charlie moved to the Kenmure development in Flat Rock, just south of Hendersonville. Charlie makes the drive to Cherryville periodically to help with the business, and he enjoys being back in the mountains in which he grew up. He lives on a golf course where he can get in occasional licks.

Charlie's attitude toward his business was the subject of a piece written in the *Asheville Citizen-Times* on Sunday, October 31, 1974, by Mary Ellen Wolcott:

> "In everything you go into, you have to have confidence," Justice says. "I had confidence in my ability to play athletics, but other people convinced me that the only thing I could do was play ball. They were always talking about dumb athletes; they didn't say it directly to me but you could feel it, see it. So I didn't have self-confidence about business until I went into the insurance business, and found out I could do other things."
>
> The thing that makes him the maddest, he says, is the word "dumb" associated with athletes. "Every ath-

lete, if he can participate on a team, can go out and make a living, because he's already used to competition, how to think on his feet in the heat of battle, how to get up from a defeat and how to get along with people. And after all, life is nothing but getting along with people."

He thinks contentment comes from "not worrying about the money you make. If people find the thing they're happiest in, then they'll have peace of mind and contentment. I'm living good and haven't starved to death; I've kept my name clean and made a living for my family. ..."

Charlie... is strong in his defense of football as character-building. "It's made men out of more boys than any one thing I know of; it taught me how to get along with people, to think on my feet, how to lose as well as to win."

That story called to mind a 1956 story in *The Charlotte Observer* by Barbara Brawley in which Charlie, addressing school kids, handed out some sage advice:

Don't neglect your studies for athletics. They're even more important than football and basketball games.

That's the advice a former All-American gridiron ace gave fifth and sixth graders at Dilworth and Wilmore schools.

Charlie Justice, University of North Carolina star, gave his views on "Sportsmanship" in a series of speeches sponsored by the Junior Woman's Club.

"Don't feel you're the only one on the team or in the classroom. Always think of the whole team working together," he said.

He urged the children to try to improve their team and not to settle for just racking up individual points and yards gained in a game. "Remember it takes a team and not just you yourself," he emphasized.

Choo Choo told the group they should take sportsmanship to the classroom when they leave the playground. "Do as the teacher asks and be considerate of other people when they want to ask questions," he illustrated.

When you're on the playground, he said, let everyone in your class play in sports, regardless of how old the child is or how well he can play.

Just as the rules in a game must be observed, stick to the rules in the school halls and classes, he said.

Charlie's health began to deteriorate around age fifty. He suffered a heart attack in 1974.

"I always had a heart murmer like my mother," he said. "Had it all the way through high school, Bainbridge, Chapel Hill, and the Redskins. It was not severe, but I thought for a while that I wouldn't have to go into service during the war. But they finally said, 'Aw, it's okay. Let him go ahead.'"

Charlie did not drink or smoke, but he loved to eat. His weight ballooned at one time to 240 pounds — seventy-five pounds above his playing weight — and he thought he looked like a beer barrel.

"Everybody thought I was drinking beer," he said, "but I wasn't. It was food. I dearly loved to eat."

Sarah and Charlie's doctors begged him to lose weight, but jokingly he would pat his ample stomach and say, "No, it cost me too much to get it up there."

When Charlie and Sarah went to Chapel Hill in 1974 to see the Tar Heels play the Pittsburgh Panthers, who featured a scatback named Tony Dorsett, Charlie weighed 225.

"Pittsburgh was beating us," Charlie said. "Bill Dooley was our coach, and he never did believe in pulling surprises."

Carolina had short yardage and the play was right in front of Charlie. Most of Pittsburgh's players were on the line, expecting a plunge. "Dooley didn't believe in throwing, and under my breath I said, 'Bill, can't you throw the ball?'"

Suddenly Justice leaped to his feet and yelled, "Throw, Bill, throw!" And when Carolina threw for a first down, Charlie had a heart attack!

"My chest began to hurt like crazy," he said, "and I was rushed to the hospital where I was diagnosed as having had a light heart attack."

Returning home to Greensboro, he began to exercise and walk two miles daily, and with great effort reduced his weight from 225 back to 165. After that, however, he began to forget his walking and exercises, and in 1978 he had a second heart attack and open heart surgery. He resumed his exercising, and drifted along working and playing golf and enjoying life and his family, and in 1994, after he had moved to Kenmure, he was diagnosed as having an irregular heartbeat.

"They put a defibrillator in me to restore the rhythm to my heart, actually put it inside me, and it's about the size of a mini tape recorder or a pocket radio. I have to go to Chapel Hill every six weeks to have it checked."

THE HAND OF PROVIDENCE

Charlie is a philosophical man. He believes that the Good Lord has looked after him all these years – in more ways than one – and that He will continue to look after him. And when his time to go comes up, he'll go.

Looking back over his life fifty years after he ran the football for North Carolina, Justice is the first to say that the hand of Providence played a great role. So many things that he would have done differently turned out for the best. Even his term in military service.

"War is awful," Justice said, "but as far as I'm concerned, I gained from it during World War II.

"I've often wondered why," he said. "The Good Lord did it. There isn't any other explanation."

Charlie can go back through his life and recount the good deeds other people did for him, and the good things that have happened accidentally.

Charlie said he "just happened to catch that ball" at Bainbridge, which he punted back and won a position on the team. He had told his mother that he would never go to the navy because he couldn't swim, yet he wound up in the navy, and that may have changed the course of his life for the better. He did not want to go to North Carolina or Duke, but South Carolina, and when he was influenced to enroll at North Carolina, he said it turned out to be the best thing for him. He decided not to play professional football, but backed himself into such a corner that he had to – and he said he should have signed professionally sooner. Finally, he vowed to have nothing to do with the insurance business, yet that was where his business success came.

"And remember," he said, "if I hadn't knocked Sarah Hunter down while scuffling in the hall in high school, she might never have noticed me. You bet that was providential!"

Always a man of faith, Charlie could see the hand of Providence in all of that. "They can't tell me that things aren't planned for us ahead of time," he said. "I think we've all got a time and when that time comes we go, but we can shorten or lengthen our days. The Bible says that. And one reason I really believe all this is because I really died when I had the heart attack in Chapel Hill, but I was brought back for some reason.

"All those things were destined," he said. "The Good Lord had already planned the whole thing and set it up for me. Maybe He wanted to slow me down. We may think we're in control of ourselves, but it isn't that way at all. Everything I didn't want to do at first turned out to be the right thing to do. What would have happened to me if I had gone the way I wanted to each time?

"I had every break in the world. If I could go back and restructure my life, I would change only two things. I would have gone pro a little earlier, and after I finished playing with the Redskins I would have stayed with Amoco.

"And the only thing I regret was that I didn't win the Heisman Trophy. I wanted that trophy so bad! I had read about it and heard about it when Frankie Sinkwich won it at Georgia, and in 1942 Sarah and I were riding in the back seat of a friend's car and something came on the radio about the Heisman, and I said to Sarah, 'I'm going to win that one of these days.' I set my goal that night, and worked toward it for years, and when I didn't get it, that was the biggest disappointment of my life. It was really the only disappointment I ever had in athletics, so I guess I'm a pretty lucky man, after all."

People often surprise themselves when they do things they didn't think they could do, but if they had enough confidence in themselves, they could do anything, regardless of the odds.

Charlie Justice is living proof of that.

The country's leading coaches who saw Justice play had only praise for his capabilities, such as:

"One of the all-time greats," Bud Wilkinson, Oklahoma.

"A coach's dream," Gen. Robert Neyland, Tennessee.

"To be such a great star, I have never seen a more unselfish player," Carl Snavely, UNC.

"He's the greatest natural football player I've ever seen," Joe Maniaci, Bainbridge.

"Charlie is one of the best runners in modern football. Too bad he didn't play the T all his career," George Preston Marshall, owner of the Washington Redskins.

Charlie's season statistics, won-lost records, All-America and All-Southern honors have been recorded in the pages of this book. Accolades are still coming for Justice after all these years. Here are some:

The University of North Caroina at Asheville named its new sports center "The Charlie Justice Sports, Health, and Physical Education Center" in February, 1975.

The Charlie "Choo Choo" Justice Lettermen's Lounge in Chapel Hill was so named in September 1988 in recognition of all Carolina football lettermen and the tradition they established.

In October 1969 Charlie and Lyn Szafaryn of the Justice Era teams were voted members of the all-time North Carolina football team: Ends Andy Bershak (1937) and Paul Severin (1939); tackles Szafaryn (1948) and Steve Maronic (1938); guards George Barclay (1934) and Bill Koman (1955); center Chris Hanburger (1964); quarterback Junior Edge (1963); halfbacks Charlie Justice (1949) and Johnny Branch (1930); and fullback Ken Willard (1964).

The University of Virginia bestowed an unusual honor on Justice, presenting him with a huge plaque that read:

> The University of Virginia presents to Charles Justice, U.N.C. '50, on the occasion of the 67th renewal, 1962, of the University of Virginia vs. University of North Carolina football game, the oldest continuous series in the South, for the greatest single performance by a U.N.C. player in this series. In 1948 at Scott Stadium you finished the greatest season of your college career in the following manner: Rushing – 167 yards on 15 carries; Passing – 87 yards on 4 completions on 6 attempts; Punting – 5 times for a 40.1 average; Touchdowns – 2 on runs of 80 and 50 yards; T.D. Passes – 2 on passes of 40 and 31 yards. Score – U.N.C. 34, U.Va. 12. You are the holder of 10 all-time records at North Carolina. In four UVa-UNC games you gained 727 yards and scored or passed for 11 T.D.'s. The U. Va. salutes the Carolina Choo-Choo, our all-time opponent.

Glenn (Pop) Warner, an aging man who had coached at Iowa State, Georgia, Cornell, Carlisle, Pittsburgh, Stanford, and Temple, the man who created the single- and double-wing formations, and a coach who had watched the best football players since before the turn of the century, picked his all-time All-America football teams in 1950.

In an odd way of picking, the coach picked a first team that included players up to and including 1925, a second team of players from 1925 to 1950, and a third team from 1926 to 1950.

He named Charlie Justice to the second team, which actually was the first team from that quarter century from 1925 to 1950.

His teams included:

FIRST TEAM
Ends – Frank Hinkey, Yale, 1891-94; and Harold (Brick)
    Muller, California, 1921-22.
Tackles – Wilbur Henry, Washington & Jefferson, 1919; and
    Duke Slater, Iowa, 1921.
Guards – William (Pudge) Heffelfinger, Yale, 1889-91; and
    Truxton Hare, Pennsylvania, 1897-99.
Center – Robert Peck, Pittsburgh, 1915-16.
Backs – Harold (Red) Grange, Illinois, 1923-25; Jim Thorpe,
    Carlisle, 1911-12; William Heston, Michigan, 1903-04;
    and Ernie Nevers, Stanford, 1925.

SECOND TEAM
Ends – Don Hutson, Alabama, 1934; and Leon Hart, Notre
    Dame, 1949.
Tackles – Ed Widseth, Minnesota, 1936; and Robert
    Suffridge, Tennessee, 1940.
Guards – Frank (Bruiser) Kinnard, Mississippi, 1940; and
    Clarence Munn, Minnesota, 1931.
Center – Charles Bednarik, Pennsylvania, 1947-48.
Backs – Charles Justice, North Carolina, 1948-49; John
    Lujack, Notre Dame, 1946-47; George Wilson, Wash-
    ington, 1925; and Bronko Nagurski, Minnesota, 1929.
    (Nagurski won All-America honors as a tackle, but
    doubled as one of Minnesota's most powerful fullbacks.)

THIRD TEAM
Ends – Benny Oosterbaan, Michigan, 1927; and Gaynell
    Tinsley, LSU, 1934-36.
Tackles – Al Wistert, Michigan, 1947; and Leo Nomellini,
    Minnesota, 1948.
Guards – Ernie Smith, Southern Cal, 1932; and John Can-
    non, Notre Dame, 1929.
Center – Ben Ticknor, Harvard, 1929-30.
Backs – Frank Albert, Stanford, 1940-41; Doak Walker,

Southern Methodist, 1948-49; Tom Harmon, Michigan, 1939-40; and Kyle Rote, Southern Methodist, 1950.

Warner said he believes that if it were possible to test the various star elevens, his third team might prove stronger than the second. He added that he possibly could pick fourth, fifth, and sixth teams that might be better than his first three, which is a good summation of all All-Star teams.

A Charlotte-based poll conducted in April 1989 asked fans to name the best college football player in the history of the Carolinas. The landslide winner was Charlie Justice. No one else received more than one vote. A half century after Justice began his career at the University of North Carolina, the 165-pound triple threat tailback remains the state's most revered sports figure.

In another poll, conducted in 1995, the 75th anniversary of the Southern Conference, Charlie was the only unanimous member of the all-time All-Southern Conference team.

His blue and white No. 22 was retired at North Carolina and will never again be worn by a Tar Heel player, and his maroon and gold No. 22 hangs in Robert F. Kennedy Stadium's Hall of Stars in Washington, placed there in ceremonies on October 13, 1985, at halftime of a Redskins-Detroit Lions game. Morris Siegel, a *Washington Post* sports reporter and chairman of the Hall of Stars selection committee, wrote of Charlie:

> ... He was a dashing, brilliant runner who was a genuine hero in this town. Although he had a relatively short career with the Redskins (1950, 1952-1954) at a time when they were really lousy, "Choo Choo" became a household name and he was very popular with Washington area fans.
>
> Next to George Allen, the biggest applause of those 55,000 fans on Sunday was for Charlie. There's probably some yuppies out there that might not know what Charlie meant to football. He wasn't just a product of Jake Wade. ...

"However, the mind's eye doesn't picture Justice with a feather on his helmet," wrote Jim Baker in the *Asheville Citizen-Times*, September 23, 1990. "He's just a streak of blue with wings on his heels."

Perhaps the accolade Charlie liked as much as anyone was told by Billy Carmichael III in a column in *The Daily Tar Heel*:

What has done more to interest the people of North Carolina in their university than the influx of Big Time Athletics at Chapel Hill? The people of the state have come to feel that great teams representing the University not only represent the 7,000 students at Chapel Hill, but the entire 3,500,000 who call themselves Tar Heels.

The effect on the youth of the state is typified by the actions of a group of second graders at the Oxford orphanage last fall. The boys – 26 in number – decided to choose by vote the most outstanding man in the country and follow his activities throughout the year.

President Harry Truman received two of the ballots, being closely followed by the Superintendent of the Orphanage who got a single vote, and the other 23 went to Charlie Justice, a fellow North Carolinian....

Few players in college football history ever won more accolades than Charlie Choo Choo. Or lived a more exciting life.

Sarah and Charlie Justice today.

THE HALL OF FAME

E lection to the College Football Hall of Fame in May 1961 by the National Football Foundation's Honors Court was a highlight of Charlie's life. Inducted with him on the evening of December 5, 1961, were Glenn Davis, Army 1947; George McAfee, Duke 1940; Bob Suffridge, Tennessee 1941; Weldon Humble, Rice 1947; Bob Reynolds, Stanford 1936; Claude Reeds, Oklahoma 1914; and Vincent Pazzetti, Lehigh 1914.

Two coaches were also taken in: Charles W. Caldwell, Jr., who coached Princeton from 1945 through 1956, and Don Faurot, University of Missouri, 1935-1956.

Justice termed his election "the greatest honor and thrill of my life" – a life replete with honors and thrills. He was the first native North Carolinian to be named to the Hall of Fame. Art Weiner, Charlie's pass-catching teammate, was elected in 1993.

"Carolina is one of few teams," Charlie said, " – maybe the only one, unless it's Notre Dame – that has two players off the same team in the Hall of Fame. I don't mean from the same school; I mean from the same team, the same group of boys. That shows the caliber of boys we had on that team. It was a pleasure, and I mean an extreme pleasure, to play with boys of that caliber. They were not just athletes, but decent human beings as well. Character has a lot to do with success, and that team had a lot of character."

The banquet was held in the Grand Ballroom of the Waldorf-Astoria Hotel in New York. Charlie looked around at all the prominent people – President John F. Kennedy; General Douglas MacArthur; Francis Cardinal Spellman, archbishop of New York; other members of the Hall of

Fame; members of *Sports Illustrated*'s 1961 Silver Anniversary Team; and Bob Hope included – and wondered, "What in the world am I doing here?"

Hugh Morton, Charlie's most ardent supporter through college and actually through the rest of his life, shot a picture of Charlie with President Kennedy and General MacArthur.

MacArthur asked him what branch of service he was in, and when Charlie told him, the general asked if he had fought in the South Pacific.

Embarrassed, Charlie told him, "Yes, sir, I got to Pearl Harbor."

"What was your job?"

"I was a Specialist-A."

"And what were your duties?"

"I exercised and trained the men," Charlie said, "and I played football."

"Hummmm," MacArthur mused. "Extra weight."

Every time Justice donned his shoulder pads, Hugh Morton was there. And on the momentous occasions in Charlie's life, like the Hall of Fame dinner, Hugh was there.

The Hall of Fame dinner was something of a reunion for Hugh. He had been a photographer during the war, and went through the South Pacific assigned to MacArthur's staff. An excellent photographer, Morton was always on the sidelines when Charlie played. He made excellent photographs not only of Charlie, but of the remainder of the team as well.

Photography was his hobby, and he followed Carolina on his own. But he sold a countless number of photographs to magazines and newspapers, and at least partially because of him and the contacts he had, the Tar Heels were certainly one of the most publicized teams in the nation.

"The first time I saw Hugh Morton was in August of 1946," Charlie said. "The weather was hot and we were practicing twice a day. Sunday was an off day and Snavely and his staff decided that was the day they'd have the press come in and take pictures, get interviews, and so forth. That day it was hot as hades. We started at two o'clock, and it seemed that everybody in the country was there to shoot our pictures. I noticed Hugh on the sidelines, paying no attention to me at all, taking pictures of everybody else.

"After two and a half hours, Coach Snavely told me I was through and could go on in.

"About that time, Morton turned and said, 'No, coach, I haven't had him. I want him.' We stayed there another two hours, hot as it was, and everything had to be just perfect.

Charlie and current UNC coach, Mack Brown, who is rebuilding Carolina's football fortunes.

Charlie's hometown honored him with a huge banquet in the Asheville City Auditorium upon his induction into the College Football Hall of Fame.

"I didn't say anything at the time," Charlie said, "but when I got in the dressing room, everybody had already left. I said, 'I hope I never see him again.' Then every time I would see him, I'd try to ignore him. I didn't want anything to do with him."

But as games passed and Charlie saw Hugh at every one of them,

blazing away from the sidelines, they began talking and soon became friends.

"I got to going down to Wilmington to the Azalea Festival," Charlie said. "Hugh ran the festival and I crowned four queens for him while I was in college.

"Then I went to Grandfather Mountain and cut the ribbon for him when the road opened up the mountain, and I was starter for his hill climb race up the mountain – and over the years he has become Mr. North Carolina to me. He loves the state of North Carolina.

"I've found that Hugh will not say one word about himself. Try to get him to talk about himself and that's it. He clams up.

"I have found Hugh to be a down-to-earth man of simple tastes, but one who can move in the circles of anyone on earth.

"Hugh should have been governor of this state, but he doesn't want any ballyhoo, no recognition; he just wants to be old Hugh Morton. But he has worked as hard for North Carolina as any governor we've ever had, yet he really didn't want to be governor. He has always been a satisfied man.

"He supported me wholeheartedly, not just at Carolina, either. When I got to the Redskins, I turned around on the field and there was Hugh, shooting pictures. Because of him, I suppose my football career was preserved on film as well as anybody's ever was.

"When I went into the Hall of Fame, he got Governor Luther Hodges's plane and flew Sarah and me and his wife to New York – and when we got there we discovered that the girls couldn't go to the banquet. It was stag. So Sarah and Hugh's wife went over to Broadway and saw 'My Fair Lady' that night. Then we flew back to Raleigh."

Charlie treasures men like Hugh Morton as his friends, and the honor is returned to him because he was one athlete who always knew how to make friends, not enemies. He never refused to give anyone the time of day.

In conjunction with Charlie's entry in the Hall of Fame, his home town of Asheville rolled out the red carpet, giving him a parade and a banquet that filled the City Auditorium, which was then managed again by his old high school coach, Ralph James, who sat proudly on the dais.

It was a bit ironic that the parade came down Patton Avenue from Pack Square, turned up Haywood Street at Pritchard Park, and ended at City Auditorium – retracing the steps Charlie and his brother Neal had made when dodging Christmas shoppers more than twenty years previously.

26

FOR THE RECORD

ASHEVILLE HIGH WON-LOST RECORDS, 1940-42

1940 (6-4-1)
32-0 Lenoir High School
19-7 loss to Kingsport, Tennessee
13-6 Columbia, South Carolina
32-0 Gaffney, South Carolina
12-0 Spartanburg, South Carolina
7-0 loss to Chattanooga Central
14-0 loss to Greenville, South Carolina
7-6 Greensboro
12-0 loss to Blue Ridge School for Boys
12-12 tie with Charlotte Central
28-0 Children's Home, Winston-Salem
142-64 Total points for season

1941 (11-0)
21-7 Children's Home, Winston-Salem
21-0 Kingsport, Tennessee
38-0 Gaffney, South Carolina
25-0 Columbia, South Carolina
54-0 Sumter, South Carolina
19-6 Greenville, South Carolina
20-6 Riverside Military Academy, Georgia
39-6 Biltmore High
39-0 Andrews High
19-0 Charlotte Central High
53-7 Blue Ridge School for Boys
348-32 Total points for season

MILK BOWL, Atlanta, Ga., January 1, 1942:
0-44 loss to Boys High, Atlanta (Boys High scored 12 more points against the Maroons than all other 1941 opponents combined).

1942 (9-0)
34-0 Tech High, Atlanta, Georgia
22-0 Kingsport, Tennessee
47-6 Columbia, South Carolina
94-0 Hickory High
35-0 Charlotte Central
55-0 Greenville, South Carolina
27-0 Knoxville, Tennessee
67-0 Brevard College
60-0 Children's Home, Winston-Salem
441-6 Total points for season

ORANGE BOWL, Miami, Florida, December 12, 1942: 7-13 loss to Miami High

SCORING FOR THREE JUSTICE SEASONS (Including Bowl Games)
Asheville 939, Opponents 159

JUSTICE'S INDIVIDUAL ASHEVILLE HIGH SCHOOL RECORD
(Note: The following statistical table, compiled by Dick Kaplan during Charlie Justice's high school career, is the only tabulation ever recorded and is reprinted from the *Asheville Citizen-Times*, Sunday, October 15, 1961)

	1940	1941	1942	Totals
Games	10	11	9	30
Runs from scrimmage	34	124	128	286
Yardage scrimmage runs	227	1393	2385	4005
Average yards per carry	6.68	11.23	18.63	14.0035
Forward passes attempted	0	36	25	61
Forward passes completed	0	23	18	41
Pass completion pct.	0	63.9	72	67.2
Yards forward passing	0	303	224	527
Punts	0	31	19	50
Yards punting	0	1214	812	2026
Avg. yards per punt	0	39.16	42.74	40.52
Touchdowns scored	3	19	27	49
Yardage on touchdowns	104	464	1117	1685
Avg. yards per touchdown	34.67	24.42	41.37	34.39
Points after touchdown	0	0	4	4
Total points scored	18	114	166	298
Touchdown passes thrown	0	4	3	7
Yardage on TD passes	0	146	64	210
Average yards TD passes	0	36.5	21.33	30
TD runs from scrimmage	1	17	22	40
TD run ydg. scrimmage	10	327	808	1145
Avg. Yds. scrimmage TD runs	10	19.24	36.73	28.63
Touchdown passes caught	1	0	0	1
Yardage TD passes caught	30	0	0	30
Touchdowns, punt returns	1	2	2	5
Yardage, TD punt returns	64	137	144	345
Avg. Yds. TD punt returns	64	68.5	72	69
TDs kickoff returns	0	0	1	1
Yardage, TD kickoff returns	0	0	85	85
Avg. Ydg. TD kickoff returns	0	0	85	85
TDs, pass interceptions	0	0	2	2
Ydg. TD pass interceptions	0	0	80	80
Avg. yds. TD pass int.	0	0	40	40

The prior table does not include two post-season bowl games. In addition, Justice made seven runs of 50 to 95 yards on non-touchdown punt and kickoff returns, and numerous others up to 50 yards. It is significant that most of the total yardage above was made while he was a regular during his junior (1941) and senior (1942) years, having had only limited service as a sophomore substitute in 1940.

UNIVERSITY OF NORTH CAROLINA

Game Scores and Records

1946 (8-1-1)
UNC 14, VPI 14
UNC 21, Miami 0
UNC 33, Maryland 0
UNC 21, Navy 14
UNC 40, Florida 19
Tennessee 20, UNC 14
UNC 21, William & Mary 7
UNC 26, Wake Forest 14
UNC 22, Duke 7
UNC 49, Virginia 14

Sugar Bowl
Georgia 20, UNC 10

1947 (8-2)
UNC 14, Georgia 7
Texas 34, UNC 0
Wake Forest 19, UNC 7
UNC 13, William & Mary 7
UNC 35, Florida 7
UNC 20, Tennessee 6
UNC 41, N. C. State 6
UNC 19, Maryland 0
UNC 21, Duke 0
UNC 40, Virginia 7

1948 (9-0-1)
UNC 34, Texas 7
UNC 21, Georgia 14
UNC 28, Wake Forest 6
UNC 14, N. C. State 0
UNC 34, LSU 7
UNC 14, Tennessee 9
UNC 7, William & Mary 7
UNC 49, Maryland 20
UNC 20, Duke 0
UNC 34, Virginia 12

Sugar Bowl
Oklahoma 14, UNC 6

1949 (7-3)
UNC 26, N.C. State 6
UNC 21, Georgia 14
UNC 28, South Carolina 13
UNC 28, Wake Forest 14
LSU 13, UNC 7
Tennessee 35, UNC 6
UNC 20, William & Mary 14
Notre Dame 42, UNC 6
UNC 21, Duke 20
UNC 14, Virginia 7

Cotton Bowl
Rice 27, UNC 13

UNC RECORDS JUSTICE AND TEAMMATES STILL HOLD IN 1995

MOST TOUCHDOWNS RESPONSIBLE FOR (SCORED AND PASSED FOR):
Season — Justice, 23, 1948, (scored 11, passed for 12)
Career — Justice, 64, 1946-49 (scored 39, passed for 25)

HIGHEST AVERAGE GAIN PER RUSH
Season — Justice, 7.2, 1946 (131 for 943)

MOST YARDS ON PUNT RETURNS
Career — Justice, 966, 1946-49 (68 returns)

HIGHEST AVERAGE GAIN PER PUNT RETURN
> Game — (minimum 3) Justice, 41.7 vs. Georgia 1948 (3 for 125)
> Season — (minimum 3) Justice, 17.5, 1948 (19 for 332)
> Career — (minimum 40) Justice, 14.2, 1946-49 (68 for 966)

MOST TOUCHDOWNS ON PUNT RETURNS
> Season — 4-way tie: 2, held by Johnny Branch (1930), Charlie Justice (1948), Norris Davis (1987), Andre Purvis (1993)
> Career — 2-way tie: 4, Johnny Branch (1929-30), Charlie Justice (1946-49)

HIGHEST AVERAGE GAIN PER KICKOFF RETURN
> Career — (minimum 30) Justice, 26.6, 1946-49 (31 for 826)

MOST TOUCHDOWNS SCORED ON KICK RETURNS
> Game — 2, Justice vs. Florida 1948 (1 punt, 1 kickoff) Record shared by Eric Blount, vs. William & Mary 1991 (1 punt, 1 kickoff) and Andre Purvis vs. Tulane 1993 (2 blocked punt recoveries in end zone).
> Season — 2, Johnny Branch 1930 (2 punts); Justice 1946 (1 punt, 1 kickoff), Justice 1948 (1 punt, 1 kickoff); Norris Davis 1987 (2 punts); Eric Blount 1991 (1 punt, 1 kickoff); Andre Purvis 1993 (2 blocked punt recoveries in end zone).
> Career — 5, Justice 1946-49 (4 punts, 1 kickoff).

RETURNING A PUNT AND KICKOFF FOR TOUCHDOWNS, SAME GAME
> Justice vs. Florida, 1948; Eric Blount vs. William & Mary, 1991.

MOST YARDS GAINED BY A FRESHMEN
> Season — 1554, Justice 1946 (943 rushing, 39 receiving, 572 returns)

MOST CONSECUTIVE GAMES SCORING A TOUCHDOWN
> 9 Justice (final 6 games of 1947, first 3 games of 1948).

MOST GAMES SCORING A TOUCHDOWN
> Career — 27 Justice 1946-49.

IN ALL TIME TOP 15

CAREER TOTAL OFFENSE
> No. 2 Justice, behind Jason Stanicek, 4883 to 5497.

CAREER SCORING
> No. 2 Justice behind Mike Voight (1973-76), 234 to 254 points. No. 15 Bob Cox (1945-48) 146 points.

CAREER RUSHING
> No. 7 Justice (2634 in 526 carries, 5.0 average, 28 TDs).
> No. 15 Hosea Rodgers (1662 in 364, 4.6 average, 13 TDs).

CAREER PASSING
> No. 14 Justice (49.5 pct., 159 of 321, 2249 yards, 25 TDs, 32 int.)

PUNTING
> No. 3 Justice, 231 punts for 9839 yards, 42.6 average (behind Harry Dunkle, 1939-41, 43.7, and Mike Cooke, 1941-42, 43.5.)

KICKOFF RETURN AVERAGE
>No. 1, Justice, 31 returns, 826 yards, 26.6 average, 1 TD.

PUNT RETURN AVERAGE
>No. 1, Justice, 68 returns, 966 yards, 14.2 average, 4 TDs.

CAREER ALL-PURPOSE YARDS
>No. 3, Justice, 2634 rushing, 234 receiving, 966 punt returns, 820 kickoff returns, 10 pass interceptions, 4670 total.

Justice led Carolina all four years in rushing, passing, punting, punt returns, kickoff returns. Led three times (1946-47-48) in All-Purpose yardage. Weiner led All-Purpose category in 1949. Interception leaders were Jim Camp 1946, Bill Flamish 1947, Bill Maceyko and Bob Kennedy 1948, and Dick Bunting 1949.

ART WEINER

MOST PASSES CAUGHT
>Season — 52, Weiner 1949, and Charlie Carr, 1966.

HIGHEST YARDAGE GAIN PER RECEPTION
>(minimum 100) 16.3, Weiner, 1946-49, (106 for 1733).

MOST GAMES GAINING 100 YARDS OR MORE RECEIVING
>Season — 3, Weiner 1949, Bob Lacey 1962, Jimmy Jerome 1974, and Corey Holliday 1993.

MOST TOUCHDOWN PASSES CAUGHT
>Career — 18, Weiner 1946-49.

CAREER PASS RECEIVING
>No. 3 Weiner, 106 for 1733 yards, 16.3 average, 18 TDs.

BILL MACEYKO

MOST YARDS ON INTERCEPTION RETURNS
>Game — 125, Maceyko 2 vs. Maryland, 1948.
>Season — 125, Maceyko 3 interceptions 1948.

MOST TOUCHDOWNS ON INTERCEPTION RETURNS
>Game — 2,Maceyko vs. Maryland 1948.
>Season — 2, Maceyko 1948, Greg Poole 1981.
>Career — 2, George Barclay 1932-34, Maceyko 1946-48, Al Goldstein 1957-59, Greg Poole 1979-82.

DICK BUNTING

CAREER INTERCEPTIONS
>Tied for 5th with 10.

TEAM

HIGHEST AVERAGE GAIN PER PUNT RETURN (5 minimum)
>30.2 vs. Georgia 1948 (5 for 151).

FEWEST FIRST DOWNS IN A WIN
    8 vs. Virginia 1949 (won 14-7)

MOST YARDS PENALIZED
    150 vs. Duke, 1947.

MOST YARDS ON INTERCEPTION RETURNS
    165 vs. Maryland, 1948.

HIGHEST AVERAGE GAIN PER RUSH
    5.2 in 1946 (447 for 2327).

HIGHEST AVERAGE GAIN PER PASS COMPLETION
    18.1 in 1946 (35 for 633).

HIGHEST PUNTING AVERAGE PER GAME
    44 in 1948.

MOST OPPONENTS PUNTS FORCED
    102 in 1948.

MOST CONSECUTIVE GAMES WITHOUT A LOSS
    17, 1947-48.

PRO FOOTBALL

22 drafted off Justice Era teams; 9 played

Name	Position	Year	Round	Team
Chan Highsmith	Center	45	15	Boston Yanks
Ralph Strayhorn	Guard	45	18	Chicago Cardinals
*Hosea Rodgers	Back	46	3	New York Giants
*Ted Hazelwood	Tackle	46	16	Chicago Bears
*Ernie Williamson	Tackle	47	8	Washington Redskins
Jack Fitch	Back	47	10	Pittsburgh Steelers
Walt Pupa	Back	47	16	Chicago Bears
Baxter Jarrell	Tackle	47	26	Green Bay Packers
*Bill Smith	Tackle	48	2	Chicago Cardinals
*Jim Camp	Back	48	2	Chicago Cardinals
*Len Szafaryn	Tackle	48	3	Washington Redskins
Bob Kennedy	Back	48	8	Washington Redskins
Mike Rubish	End	49	8	Boston Yanks
Bob Mitten	Guard	49	19	Chicago Bears
Joe Romano	Tackle	49	20	Detroit Lions
Bob Cox	End	49	23	Chicago Cardinals
Stan Marczyk	Tackle	49	25	Chicago Bears
*Art Weiner	End	50	2	New York Bulldogs
*Charlie Justice	Back	50	16	Washington Redskins
Ken Powell	End	50	18	Pittsburgh Steelers
Irv Holdash	Center	51	7	Cleveland Rams
*Roscoe Hansen	End	51	29	Philadelphia Eagles

(* indicates those who played professional football. Szafaryn had the longest career, playing eight seasons for Washington, Green Bay, and Philadelphia.)

PLAYED IN COLLEGE ALL-STAR GAME

William Smith 1948; Len Szafaryn 1949; Charlie Justice and Art Weiner 1950; Irv Holdash 1951.

PLAYED IN SENIOR BOWL

Justice, Powell, Weiner 1950; Billy Hayes 1951.

ALL-SOUTHERN CONFERENCE SELECTIONS

(All first team choices)

1943 — Hosea Rodgers.
1946 — Charlie Justice.
1947 — Charlie Justice, Art Weiner, Len Szafaryn.
1948 — Justice, Weiner, Szafaryn (Justice player of the year).
1949 — Justice, Weiner, Irv Holdash (Justice player of the year).
1950 — Holdash.

JUSTICE'S ALL-AMERICA SELECTIONS

1946 — 2nd Team: PIC Scouts, UP, NEA, Gridiron Weekly; 3rd Team: Coaches (Saturday Evening Post), AP, Sports Week.

1947 — 2nd Team: AP, NEA; 3rd Team: INS, Central Press.

1948 — 1st Team: UP, AP, Coaches (Collier's), Central Press, NEA, New York News, All-Players (Chicago Tribune), INS, All-America Board, Bill Stern, Sports Week, Police Gazette, Boston Record, Football Digest, Complete Football, College Football Illustrated, Houlgate, The Sporting News; 2nd Team: Grantland Rice (Look).

1949 — 1st Team: Coaches (Collier's), AP, All-Players (Chicago Tribune), The Sporting News, INS, All-America Board, Paramount, Police Gazette, Sports Review, Williamson, Football Digest; 2nd Team: Central Press, UP; 3rd Team: Grantland Rice (Look).

JUSTICE ERA PLAYERS WHO BECAME UNC COACHES

Jim Camp — backfield 49, freshmen 50, backs 51-52.
Emmett Cheek — scout 56-58, admin. asst. 59-64, defensive line 64-66.
Bob Cox — freshmen 50, backs, ends 51.
Ted Hazelwood — line 50-51, jayvees 52.
Charlie Justice — backs 51.
Walt Pupa — asst. freshmen 48-49, backs 50-51, jayvees 52.

ASSISTANTS UNDER CARL SNAVELY DURING JUSTICE YEARS

1946
Max Reed, line
Russ Murphy, backs
Jim Gill, ends
George (Snuffy) Stirnweiss, backs *
Eddie Teague, line
Crowell Little, jayvees

1947
Max Reed, line
Russ Murphy, backs
Jim Gill, ends
George Radman, ends
Crowell Little, jayvees

1948
Max Reed, line
Russ Murphy, backs
Jim Gill, ends
George Radman, ends
Crowell Little, freshmen
Walt Pupa, freshmen asst.

1949
Russ Murphy, backs
Jim Camp, backs
Marvin Bass, line
Jim Gill, ends
George Radman, ends
Crowell Little, freshmen
Walt Pupa, freshmen asst.

* Stirnweiss played 129 baseball games with the New York Yankees in 1946 and returned to Chapel Hill to coach. He returned to play the full schedule with the Yankees the following year.